PENGUIN HANDBOOKS

THE BEST OF ELIZA ACTON

Eliza Acton was born in 1799 and lived in Tonbridge, where she kept house for her mother.
Modern Cookery, published in 1845, was her first
cookery book – a book which she worked on for the
best part of seven years. Apart from a somewhat
enlarged and very cheaply produced popular edition
of *Modern Cookery*, her only other cookery publication was a work about bread-making. She died
in 1860,

D0474876

THE BEST OF

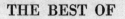

Eliza Acton

Recipes from her classic
MODERN COOKERY
FOR PRIVATE FAMILIES
first published in 1845
selected and edited by
ELIZABETH RAY
with an introduction by
ELIZABETH DAVID

PENGUIN BOOKS

Penguin Books Ltd, Harmondsworth, Middlesex, England
Penguin Books Inc., 7110 Ambassador Road, Baltimore, Maryland 21207, U.S.A.
Penguin Books Australia Ltd, Ringwood, Victoria, Australia
Penguin Books Canada Ltd, 41 Steelcase Road West, Markham, Ontario, Canada

—

First published by Longmans, Green & Co. 1968
Published in Penguin Books 1974

—

This edition copyright © Longmans, Green & Co. Ltd, 1968
Introduction copyright © Elizabeth David, 1968

Made and printed in Great Britain by
Cox & Wyman Ltd
London, Reading and Fakenham
Set in Linotype Georgian

CONTENTS

Chapter 3: Dishes of Shell-Fish

Chapter 4: Gravies

Chapter 5: Sauces

Chapter 6: Cold Sauces and Salads

Chapter 7: Store Sauces

Chapter 8: Forcemeats

Chapter 9: Boiling, Roasting, etc.

Chapter 10: Beef

Chapter 11: Veal

x

Chapter 15: Game

Chapter 16: Curries, Potted Meats, etc.

Chapter 17: Vegetables

Chapter 18: Pastry

Chapter 19: Soufflés, Omlets, etc.

Chapter 20: Boiled Puddings

xiii

Chapter 21: Baked Puddings

Chapter 22: Eggs and Milk

Chapter 23: Sweet Dishes, or Entremets

xvi

Chapter 27: Confectionary

Chapter 28: Dessert Dishes

Chapter 29: Syrups, Liqueurs, etc.

Chapter 30: Coffee, Chocolate, etc.

Chapter 31: Bread

Chapter 32: Foreign and Jewish Cookery

PREFACE

'It cannot be denied that an improved system of practical domestic cookery, and a better knowledge of its first principles, are still much needed in this country.' This was written in the middle of the last century by Eliza Acton, and if it remains, alas, all too true today the fault is not Miss Acton's. Her *Modern Cookery for Private Families* was first published by Longmans in 1845, and remained in print for more than half a century, although it is Mrs Beeton, whose now more famous book was published in the 1860s, who is remembered as the cookery writer of the century.

Miss Acton's book is devoted entirely to cookery, unlike Mrs Beeton's, which included branches of Household Management, and it is so practical and well planned that it can still be used very readily.

In this edition of the book I have kept the receipts exactly as they were written, spelling and all, and have selected only those which I believe are manageable today, or which have a special appeal, either because of some charm or oddity in the writing, or because they serve as footnotes to the social history of the last century. I have also added a few notes of my own where such seemed appropriate. Eliza Acton's own '*Obs.*' (observations) follow many of the receipts. The Vocabulary of Terms has been enlarged.

Eliza Acton was born in Sussex in 1799, the daughter of a brewer, but her early life was spent in Suffolk, where her father's family originated. She also spent some time in France, as she was said to be delicate, and it may well be that it was here that her interest in cooking was aroused, for although she is basically a very English cook, many of her receipts are labelled 'French', and appear as a matter of course in the main body of the book, whereas 'Foreign Cookery' is given a chapter to itself, and covers any receipt that does not come from England or from France.

She also refers frequently to Jewish cookery, mentioning several times a 'certain Jewish lady' to whom she is indebted for these receipts. Such an interest, so early in the century, is unexpected, as it was not until nearer the end of the nineteenth century that the great wave of Jewish immigrants settled in this country, bringing with them their dietary laws and their own cooking. One would have thought that in Eliza Acton's time it would still be the Sephardic Jews – those from Spain, Portugal, and Italy, perhaps by way of Holland: Jews, in fact, of the same background as Disraeli or Mendoza or Montefiore – who, if any, would have a modest influence on the cooking of middle-class Londoners. But Eliza Acton's receipts are undoubtedly those of the Jews of Central and Eastern Europe, as are those of a *Little Book of Jewish Cookery* that appeared about the end of the century.

Eliza Acton's muse had once flown further than the kitchen: the story has often been written of how the maiden lady of the eighteen-thirties, already a poet with a modest reputation, took 'further fugitive verses' to her publishers – to be told that they would rather have a cookery book instead. *Modern Cookery for Private Families* was the result, and posterity has agreed with her publishers: the cookery book survives, but not the verses.

Nevertheless, an unmistakable literary talent appears even in her receipts, in the style itself, and in the engaging titles she bestows on some of her dishes. 'The Elegant Economist's Pudding' for example, is an appetising name indeed for what is, in fact, a way of using up left-over Christmas pudding. 'Poor Author's Pudding' is contrasted with 'The Publisher's Pudding', which 'can scarcely be made *too rich*'. The italics are her own, the poor author's. Titles such as these would seem to be her own and not traditional – she certainly admits to 'The Good Daughter's Mincemeat Pudding', and 'The Welcome Guest's Own Pudding'. The encouraging asides such as 'Good and Wholesome' or 'excellent', are hers too. 'Common' is used in the sense of 'ordinary'.

She must have been a remarkable woman. To be an unmarried

woman (there were dark hints of an equivocal past) who wrote signed poetry and newspaper articles was to be not particularly respectable in those Victorian times, and it must have taken some strength of character to withstand the pressures of the conventions. Perhaps that was the reason that she so readily accepted the invitation to write about cooking, a 'womanly' occupation that might stifle some of the criticism. Poet though she might have been, she is practical indeed in some of her comments in her writing on cookery – on potatoes, for example (her book was published at the height of the Irish famine). And she can observe sharply that 'it is not so much cookery books which we need half so much as cooks really trained to a knowledge of their duties, and suited ... to families of different grades', while being prepared to suggest that 'innovation on established usages is, however, sometimes to be recommended'.

She was writing at a particularly interesting time. The Industrial Revolution was changing England from an almost completely rural to a largely urban nation, there were great contrasts between plenty and want, and the new railways were beginning to distribute goods over the entire country in a way hitherto unknown. It is noticeable how many commodities she mentions were to be bought in shops, that until then had either not been available or were expected to be made at home, including preserves, bottled sauces, and even bread; and a wide range of fruits was already being imported. Eliza Acton lived her adult life in Tonbridge and Hampstead, both sophisticated places where a variety of goods would be readily available, and this in itself helps to make her book seem more up to date and less merely 'quaint' than those of many of her contemporaries. Also, as she was unmarried, and catering presumably for a small adult household, her receipts seem better geared to the households of today.

But in spite of the change in urban habits, it was still a period of eating at home: restaurants as we know them now had not yet come into existence. There were clubs, chop houses, and inns for the men or for travellers, but women did not dine out, and the habit of dining out for pleasure had not been formed. The many cookery books of the period were not written for the grand houses, nor for servants, many of whom could not read or write, but for the rising and expanding middle classes, and *Modern Cookery* is dedicated to 'the young housekeepers of England', and written simply and clearly for those who ran a modest household.

'It is a popular error to imagine that what is called good cookery is adapted only to the establishments of the wealthy, and that it is beyond the reach of those who are not affluent ... merely to please the eye by such fanciful and elaborate decorations as distinguish many modern dinners, or to flatter the palate by the production of new and enticing dainties ought not to be the *principal* aim, at least, of any work on cookery.

'Why should not *all* classes participate in the benefit to be derived from nourishment calculated to sustain healthfully the powers of life? And why should the English, as a people, remain more ignorant than their continental neighbours of so simple a matter as that of preparing it for themselves?'

These are remarks as apt now as when they were written, and in the Preface to the first edition of *Modern Cookery* she points out that she tries, 'to supply, by such thoroughly explicit and minute instructions as, may we trust, be readily comprehended and carried out by any class of learners', mentioning proudly the 'summary appended to the receipts, of the different ingredients which they contain, with the exact proportions of each, and the precise time required to dress the whole. This shows at a glance what articles have to be prepared beforehand, and the hour at which they must be ready; while it affords great facility as well, for an estimate of the expense attending them.'

Indeed, she may well be proud of this, for the receipts are set out as well and as clearly as any I have come across, and while allowance may have to be made for the differences in cooking times associated by the use of modern cookers, they 'may be *perfectly depended on*'.

There is a short chapter in this book on Bread Making, a subject that so interested Eliza Acton as to cause her to publish her *English Bread Book* in 1857; and there is some evidence that she was also preparing, though she never finished, another cookery book.

Eliza Acton died in 1859, and although we can say as she did a century ago, that writers on cookery, 'happily for us, abound at the present day', she is still worthy of her place in the honourable line of their predecessors – proud of the best plain English dishes, yet not ashamed to learn from abroad; frugal, practical and, as I hope will be apparent in the following pages, always lucid and readable.

ELIZABETH RAY

Note. Editorial introductions to certain chapters, interpolations in the text, and footnotes are printed in italic. Miss Acton's footnotes are distinguished by an asterisk*, the editor's by a dagger†.

INTRODUCTION

by Elizabeth David

Eliza Acton's *Modern Cookery*, first published in 1845 by Long-mans, preceded Mrs Beeton's *Household Management* by sixteen years; during the following half-century Miss Acton's work – she herself died in 1859 – was perhaps more plagiarized than even Mrs Beeton's. She refers in scathing terms in her 1855 edition to 'the unscrupulous manner in which large portions of my volume have been appropriated by contemporary authors' and indeed it is difficult to find any standard cookery compendium of the latter part of the Victorian era – works such as Warne's series of *Model Cookery* books and Cassells' *Dictionaries of Cookery*, not to mention the Beeton volumes – which do not include a quantity of Miss Acton's recipes. Although *Modern Cookery* was rarely acknowledged as the source from which these recipes stemmed, to anyone familiar with the original, every paragraph lifted from Miss Acton is unmistakable.

With rare exceptions, given as coming from sources she considered reliable beyond question, every recipe Eliza Acton wrote had been tested in her own kitchen at Bordyke House in Tonbridge, where she lived and kept house for her mother. Details which few cookery writers think important enough to include in their instructions are meticulously noted down by Miss Acton. When, for example, she gives jam and jelly recipes she tells how the results differ from year to year according to whether the summer was wet or dry, whether the fruit was picked early or late.

Not for her the all-purpose jam recipes – a pound of fruit to a pound of sugar – of today's cookery books. For each preserve she specifies the precise variety of fruit suitable, the methods and sugar content differing widely. The Orange or Stonewood plum, she says, is very insipid when ripe but makes an excellent preserve if used at its full growth, but while still hard and green. For this jam she orders 4½ lb of sugar to 6 lb of fruit. Red Imperatrice plums, a very sweet variety, require only 2 lb of sugar to 6 lb of the fruit to make 'a very rich preserve'. Mogul or Magnum Bonum plums, Bullace plums, Mussel plums, greengages, each has its separate formula. She thinks red gooseberries the only ones worth bothering with for jams, and likes them mixed with raspberries or greengages. She studies the making of strawberry jelly every season following the first appearance of her book and in the revised 1855 edition devotes a whole page to fresh explanations; some varieties of strawberry yield thinner juice than others, and jelly from these will require longer boiling than that from a rich fruit, is therefore not so brilliant in colour and will retain less of the authentic flavour. There is much in all this to explain the apparently inexplicable – why a recipe which has worked successfully several years running should suddenly produce a failure.

Miss Acton knew, and by instinct and sheer intelligence rather than by experience (this was her first cookery book, she must have worked on it for the best part of seven years, and apart from a somewhat enlarged and very cheaply produced, popular edition of *Modern Cookery*,* her only other cookery publication was a crusading little work about bread making) that many people who use cookery books tend to pay attention only to the broad outline of a recipe, rejecting, because they think it of no importance, just some finer point which makes the whole difference. So she set about making as sure as she could that the smaller details were rammed home. Having learned from her failures (anybody who does not care to admit them could not, or should not, write a cookery book) she uses them as warnings. Appended to her instructions for *Superior Pine-Apple Marmalade* is a paragraph explaining how, by placing the preserving pan on a trivet which raises it above direct contact with the burning coals or charcoal, to avoid turning your jam to 'a strange sort of compound, for which it is difficult to find a name, and which results from the sugar being subjected – when in combination with the acid of the

---

* *The People's Book of Modern Cookery*. Simpkin, Marshall, Hamilton, Kent and Co. My copy is the 35th edition, undated.

fruit – to a degree of heat which converts it into caramel or highly boiled barley sugar'. Nobody could so accurately describe this unnerving occurrence if they had not actually seen it happening; and the preventative is still applicable today.

One example of the Acton technique which I have always admired is demonstrated by the simplest possible recipe for sole cooked in cream. After first preparing some very fresh middling sized sole with 'exceeding nicety' you are to simmer them for two minutes only in boiling salted water; you lift them out, drain them, and put them in a wide pan with as much sweet rich cream as will nearly cover them; the dish is seasoned with pounded mace, cayenne, and salt. You cook the fish 'softly, from six to ten minutes or until the flesh parts readily from the bones'. She directs then that you at once 'remove them to the serving dish, stir the juice of half a lemon to the sauce, pour it over the soles and send them immediately to table'. She gives an alternative flavouring for the sauce, 'some lemon rind may be boiled in the cream, if approved', and says that you can thicken it should you think necessary (Miss Acton, one fancies, did not) with a small teaspoonful of arrowroot very smoothly mixed with a little milk *before* the lemon juice is added. Now, in two lines, comes a recapitulation of the whole recipe: 'Soles, 3 or 4; boiled in water for 2 minutes. Cream, ½ to whole pint; salt, mace, cayenne; fish stewed 6 to 10 minutes. Juice of half a lemon.'

These summings up at the end of a recipe, entirely Miss Acton's own invention and at the time quite revolutionary in English cookery writing, were subsequently copied by Mrs Beeton, who chose to place them at the head of each recipe, where they carry much less impact. What Miss Acton then does, in a final brief paragraph, is to throw out a fresh piece of information. 'In Cornwall, the fish is laid at once into thick clotted cream and stewed entirely in it' – and uses it to bring the reader back to what she considered the vital initial instruction – 'but this method gives to the sauce, which ought to be extremely delicate, a coarse fishy flavour which the previous boil in water prevents.'

Those final lines provide a clue to what makes good cookery instruction. The author's little piece of knowledge about Cornish regional recipes opens up new possibilities for us; she lets us know that she has tried variations and tested the Cornish cream recipe, she warns us that she thinks it slovenly, she prefers her own, she tells us why. If we can't be bothered with the processes she recommends, we know what to expect.

Over and over again, reading *Modern Cookery* – for twenty years the book has been my beloved companion – I have marvelled at the illuminating and decisive qualities of Miss Acton's recipes. Remark these directions for the beating of egg whites for a sponge cake:

> The excellence of the whole depends much on the manner in which the eggs are whisked; this should be done as lightly as possible, but it is a mistake to suppose that they cannot be too long beaten, as after they are brought to a state of perfect firmness they are injured by a continuation of the whisking and will at times curdle, and render a cake heavy from this cause.

There you have, in under one hundred words (Madame Saint-Ange, in some ways the twentieth-century French equivalent of Eliza Acton, devotes eight closely written pages to the explanation of these little facts of kitchen life) the simple explanation of a million leaden sponge cakes – and for that matter of several million failed soufflés.

And again, a piece of cookery lore no doubt well known in the mid-nineteenth century but in our own day almost forgotten:

> When in very sultry weather cream becomes acid ... it may still be made available for delicate pastry-crust, and superlative cakes, biscuits and bread; but if ever so slightly putrid it will be fit only to be thrown away.

Now, plenty of less meticulous writers may tell you to use sour milk or cream for scone or pancake mixtures, although they may not appreciate that cream is often better than butter for pastry (particularly for brioche dough) but what especially we learn from that paragraph of Eliza Acton's is one of the most valuable of all lessons in the conduct of the kitchen: avoid waste when it is avoidable; when it is not, we must face up to the rejection of any ingredient which is in the least degree dubious.

For points upon which she wishes to express criticism Eliza Acton reserves an irony formidable in its balanced brevity. Here she is commenting upon the wilfully haphazard cook:

Many indifferent cooks pique themselves on never doing anything by rule ... the consequence is repeated failure in all they attempt to do ...

and on a popular misconception regarding the process of braising:

Common cooks sometimes stew meat in a mixture of butter and water, and call it braising ...

Then comes the constructive, the positive direction:

No attempt should be made to braise a joint in any vessel that is not very nearly of its own size.

How was it then that this peerless writer came to be superseded by imitators so limited in experience, and in capacity of expression so inferior?

I think that Miss Acton's eclipse came about because, born in 1799, she was in taste and in spirit, a child of the eighteenth century. Although so masterly an innovator in style and method she was, in full mid-nineteenth century, living in the manner and writing of a style of English domestic life already doomed. Her book was the final expression, the crystallization, of pre-Industrial England's taste in food and attitude to cookery. The dishes she describes and the ingredients which went into them would have been familiar to Jane Austen and Lord Byron, to Fanny Burney and Tobias Smollett. They would have been served at the tables of great political hostesses such as Lady Melbourne, and of convivial country gentlemen like Parson Woodforde.

By 1845, when Eliza Acton's book first saw the light of day, this rural England was vanishing fast. Radical changes were about to overtake English cooking. To some of them, such as the influence exercised by Baron Liebig's chemical and nutritional theories, Miss Acton paid admiring tribute when in 1855 she revised her book. Others, less edifying, she ignored. In 1840 for example, there had been launched a commercial product called Birds Custard Powder. What we know as modern cookery, and it had little to do with Eliza Acton's version, was on its way.

In 1861, two years after Miss Acton's death, appeared Mrs Beeton's *Household Management*. By 1906, when the most voluminous and the most famous of all the Beeton editions came out (Mrs Beeton herself had been dead for forty years and this volume, edited and very largely re-written by a professional chef of Swiss origin, contained little of the original work), the Beeton books and their competitors, Cassell's and Warne's series of Cookery dictionaries and compendiums directed at all classes of the community, were the kitchen manuals to be found in every literate household in the land.

Although until 1914 Eliza Acton's book was still selling, and in the face of heavy competition, after 1918 Messrs Longmans allowed the book to lapse. No doubt their judgement was correct. The English public had become accustomed to cookery books put together by syndicates of editors and recipe compilers rather than written as the expression of one author's experience and beliefs. In other words, housewives and cooks did not read cookery books, they merely looked up recipes. A book such as Miss Acton's written as a coherent whole, is essentially one to be read, as it is written, with intelligence and understanding and application.

The young women of today, who love good cooking and strive to understand its technical complexities in a way in which their grandmothers did not because they simply were unaware of them, will bless Miss Acton for her clarity, for her positive attitude and for the memorable comments and instructions which bejewel her pages.

We also have cause to be grateful to Messrs Longmans, and to Elizabeth Ray whose notes and comments are expressed with an economy which even Eliza Acton might have envied. They have brought back to us the greatest cookery book in our language in a form which makes us see that after all Eliza Acton was not, and has never been, superseded. She was simply, for a generation or two, eclipsed. Temporary eclipse has often been the fate of great innovators. In a way it is posterity's compliment to genius.

London   ELIZABETH DAVID
June 1968

VOCABULARY OF TERMS
USED IN MODERN COOKERY

ASPIC – fine transparent jelly, in which cold game, poultry, fish, etc., are moulded; and which serves also to decorate or garnish them.

ASSIETTE VOLANTE – a dish which is handed round the table without ever being placed upon it. Small *fondus* in paper cases are often served thus; and various other preparations, which require to be eaten very hot.

BAY SALT – a coarse-grained, very pure salt. Nowadays this can be bought in fine powdered form, and is much saltier than 'table' salt. In general, the kind of salt used in the following receipts, unless otherwise stated, would be like 'cooking' salt.

BAIN MARIE – a vessel containing water, in which smaller dishes are placed to keep hot, or to cook more gently than when placed directly on the stove or in the oven.

BLANQUETTE – a kind of fricassee.

BOUDIN – a somewhat expensive dish, formed of the French forcemeat called *quenelles,* composed either of game, poultry, butcher's meat, or fish, moulded frequently into the form of a *rouleau,* or sausage, and gently poached until it is firm; then sometimes broiled or fried, but as frequently served plain.

BOUILLI – boiled beef, or other meat, beef being more generally understood by the term.

BOUILLIE – a sort of hasty pudding.

BOUILLON – broth.

CASSEROLE – a stewpan; and the name also given to a rice-crust, when moulded in the form of a pie, then baked and filled with a mince or *purée* of game, or with a *blanquette* of white meat.

COCHINEAL – a red colouring liquid, without flavour.

COLLOPS – dishes made of minced or small pieces of meat.

CONSOMMÉ – very strong rich stock, or gravy.

COURT BOUILLON – a preparation of vegetables and wine, in which (in expensive cookery) fish is boiled.

CRIMP – 'to crimp fish' is to cut the edges of the slices to make the fish cook more crisply, and is done only when the fish is very fresh, so also implies freshness.

CROUSTADE – a case or crust formed of bread, in which minces, *purées* of game, and other preparations are served. (Also made of pastry, and similar to, but larger than, a *vol-au-vent*.)

CROÛTON – a sippet of bread, usually fried, to add to soups as a garnish.

DUTCH OVEN – a metal box, the open side of which is placed towards an open fire which heats it.

ENTRÉE – a first-course side or corner dish. (Neither roasts nor removes come under the denomination of *entrées*; and the same remark applies equally to the *entrements* in the second course.)

ENTREMETS – a second-course side or corner dish.

ESPAGNOLE – or Spanish sauce – a brown gravy of high savour.

FAGGOT – a bunch of herbs for flavouring stews, etc.

FARCE – forcemeat.

FLAPS – flat mushrooms.

FONDU – a cheese *soufflé*.

GÂTEAU – a cake, also a pudding, as *Gâteau de Riz;* sometimes also a kind of tart.

HORS D'ŒUVRES – small dishes of anchovies, sardines, and other relishes of the kind, served in the first course.

ISINGLASS – a substance used for making jelly, when calves feet were not used. Nowadays gelatine, in leaf or powdered form is used instead.

LARDING – strips of bacon or pork fat threaded with a special needle through a joint of lean meat. More commonly done in France than in England, and now mostly done by the butcher.

LARDOONS – the strips of fat used in larding.

LISBON SUGAR – fine white sugar in powder form.

MACARONCINI – a small kind of macaroni.

MAIGRE – made without meat (a *Jour Maigre* is a fast day or meatless day).

MATELOTE – a rich and expensive stew of fish with wine, generally of carp, eels, or trout.

MERINGUE – a cake or icing, made of sugar and whites of egg beaten to a snow.

MERINGUÉ – covered or iced with a meringue mixture.

MERRYTHOUGHT – the wishbone of a bird.

NOUILLES – a paste made of yolks of eggs and flour, then cut small like vermicelli.

PANADA – bread soaked in milk or gravy and squeezed dry, and which forms the base for many forcemeats. From the French *pain*.

PURÉE – meat or vegetables, reduced to a smooth pulp, and then mixed with sufficient liquid to form a thick sauce or soup.

QUENELLES – French forcemeat.

RATAFIA – a strong, sweet *apéritif* wine from France, not in much use today, but was very popular in the last century as a mid-morning drink, with which were eaten small biscuits, rather like macaroons, also called Ratafias.

RISSOLES – small fried pastry, either sweet or savoury.

SALAMANDER – a metal utensil, with a flat round head, which was heated over the fire until thoroughly hot, then used to brown the top of a dish without cooking it further. They are still obtainable but not so much used now, as the grill of a modern cooker is often used instead.

STOCK – the unthickened broth or gravy which forms the basis of soups and sauces.

TAMMY – a strainer made of fine, thin, woollen canvas.

TIMBALE – a sort of pie made in a mould.

TOURTE – a delicate kind of tart baked generally in a shallow tin pan, or without any.

TRIVET – a stand upon which a saucepan is placed in the stove to keep it a little distance from the fiercest heat of the fire.

TOUS-LES-MOIS – a superior version of arrowroot.

WATER-SOUCHY – a fish soup.

WEIGHTS AND MEASURES

Although there is a difference between the British and American standard cup measures, the proportion of teaspoon to tablespoon is the same in both. Therefore as cup measures are not generally used in these receipts, which are given in measurements of ounces and spoonsful, the receipts can be used quite easily, the difference being that the use of the British spoon will give a slightly larger yield than the American.

The drachm is a measure referred to occasionally in the receipts. This is now hardly ever used in cookery as a measure, and is so small that it can best be described as a very small pinch, or a drop.

1½ teaspoons	= 1 dessertspoon
3 teaspoons	= 1 tablespoon
1½ dessertspoons	= 1 tablespoon
2 tablespoons	= 1 ounce (liquid)
8 ounces	= 1 American cup
10 ounces	= 1 British cup
5 ounces (liquid)	= 1 gill
16 ounces (liquid)	= 1 American pint
20 ounces (liquid)	= 1 Imperial pint
16 ounces	= 1 pound

[Note: Eliza Acton was writing before the introduction of the Imperial pint into England, therefore, in the receipts that follow, her pint was 16 liquid ounces, the same as the American pint today.]

It must be remembered that the cooking stove upon which these receipts were prepared would be a solid fuel range, probably fired with wood. Consequently, allowance must be made in timing if they are to be used on modern electric or gas cookers, which are much quicker to heat and more flexible to adjust.

Dishes of vegetables, for instance, will take less time, as the time allowed in bringing cold water to the boil can easily be halved.

A 'clear' fire for boiling, and a 'brisk' oven for baking will be hot, the oven at about 400°–450°.

1

SOUPS

This opening chapter of Eliza Acton speaks for itself, and although some of the receipts which follow may be too elaborate or complicated for the smaller households of today, many, particularly those based on vegetables, will be found to be easy and good.

Baron Liebig, referred to many times, was the Baron Justus Liebig, whose 'Researches on the Chemistry of Food' appeared in 1847, and who obviously influenced Eliza Acton very strongly.

The longest and most complicated are omitted, among them those for Mock Turtle, as no one nowadays is likely to make such an elaborate affair, involving a whole calf's head and 8 lb of beef cooked for 8 hours. The Mock Turtle is best remembered by Tenniel's drawings.

In Eliza Acton's day 'soup' was the food for the poor, and the charitable would make gruel to give to the less fortunate. Too often, it would be mostly hot water with a few vegetables floating in it, but any of the cheaper soups in this book would have been good and nourishing.

INGREDIENTS WHICH MAY ALL BE USED FOR MAKING SOUP OF VARIOUS KINDS

Beef – Mutton – Veal – Hams – Salted Pork – Fat Bacon – Pigs' Ears and Feet – Venison – Black and Moor Game – Partridges – Pheasants – Wild Pigeons – Hares – Rabbits – Turkeys – Fowls – Tame Pigeons – Sturgeon – Conger Eel, with all sorts of Fish usually eaten – All Shell-Fish – Every kind of Vegetable and Herb fit for food – Butter – Milk – Eggs – Sago – Arrowroot – Indian Corn – Hominy – Soujee – Tapioca – Pearl Barley – Oatmeal – Polenta – Macaroni – Vermicelli – Semoulina, and other Italian Pastes.

The art of preparing good, wholesome, palatable soups, *without great expense*, which is so well understood in France, and in other countries where they form part of the daily food of all classes of the people, has hitherto been very much neglected in England;* yet it really presents no difficulties which a little practice, and the most common degree of care, will not readily overcome; and we strongly recommend increased attention to it, not only on account of the loss and inconvenience which ignorance of it occasions in many households, but because a better knowledge of it will lead naturally to improvement in other branches of cookery connected with it in which our want of skill is now equally apparent.

We have endeavoured to show by the list at the beginning of this chapter the immense number of different articles of which soup may be in turn compounded. It is almost superfluous to add, that it may be rendered at pleasure exceedingly rich, or simple in the extreme; composed, in fact, of all that is most choice in diet, or of little beyond herbs and vegetables.

From the varied produce of a well-stored kitchen garden, it may be made excellent at a very trifling cost; and where fish is fresh and abundant it may be cheaply supplied nearly equal in quality to that for which a full proportion of meat is commonly used.

It is best suited to the colder seasons of the year when thickened well with rice, semoulina, pearl barley, or other ingredients of the same nature; and adapted to the summer months when lighter and more refreshing. Families who have resided much abroad, and those accustomed to continental modes of service, prefer it usually *in any form* to the more solid and heavy dishes which still often supersede it altogether at our tables (except at those of the more affluent classes of society, where it appears, as a matter of course, in the daily bills of fare), and which are so *oppressive*, not only to foreigners, but to all persons generally to whom circumstances have rendered them unaccustomed diet; and many a housekeeper who is compelled by a narrow income to adopt a system of rigid domestic economy, would find it assists greatly in furnishing comfortable meals in a very frugal manner, if the proper modes of making it were fully comprehended as they ought to be.

* The inability of servants to prepare delicately and well even a little broth suited to an invalid, is often painfully evident in cases of illness, not only in common English life, but where the cookery is supposed to be of a superior order.

TO MAKE NOUILLES
(*An elegant substitute for Vermicelli*)

Wet with the yolks of four eggs, as much fine dry sifted flour as will make them into a firm but very smooth paste. Roll it out as thin as possible, and cut into bands of about an inch and a quarter in width. Dust them lightly with flour, and place four of them one upon the other. Cut them obliquely into the finest possible strips; separate them with the point of a knife, and spread them upon writing paper, so that they may dry a little before they are used. Drop them gradually into the boiling soup, and in ten minutes they will be done.

Various other forms may be given to this paste at will. It may be divided into a sort of ribbon macaroni; or stamped with small confectionary cutters into different shapes. It is much used in the more delicate departments of cookery, and when cut as for soup, and prepared as for the *Genoises à la Reine* makes very superior puddings, pastry, fritters, and other sweet dishes.

TO FRY BREAD TO SERVE WITH SOUP

Cut some slices a quarter of an inch thick from a stale loaf; pare off the crust and divide the bread into dice, or cut it with a small paste-cutter into any other form. For half a pound of bread put two ounces of the best butter into a frying-pan, and when it is quite melted, add the bread; keep it turned over a gentle fire until it is equally coloured to a very pale brown, then drain it from the butter, and dry it on a soft cloth, or on a sheet of paper placed before a clear fire upon a dish, or upon a sieve reversed.

SIPPETS À LA REINE

Having cut the bread as for common sippets [*see preceding receipt*], spread it on a dish, and pour over it a few spoonsful of thin cream, or of good milk: let it soak for an hour, then fry it in fresh butter of a delicate brown, drain and serve the sippets very hot.

EXTRACT OF BEEF, OR,
VERY STRONG PLAIN BEEF GRAVY SOUP
(*Baron Liebig's Receipt*)

Take a pound of good, juicy beef (rumpsteak is best for the purpose), from which all the skin and fat that can possibly be separated from it, has been cut away. Chop it up small like sausage-meat; then mix it thoroughly with an exact pint of cold water, and place it on the side of the stove to heat *very slowly indeed*; and give it an occasional stir. It may stand two or three hours before it is allowed to simmer, and will then require at the utmost but fifteen minutes gentle boiling. Professor Liebig directs even less time than this, but the soup then occasionally retains a raw flavour which is distasteful. Salt should be added when the boiling first commences, and for invalids, this, in general, is the only seasoning required. When the extract is thus far prepared, it may be poured from the meat into a basin, and allowed to stand until any particles of fat it may exhibit on the surface can be skimmed off entirely, and the sediment has subsided and left the soup quite clear (which it speedily becomes), when it may be poured gently off, heated in a clean saucepan, and served at once. It will contain all the nutriment which the meat will yield. The scum should always be well cleared from the surface of the soup as it accumulates.

To make light beef tea or broth, merely increase the proportion of water to a pint and a half or a quart; but in all else proceed as above.

Meat (without fat or skin), 1 lb; cold water, exact pint: heating 2 hours or more; to boil 15 minutes at the utmost. Beef tea or broth – Beef, 1 lb; water, 1½ pint or 1 quart.

CLEAR, PALE GRAVY SOUP OR CONSOMMÉ

Rub a deep stewpan or soup-pot with butter, and lay into it three quarters of a pound of ham freed entirely from fat, skin, and rust [*crusted salt*], four pounds of leg or neck of veal, and the same

5

weight of lean beef, all cut into thick slices; set it over a clear and rather brisk fire, until the meat is of a fine amber-colour; it must be often moved, and closely watched, that it may not stick to the pan, nor burn. When it is equally browned, lay the bones upon it, and pour in gradually four quarts of boiling water. Take off the scum carefully as it rises, and throw in a pint of cold water at intervals to bring it quickly to the surface. When no more appears, add two ounces of salt, two onions, two large carrots, two turnips, one head of celery, a faggot of savoury herbs, a dozen cloves, half a teaspoonful of whole white pepper, and two large blades of mace. Let the soup boil gently from five hours and a half to six hours and a half: then strain it through a very clean fine cloth, laid in a hair sieve. When it is perfectly cold, remove every particle of fat from the top; and, in taking out the soup, leave the sediment untouched; heat in a clean pan the quantity required for table, add salt to it if needed, and a few drops of chili or of cayenne vinegar. Harvey's sauce, or very fine mushroom catsup, may be substituted for these. When thus prepared the soup is ready to serve: it should be accompanied by pale sippets of fried bread, or sippets *à la reine* (At tables where English modes of service entirely prevailed, clear gravy-soup, until very recently, was always accompanied by dice, or sippets as they are called, of delicately toasted bread. These are now seldom seen, but some Italian paste, or nicely prepared vegetable, is served *in* the soup instead.) Rice, maccaroni in lengths or in rings, vermicelli, or *nouilles*, may in turn be used to vary it; but they must always be boiled apart, till tender, in broth or water, and well drained before they are slipped into it. The addition of young vegetables, too, and especially of asparagus, will convert it into superior spring-soup; but they, likewise, must be separately cooked.

VERMICELLI SOUP
(*Potage au Vermicelle*)

Drop very lightly, and by degrees, six ounces of vermicelli, broken rather small, into three quarts of boiling bouillon, or clear gravy soup; let it simmer for half an hour over a gentle fire, and stir it often. This is the common French mode of making vermicelli soup, and we can recommend it as a particularly good one for family use. In England it is customary to soak, or to blanch the vermicelli, then to drain it well, and to stew it for a shorter time in the soup; the quantity also must be reduced quite two ounces, to suit modern taste.

Bouillon, or gravy soup, 3 quarts; vermicelli, 6 oz; 30 minutes. Or, soup, 3 quarts; vermicelli, 4 oz.; blanched in boiling water 5 minutes; stewed in soup 10 to 15 minutes.

MADEMOISELLE JENNY LIND'S SOUP
(*Authentic Receipt*)

This receipt does not merely bear the name of 'Mademoiselle Lind', but is in reality that of the soup which was constantly served to her, as it was prepared by her own cook. We are indebted for it to the kindness of the very popular Swedish authoress, Miss Bremer, who received it direct from her accomplished countrywoman.

The following proportions are for a tureen of this excellent *potage*: Wash a quarter of a pound of the best pearl sago until the water poured from it is clear; then stew it quite tender and very thick in water or thick broth (it will require nearly or quite a quart of liquid, which should be poured to it cold, and heated slowly): then mix gradually with it a pint of good boiling cream, and the yolks of four fresh eggs, and mingle the whole carefully with two quarts of strong veal or beef stock, which should always be kept ready boiling. Send the soup immediately to table.

THE LORD MAYOR'S SOUP
(*Author's Receipt*)

We prefer to have this soup made, in part, the evening before it is wanted. Add five quarts of water to the ears and feet [*see ingredients below*]; skim it thoroughly when it first boils, and throw in a tablespoonful of salt, two onions of moderate size, a small head of celery, a bunch of herbs, two whole carrots, a small teaspoonful of white peppercorns, and a blade of mace. Stew these softly until the ears and feet are perfectly tender, and, after they are lifted out, let the liquor be kept *just simmering* only, while they are being boned, that it may not be too much reduced. Put the bones back into it, and stew them as gently as possible for an hour, then strain the soup into a clean pan, and set it by until the morrow in a cool place. The flesh should be cut into dice while it is still warm and covered with the cloth before it becomes *quite* cold. To prepare the soup for table clear the stock from fat and sediment, put it into a very clean stewpan, or deep saucepan, and stir to it when it boils, six ounces of the finest rice-flour smoothly mixed with a quarter of a teaspoonful of cayenne, three times as much of mace and salt, the strained juice of a lemon, three tablespoonsful of Harvey's sauce, and half a pint of good sherry or Madeira. Simmer the whole for six or eight minutes, add more salt if needed, stir the soup often, and skim it thoroughly; put in the meat and herbs, and after they have boiled gently for five minutes, dish the soup, add forcemeat-balls or not, at pleasure, and send it to table quickly.

Moderate-sized pigs' feet, 8; ears, 4; water, 5 quarts; salt, 1 tablespoonful; onions, 2; celery, 1 head; carrots, 2; bunch of herbs; peppercorns, 1 small teaspoonful; mace, 1 blade: 3½ to 4½ hours. Stock, 5 pints; rice-flour, 6 oz; cayenne, ¼ teaspoonful; mace and salt, each ¾ of a teaspoonful; juice of 1 lemon; Harvey's sauce, 3 tablespoonsful; sherry or Madeira, ½ pint: 6 to 8 minutes. Savoury herbs, 2 tablespoonsful: 5 minutes.

Obs. 1. Should the quantity of stock exceed five pints, an additional ounce or more of rice must be used, and the flavouring be altogether increased in proportion. Of the minced herbs, two-thirds should be parsley, and the remainder equal parts of lemon thyme and winter savoury, unless sweet basil should be at hand, when a teaspoonful of it may be substituted for half of the parsley. To some tastes a seasoning of sage would be acceptable; and a slice or two of lean ham will much improve the flavour of the soup.

Obs. 2. Both this soup, and the preceding one, may be rendered very rich by substituting strong *bouillon* or good veal broth for water, in making them.

CHESTNUT SOUP

Strip the outer rind from some fine, sound Spanish chestnuts, throw them into a large pan of warm water, and as soon as it becomes too hot for the fingers to remain in it, take it from the fire, lift out the chestnuts, peel them quickly, and throw them into cold water as they are done; wipe and weigh them; take three-quarters of a pound for each quart of soup, cover them with good stock, and stew them gently for upwards of three-quarters of an hour, or until they break when touched with a fork; drain, and pound them smoothly, or bruise them to a mash with a strong spoon, and rub them through a fine sieve; mix with them by slow degrees the proper quantity of stock; add sufficient mace, cayenne, and salt to season the soup, and stir it often until it boils. Three-quarters of a pint of rich cream, or even less will greatly improve it. The stock in which the chestnuts are boiled can be used for the soup when its sweetness is not objected to; or it may in part be added to it.

Chestnuts, 1½ lb: stewed from ¾ to 1 hour. Soup, 2 quarts; seasoning of salt, mace, and cayenne: 1 to 3 minutes. Cream, ¾ pint (when used).

JERUSALEM ARTICHOKE, OR PALESTINE SOUP

Wash and pare quickly some freshly-dug artichokes, and to preserve their colour, throw them into spring water as they are done, but do not let them remain in it after all are ready. Boil three pounds of them in water for ten minutes; lift them out, and slice them into three pints of boiling stock; when they have stewed gently in this from fifteen to twenty minutes, press them with the soup, through a fine sieve, and put the whole into a clean sauce-

9

pan with a pint and a half more of stock; add sufficient salt and cayenne to season it, skim it well, and after it has simmered for two or three minutes, stir it to a pint of rich boiling cream. Serve it immediately.

Artichokes, 3 lb, boiled in water: 10 minutes. Veal stock, 3 pints: 15 to 20 minutes. Additional stock, 1½ pints; little cayenne and salt: 2 to 3 minutes. Boiling cream, 1 pint.

Obs. The palest veal stock, as for white soup, should be used for this; but for a family dinner, or where economy is a consideration, excellent mutton-broth, made the day before and perfectly cleared from fat, will answer very well as a substitute; milk too may in part take the place of cream when this last is scarce: the proportion of artichokes should then be increased a little.

Vegetable-marrow, when young, makes a superior soup even to this, which is an excellent one. It should be well pared, trimmed, and sliced into a small quantity of boiling veal stock or broth, and when perfectly tender, pressed through a fine sieve, and mixed with more stock and some cream. In France the marrow is stewed, first in butter, with a large mild onion or two also sliced; and afterwards in a quart or more of water, which is poured gradually to it; it is next passed through a tammy,* seasoned with pepper and salt, and mixed with a pint or two of milk and a little cream.

* Derived from the French *tamis*, which means a sieve or strainer.

COMMON CARROT SOUP

The most easy method of making this favourite English soup is to boil some highly coloured carrots quite tender in water slightly salted, then to pound or mash them to a smooth paste and to mix with them boiling gravy soup or strong beef broth in the proportion of two quarts to a pound and a half of the prepared carrots; then to pass the whole through a strainer, to season it with salt and cayenne, to heat it in a clean stewpan, and to serve it immediately. If only the red outsides of the carrots be used, the colour of the soup will be very bright; they should be weighed after they are mashed. Turnip soup may be prepared in the same manner.

Obs. An experienced and observant cook will know the proportion of vegetables required to thicken this soup appropriately, without having recourse to weights and measures; but the learner had always better proceed by *rule*.

Soup, 2 quarts; pounded carrot, 1½ lb; salt, cayenne: 5 minutes.

A FINER CARROT SOUP

Scrape very clean, and cut away all blemishes from some highly-flavoured red carrots; wash, and wipe them dry, and cut them into quarter-inch slices. Put into a large stewpan three ounces of the best butter, and when it is melted, add two pounds of the sliced carrots, and let them stew gently for an hour without browning; pour to them then four pints and a half of brown gravy soup, and when they have simmered from fifty minutes to an hour, they ought to be sufficiently tender. Press them through a sieve or strainer with the soup; add salt, and cayenne if required; boil the whole gently for five minutes, take off all the scum, and serve the soup as hot as possible.

Butter, 3 oz; carrots, 2 lb; 1 hour. Soup, 4½ pints: 50 to 60 minutes. Salt, cayenne: 5 minutes.

BUCHANAN CARROT SOUP
(*Excellent*)

Make two quarts of soup by either of the foregoing receipts, using for it good brown stock (for a common family dinner strong beef broth will do). Mix smoothly with a little liquid, a tablespoonful of fine currie-powder, and boil it in the soup for ten minutes; or instead of this, season it rather highly with cayenne pepper, and then stir into it from six ounces to half a pound of Patna rice boiled dry and tender as for a currie. The whole may then remain by the side of the fire without even simmering for ten minutes longer, and then be served immediately. As a winter *potage* this is generally much liked. A spoonful of *Captain White's* currie-paste will flavour it very agreeably if smoothly diluted, and simmered in it for two or three minutes: we prefer it always to the powder. Three or four ounces of pearl barley well washed, soaked for some hours, and boiled extremely tender in broth or water, may on occasion be substituted for the rice.

A QUICKLY MADE TURNIP SOUP

Pare and slice into three pints of veal or mutton stock or of good broth, three pounds of young mild turnips; stew them gently from twenty-five to thirty minutes, or until they can be reduced quite to pulp; rub the whole through a sieve, and add to it another quart of stock, a seasoning of salt and white pepper, and one lump of sugar; give it two or three minutes' boil, skim and serve it. A large white onion when the flavour is liked may be sliced and stewed with the turnips. A little cream improves much the colour of this soup.

Turnips, 3 lb; soup, 5 pints: 25 to 30 minutes.

POTATO SOUP

Mash to a smooth paste three pounds of good mealy potatoes, which have been steamed, or boiled very dry; mix with them by degrees, two quarts of boiling broth, pass the soup through a strainer, set it again on the fire, add pepper and salt, and let it boil for five minutes. Take off entirely the black scum that will rise upon it, and serve it very hot with fried or toasted bread. Where the flavour is approved, two ounces of onions minced and fried a light brown, may be added to the soup, and stewed in it for ten minutes before it is sent to table.

Potatoes, 3 lb; broth, 2 quarts: 5 minutes. (With onions, 2 oz): 10 minutes.

APPLE SOUP

(*Soupe à la Bourguignon*)

Clear the fat from five pints of good mutton broth, *bouillon*, or shin of beef stock, and strain it through a fine sieve; add to it when it boils, a pound and a half of good cooking apples, and stew them down in it very softly to a smooth pulp; press the whole through a strainer, add a small teaspoonful of powdered ginger and plenty of pepper, simmer the soup for a couple of minutes, skim, and serve it very hot, accompanied by a dish of rice, boiled as for curries.

Broth, 5 pints; apples, 1½ lb: 25 to 40 minutes. Ginger, 1 teaspoonful; pepper, ½ teaspoonful: 2 minutes.

PARSNEP SOUP

Dissolve, over a gentle fire, four ounces of good butter, in a wide stewpan or saucepan, and slice in directly two pounds of sweet tender parsneps; let them stew very gently until all are quite soft, then pour in gradually sufficient veal stock or good broth to cover them, and boil the whole slowly from twenty minutes to half an hour; work it with a wooden spoon through a fine sieve, add as much stock as will make two quarts in all, season the soup with salt and white pepper or cayenne, give it one boil, skim, and serve it very hot. Send pale fried sippets to table with it.

Butter, 4 oz; parsnep, 2 lb: ¾ hour, or more. Stock, 1 quart: 20 to 30 minutes; 1 full quart more of stock; pepper, salt: 1 minute.

Obs. We can particularly recommend this soup to those who like the peculiar flavour of the vegetable.

SUPERLATIVE HARE SOUP

Cut down a hare into joints, and put into a soup-pot, or large stewpan, with about a pound of lean ham, in thick slices, three moderate-sized mild onions, three blades of mace, a faggot of thyme, sweet marjoram, and parsley, and about three quarts of good beef stock. Let it stew very gently for full two hours from the time of its first beginning to boil, and more, if the hare be old. Strain the soup and pound together very fine the slices of ham and all the flesh of the back, legs, and shoulders of the hare, and put this meat into a stewpan with the liquor in which it was boiled, the crumb of two French rolls, and half-pint of port wine. Set it on the stove to simmer twenty minutes; then rub it through a sieve, place it again on the stove till very hot, but do not let it boil; season it with salt and cayenne, and send it to table directly.

Hare, 1; ham, 12 to 16 oz; onions, 3 to 6; mace, 3 blades; faggot of savoury herbs; beef stock, 3 quarts: 2 hours. Crumb of 2 rolls; port wine, ½ pint; little salt and cayenne: 20 minutes.

A LESS EXPENSIVE HARE SOUP*

Pour on two pounds of neck or shin of beef and a hare well washed and carved into joints, one gallon of cold water, and when it boils and has been thoroughly skimmed, add an ounce and a half of salt, two onions, one large head of celery, three moderate-sized carrots, a teaspoonful of black peppercorns, and six cloves.

Let these stew very gently for three hours, or longer, should the hare not be perfectly tender. Then take up the principal joints, cut the meat from them, mince, and pound it to a fine paste, with the crumb of two penny rolls (or two ounces of the crumb of household bread) which has been soaked in a little of the boiling soup, and then pressed very dry in a cloth; strain, and mix smoothly with it the stock from the remainder of the hare; pass the soup through a strainer, season it with cayenne, and serve it when at the point of boiling; if not sufficiently thick, add to it a tablespoonful of arrowroot moistened with a little cold broth, and let the soup simmer for an instant afterwards. Two or three glasses of port wine, and two dozens of small forcemeat-balls, may be added to this soup with good effect.

Beef, 3 lb; hare, 1; water, 1 gallon; salt, 1½ oz; onions, 2; celery, 1 head; carrots, 3; bunch of savoury herbs; peppercorns, 1 teaspoonful; cloves, 6: 3 hours, or more. Bread, 2 oz; cayenne, arrowroot (if needed), 1 tablespoonful.

* The remains of a roasted hare, with the forcemeat and gravy, are admirably calculated for making this soup.

ECONOMICAL TURKEY SOUP

The remains of a roast turkey, even after they have supplied the usual mince and broil, will furnish a tureen of cheap and excellent soup with the addition of a little fresh meat. Cut up rather small two pounds of the neck or other lean joint of beef, and pour to it five pints of cold water. Heat these very slowly; skim the liquor when it begins to boil, and add to it an ounce of salt, a small, mild onion (the proportion of all the vegetables may be much increased when they are liked), a little celery, and the flesh and bones of the turkey with any gravy or forcemeat that may have been left with them. Let these boil gently for about three hours; then strain off the soup through a coarse sieve or cullender, and let it remain until the fat can be entirely removed from it. It may then be served merely well thickened with rice which has previously been boiled very dry as for currie, and stewed in it for about ten minutes; and seasoned with one large heaped tablespoonful or more of minced parsley, and as much salt and pepper or cayenne as it may require. This, as the reader will perceive, is a somewhat frugal preparation, by which the residue of a roast turkey may be turned to economical account; but it is a favourite soup at some good English tables, where its very simplicity is a recommendation. It can always be rendered *more expensive*, and of richer quality by the addition of lean ham or smoked beef, a larger weight of fresh meat, and catsup or other store-sauces.

The Patna, or small-grained rice, which is not so good as the Carolina, for the general purposes of cookery, ought to be served with currie. First take out the unhusked grains, then wash the rice in several waters, and put it into a large quantity of cold water: bring it gently to boil, keeping it uncovered, and boil it softly for fifteen minutes, when it will be perfectly tender, and every grain will remain distinct. Throw it into a *large* cullender, and let it drain for ten minutes near the fire; should it not then appear *quite* dry, turn it into a dish, and set it for a short time into a gentle oven, or let it steam in a clean saucepan near the fire. It should neither be stirred, except just at first, to prevent its lumping while it is still quite hard, nor touched with either fork or spoon; the stewpan may be shaken occasionally, should the rice seem to require it, and it should be thrown lightly from the cullender upon the dish. A couple of minutes before it is done, throw in some salt, and from the time of its beginning to boil remove the scum as it rises.

Patna rice, ½ lb; cold water, 2 quarts: boiled slowly, 15 minutes. Salt, 1 large teaspoonful.

Obs. This, of all the modes of boiling rice which we have tried, and they have been very numerous, is indisputably the best. The Carolina rice answers well dressed in the same manner, but requires four or five minutes longer boiling: it should never be served until it is quite tender. One or two minutes, more or less, will sometimes, from the varying quality of the grain, be requisite to render it tender.

GOOD VEGETABLE MULLAGATAWNY

Dissolve in a large stewpan or thick iron saucepan, four ounces of butter, and when it is on the point of browning, throw in four large mild onions sliced, three pounds' weight of young vegetable marrow cut in large dice and cleared from the skin and seeds, four large or six moderate-sized cucumbers, pared, split, and emptied likewise of their seeds, and from three to six large acid apples, according to the taste; shake the pan often, and stew these over a gentle fire until they are tolerably tender; then strew lightly over and mix well amongst them, three heaped table-spoonsful of mild currie powder, with nearly a third as much of salt, and let the vegetables stew from twenty to thirty minutes longer; then pour to them gradually sufficient boiling water (broth or stock if preferred) to just cover them, and when they are reduced almost to a pulp press the whole through a hair-sieve with a wooden spoon, and heat it in a clean stewpan, with as much additional liquid as will make two quarts with that which was first added. Give any flavouring that may be needed, whether of salt, cayenne, or acid, and serve the soup extremely hot. Should any butter appear on the surface, let it be carefully skimmed off, or stir in a small dessertspoonful of arrowroot (smoothly mixed with a little cold broth or water) to absorb it. Rice may be served with this soup at pleasure, but as it is of the consistence of winter peas soup, it scarcely requires any addition. The currie powder may be altogether omitted for variety, and the whole converted into a plain vegetable *potage*; or it may be rendered one of high savour, by browning all the vegetables lightly, and adding to them rich brown stock. Tomatas, when in season, may be substituted for the apples, after being divided, and freed from their seeds.

Butter, 4 oz; vegetable marrow, pared and scooped, 3 lb; large mild onions, 4; large cucumbers, 4; or middling-sized, 6; apples, or large tomatas, 3 to 6: 30 to 40 minutes. Mild currie-powder, 3 heaped tablespoonsful; salt, one small tablespoonful: 20 to 32 minutes. Water, broth, or good stock, 2 quarts.

GREEN PEAS SOUP, WITHOUT MEAT

Boil tender in three quarts of water, salted, one quart of large, full grown peas; drain and pound them in a mortar, mix with them gradually five pints of the liquor in which they were cooked, put the whole again over the fire, and stew it gently for a quarter of an hour; then press it through a hair-sieve. In the mean time, simmer in from three to four ounces of butter,* three large, or four small cucumbers pared and sliced, the hearts of three or four lettuces shred small, from one to four onions, according to the taste, cut thin, a few small sprigs of parsley, and, when the flavour is liked, a dozen leaves or more of mint roughly chopped: keep these stirred over a gentle fire for nearly or quite an hour, and strew over them a half-teaspoonful of salt, and a good seasoning of white pepper or cayenne. When they are partially done drain them from the butter, put them into the strained stock, and let the whole boil gently until all the butter has been thrown to the surface, and been entirely cleared from it; then throw in from half to three-quarters of a pint of young peas boiled as for eating, and serve the soup immediately.

When more convenient, the peas, with a portion of the liquor, may be rubbed through a sieve, instead of being crushed in a mortar; and when the colour of the soup is not so much a consideration as the flavour, they may be slowly stewed until perfectly tender in four ounces of good butter, instead of being boiled: a few green onions, and some branches of parsley may then be added to them.

Green peas, 1 quart; water, 5 pints; cucumbers, 3 to 6; lettuces, 3 or 4; onions, 1 to 4; little parsley; mint (if liked), 12 to 20 leaves; butter, 3 to 4 oz; salt, half-teaspoonful; seasoning of white pepper or cayenne: 50 to 60 minutes. Young peas, ½ to ¾ of a pint.

Obs. We must repeat that the peas for these soups must not be *old*, as when they are so, their fine sweet flavour is entirely lost, and the dried ones would have almost as good an effect; nor should they be of inferior kinds. Freshly gathered marrowfats, taken at nearly or quite their full growth, will give the best quality of soup. We are credibly informed, but cannot assert it on our own authority, that it is often made for expensive tables in early spring, with the young tender plants or 'halms' of the peas, when they are about a foot in height. They are cut off close to the ground, like small salad, we are told, then boiled and pressed through a strainer and mixed with the stock. The flavour is affirmed to be excellent.

* Some persons prefer the vegetables slowly fried to a fine brown, then drained on a sieve, and well dried before the fire; but though more savoury so, they do not improve the colour of the soup.

A CHEAP GREEN PEAS SOUP

Wash very clean and throw into an equal quantity of boiling water salted as for peas, three quarts of the shells, and leave in from twenty to thirty minutes, when they will be quite tender, turn the whole into a large strainer, and press the pods strongly with a wooden spoon. Measure the liquor, put two quarts of it into a clean deep saucepan, and when it boils add to it a quart of full grown peas, two or even three large cucumbers, as many moderate-sized lettuces freed from the coarser leaves and cut small, one large onion (or more if liked) sliced extremely thin and stewed for half an hour in a morsel of butter before it is added to the soup, or gently fried without being allowed to brown; a branch or two of parsley, and, when the flavour is liked, a dozen leaves of mint. Stew these softly for an hour, with the addition of a small teaspoon, or a larger quantity if required of salt, and a good seasoning of fine white pepper or of cayenne; then work the whole of the vegetables with the soup through a hair-sieve, heat it afresh, and send it to table with a dish of small fried sippets. The colour will not be so bright as that of the more expensive soups which precede it, but it will be excellent in flavour.

Pea-shells, 3 quarts; water, 3 quarts: 20 to 30 minutes. Liquor from these, 2 quarts; full-sized green peas, 1 quart; large cucumbers, 2 or 3; lettuces, 3 onion, 1 (or more); little parsley; mint, 12 leaves; seasoning of salt and pepper or cayenne: stewed 1 hour.

Obs. The cucumber should be pared, quartered, and freed from the seeds before they are added to the soup. The peas, as we have said already more than once, should not be *old*, but taken at their full growth, before they lose their colour: the youngest of the shells ought to be selected for the liquor.

19

Put from four to five pounds of the gristly part of the shin of beef into three quarts of cold water, and stew it very softly indeed, with the addition of the salt and vegetables directed for *bouillon* until the whole is very tender; lift out the meat, strain the liquor, and put it into a large clean saucepan, add a thickening of rice-flour or arrowroot, pepper and salt if needed, and a tablespoonful of mushroom catsup. In the mean time, cut all the meat into small, thick slices, add it to the soup, and serve it as soon as it is very hot. The thickening and catsup may be omitted, and all the vegetables, pressed through a strainer, may be stirred into the soup instead, before the meat is put back into it.

SOUP IN HASTE

Chop tolerably fine a pound of lean beef, mutton, or veal, and when it is partly done, add to it a small carrot and one small turnip cut in slices, half an ounce of celery, the white part of a moderate-sized leek or a quarter of an ounce of onion. Mince all these together, and put the whole into a deep saucepan with three pints of cold water. When the soup boils take off the scum, and add a little salt and pepper. In half an hour it will be ready to serve with or without straining: it may be flavoured at will, with cayenne, catsup, or aught else that is preferred, or it may be converted into French spring broth, by passing it through a sieve, and boiling it again for five or six minutes, with a handful of young and well washed sorrel.

Meat, 1 lb; carrot, 2 oz; celery, ½ oz; onion, ¼ oz; water, 3 pints: half an hour. Little pepper and salt.

Obs. Three pounds of beef or mutton, with two or three slices of ham, and vegetables in proportion to the above receipt, all chopped fine, and boiled in three quarts of water for an hour and a half, will make an excellent family soup on an emergency: additional boiling will of course improve it, and a little spice should be added after it has been skimmed and salted. It may easily be converted into carrot, turnip, or ground-rice soup after it is strained.

CHEAP RICE SOUP

Place a gallon of water on the fire (more or less according to the quantity of soup required), and when it boils, throw in a moderate-sized tablespoonful of salt, and two or three onions, thickly sliced, a faggot of sweet herbs, a root of celery, and three or four large carrots split down into many divisions, and cut into short lengths. Boil these gently for an hour and a half, or two hours, and then strain the liquor from them. When time will permit, let it become cold; then for each quart, take from three to four ounces of well washed rice, pour the soup on it, heat it *very* slowly, giving it an occasional stir, and stew it gently until it is perfectly tender, and the potage quite thick. A moderate seasoning of pepper, and an ounce or two of fresh butter well blended with a teaspoonful of flour, may be thoroughly stirred up with the soup before it is served; or, in lieu of the butter, the yolks of two or three new-laid eggs, mixed with a little milk, may be carefully added to it.

It may be more quickly prepared by substituting vermicelli, semoulina, or soujee for the rice, as this last will require three-quarters of an hour or more of stewing after it begins to boil, and the three other ingredients – either of which must be dropped gradually into the soup when it is in full ebullition – will be done in from twenty to thirty minutes; and two ounces will thicken sufficiently a quart of broth.

A large tablespoonful of Captain White's currie-paste, and a small one of flour, diluted with a spoonful or two of the broth, or with a little milk or cream, if perfectly mixed with the rice and stewed with it for fifteen or twenty minutes before it is dished, render it excellent; few eaters would discover that it was made without meat.

Good beef or mutton broth can be used instead of water for the above soup, and in that case the vegetables sliced small, or rubbed through a strainer, may be added to it before it is served.

An infinite variety of excellent soups may be made of fish, which may be stewed down for them in precisely the same manner as meat, and with the same addition of vegetables and herbs. When the skin is coarse or rank it should be carefully stripped off before the fish is used; and any oily particles which may float on the surface should be entirely removed from it.

In France, Jersey, Cornwall, and many other localities, the conger eel, divested of its skin, is sliced up into thick cutlets and made into soup, which we are assured by English families who have it often served at their tables, is extremely good. A half-grown fish is best for the purpose. After the soup has been strained and allowed to settle, it must be heated afresh, and rice and minced parsley may be added to it as for the turkey soup of page 15; or it may be thickened with rice-flour only, or served clear. Curried fish-soups, too, are much to be recommended.

When broth or stock has been made as above with conger eel, common eels, whitings, haddocks, codlings, fresh water fish, or any common kind, which may be at hand, flakes of cold salmon, cod fish, John Dories, or scallops of cold soles, plaice, etc.,* may be heated and served in it; and the remains of crabs or lobsters mingled with them. The large oysters sold at so cheap a rate upon the coast, and which are not much esteemed for eating raw, serve admirably for imparting flavour to soup, and the softer portions of them may be served in it after a few minutes of gentle simmering. Anchovy or any other store fish-sauce may be added with good effect to many of these pottages if used with moderation. Prawns and shrimps likewise would generally be considered an improvement to them.

For more savoury preparations, fry the fish and vegetables, lay them into the soup-pot, and add boiling, instead of cold water to them.

* Cold vegetables, cut up small, may be added with these at pleasure.

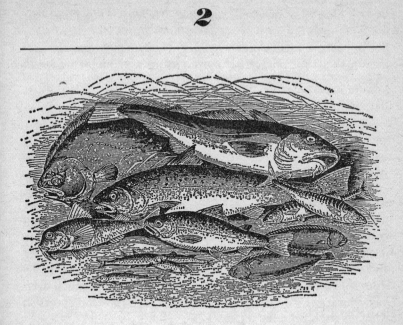

2

FISH

*As always, Eliza Acton's general directions are well worth fol-
lowing, though unfortunately many of the fish she mentions are
difficult to find nowadays, when so much of our fish eating is
confined to sole, plaice and frozen foods.*

*The receipts she gives for plain boiled fish are really only good
if the fish is very fresh, in which case they are delicious.*

*It is interesting to note how much she uses meat and fish
together – fish cooked in meat stock, meat stuffed with oysters, as
well as fish cooked in red wine.*

*Oysters are used very frequently both as dishes on their own,
or as forcemeat for other dishes, in a way that nowadays
would be wildly extravagant. But eightpence a bushel was the
price in those days and, as Sam Weller observed, 'poverty and*

oysters always seem to go together'. On the other hand, she
makes no mention of mussels or scallops, although both of these
fish are mentioned in contemporary receipt books, and she uses
scallop shells for one of her oyster receipts. It might be worth
trying some of the Acton oyster dishes with mussels.

TO CHOOSE FISH

The cook should be well acquainted with the signs of freshness
and good condition in fish, as they are most unwholesome
articles of food when stale, and many of them are also dangerous
eating when they are out of season. The eyes should always be
bright, the gills of a fine clear red, the body stiff, the flesh firm,
yet elastic to the touch, and the smell not disagreeable. When all
these marks are reversed, and the eyes are sunken, the gills very
dark in hue, the fish itself flabby and of offensive odour, it is bad,
and should be avoided. The chloride of soda, will, it is true, re-
store it to a tolerably eatable state,* if it be not very much overkept, but it will never resemble in quality and wholesomeness fish
which is fresh from the water.

A good turbot is thick and full fleshed, and the under side is of
a pale cream colour or yellowish white; when this is of a bluish
tint, and the fish is thin and soft, it should be rejected. The same
observations apply equally to soles.

The best salmon and cod fish are known by a small head, very
thick shoulders, and small tail; the scales of the former should be
bright, and its flesh of a fine red colour; to be eaten in perfection
it should be dressed as soon as it is caught, before the curd (or
white substance which lies between the flakes of flesh) has melted
and rendered the fish oily. In that state it is really crimp,† but
continues so only for a very few hours; and it bears therefore a
much higher price in the London market then, than when mellowed by having been kept a day or two.

The flesh of cod fish should be white and clear before it is
boiled, white still after it is boiled, and firm though tender, sweet
and mild in flavour, and separated easily into large flakes. Many
persons consider it rather improved than otherwise by having a

24

little salt rubbed along the inside of the backbone and letting it lie from twenty-four to forty-eight hours before it is dressed. It is sometimes served crimp like salmon, and must then be sliced as soon as it is dead, or within the shortest possible time afterwards.

Herrings, mackerel, and whitings, unless newly caught, are quite uneatable. When they are in good condition their natural colours will be very distinct and their whole appearance glossy and fresh. The herring when first taken from the water is of a silvery brightness; the back of the mackerel is of a bright green marked with dark stripes; but this becomes of a coppery colour as the fish grows stale. The whiting is of a pale brown or fawn colour with a pinkish tint; but appears dim and leaden-hued when no longer fresh.

Eels should be alive and brisk in movement when they are purchased, but the 'horrid barbarity,' as it is truly designated, of skinning and dividing them while they are so, is without excuse, as they are easily destroyed 'by piercing the spinal marrow close to the back part of the skull with a sharp pointed knife or skewer. If this is done in the right place all motion will instantly cease'. We quote Dr Kitchener's assertion on this subject; but we know that the mode of destruction which he recommends is commonly practised by the London fishmongers. Boiling water also will immediately cause vitality to cease, and is perhaps the most humane and ready method of destroying the fish.

Lobsters, prawns, and shrimps, are very stiff when freshly boiled, and the tails turn strongly inwards; when these relax, and the fish are soft and watery, they are stale; and the smell will detect their being so, instantly, even if no other symptoms of it be remarked. If bought alive, lobsters should be chosen by their weight and 'liveliness'. The hen lobster is preferred for sauce and soups, on account of the coral; but the flesh of the male is generally considered of fine flavour for eating. The vivacity of their leaps will show when prawns and shrimps are fresh from the sea.

Oysters should close forcibly on the knife when they are opened: if the shells are apart ever so little they are losing their condition, and when they remain far open the fish are dead and fit only to be thrown away. Small plump natives are very preferable to the larger and coarser kinds.

*We have known this applied very successfully to salmon which from some hours' keeping in sultry weather had acquired a slight degree of taint, of which no trace remained after it was dressed; as a general rule, however, fish which is not *wholesomely fresh* should be rejected for the table.

† [*'Crimp' fish is very fresh, and 'crimped' slices are slashed at the edges to make them cook more crisply.*]

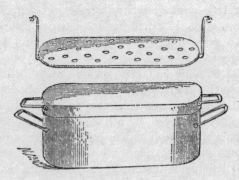

Copper Fish or Ham Kettle

THE MODE OF COOKING BEST ADAPTED TO DIFFERENT KINDS OF FISH

It is not possible, the reader will easily believe, to insert in a work of the size of the present volume, all the modes of dressing the many varieties of fish which are suited to our tables; we give, therefore, only the more essential receipts in detail, and add to them such general information as may, we trust, enable even a moderately intelligent cook to serve all that may usually be required, without difficulty.

There is no better way of dressing a good turbot, brill, John Dory, or cod's head and shoulders, than plain but careful boiling. Salmon is excellent in almost every mode in which it can be cooked or used. Boiled entire or in crimped slices; roasted in a cradle-spit or Dutch oven; baked; fried in small collops; collared; potted; dried and smoked; pickled or soused (this is the coarsest and least to be recommended process for it, of any); made into a raised or common pie, or a potato-pastry; served cold in or with savoury jelly, or with a *Mayonnaise* sauce; or laid on potatoes and baked, as in Ireland, it will be found GOOD.

Soles may be either boiled, or baked, or fried entire, or in fillets; curried; stewed in cream; or prepared by any of the directions given for them in the body of this chapter.

Plaice, unless when in full season and very fresh, is apt to be watery and insipid; but taken in its perfection and carefully cooked, it is very sweet and delicate in flavour. If large, it may be boiled with advantage either whole or in fillets; but to many tastes it is very superior when filleted, dipped into egg and breadcrumbs, and fried. The flesh may also be curried; or the plaice may be converted into water-souchy, or *soupe-maigre*: when small it is often fried whole.

Red mullet should always be *baked, broiled*, or *roasted*: it should on no occasion be boiled.

Mackerel, for which many receipts will be found in this chapter, when broiled *quite whole*, as we have directed, or freed from the bones, divided, egged, crumbed, and fried, is infinitely superior to the same fish cooked in the ordinary manner.

The whiting, when *very fresh* and in season, is always delicate and good; and of all fish is considered the best suited to invalids. Perhaps *quite* the most wholesome mode of preparing it for them, is to open it as little as possible when it is cleansed, to leave the skin on, to dry the fish well, and to broil it gently. It should be sent very hot to table, and will require no sauce: twenty minutes will usually be required to cook it, if of moderate size.

The haddock is sometimes very large. We have had it occasionally from our southern coast between two and three feet in length, and it was then remarkably good when simply boiled, even the day after it was caught, the white curd between the flakes of flesh being like that of extremely fresh salmon. As it is in full season in mid-winter, it can be sent to a distance without injury. It is a *very* firm fish when large and in season; but, as purchased commonly at inland markets, is often neither fine in size nor quality. *One* of the best modes of cooking it is, to take the flesh entire from the bones, to divide it, dip it into egg and bread-crumbs, mixed with savoury herbs finely minced, and a seasoning of salt and spice, and to fry it like soles.

TO BAKE FISH

A gentle oven may be used with advantage, for cooking almost every kind of fish, as we have ascertained from our own observation; but it must be subjected to a mild degree of heat only. This penetrates the flesh gradually, and converts it into wholesome succulent food; whereas, a *hot oven* evaporates all the juices rapidly, and renders the fish hard and dry. When small, they should be wrapped in oiled or buttered paper before they are baked; and when filleted, or left in any other form, and placed in a deep dish with or without any liquid before they are put into the oven, a buttered paper should still be laid closely upon them to keep the surface moist. Large pieces of salmon, conger eel, and other fish of considerable size are sometimes in common cookery baked like meat over potatoes pared and halved.

FAT FOR FRYING FISH

This, whether it be butter, lard, or oil should always be excellent in quality, for the finest fish will be rendered unfit for eating if it be fried in fat that is rancid. When good, and used in sufficient quantity, it will serve for the same purpose several times, if strained after each frying, and put carefully away in a clean pan, provided always that it has not been smoked nor burned in the using.

Lard renders fish more crisp than butter does; but fresh, pure olive-oil (*salad oil*, as it is commonly called in England) is the *best* ingredient which can be used for it, and as it will serve well for the same purpose, many times in succession, if strained and carefully stored as we have already stated, it is not in reality so expensive as might be supposed for this mode of cooking. There should always be an ample quantity of it (or of any other *friture*)* in the pan, as the fish should be nearly covered with it, at the least; and it should cease to bubble before either fish or meat is laid into it, or it will be too much absorbed by the flesh, and will impart neither sufficient firmness, nor sufficient colour.

* The French term for fat of all kinds used in frying.

TURBOT À LA CRÊME

Raise carefully from the bones the flesh of a cold turbot, and clear it from the dark skin; cut it into small squares, and put it into an exceedingly clean stewpan or saucepan; then make and pour upon it the cream sauce of Chapter 5, or make as much as may be required for the fish by the same receipt, with equal proportions of milk and cream and a little additional flour. Heat the turbot slowly in the sauce, but do not allow it to boil, and send it very hot to table. The white skin of the fish is not usually added to this dish, and it is of better appearance without it; but for a family dinner, it may be left on the flesh, when it is much liked. No acid must be stirred to the sauce until the whole is ready for table.

TURBOT AU BÉCHAMEL, OR, IN BÉCHAMEL SAUCE

Prepare the cold turbot as for the preceding receipt, but leave no portion of the skin with it. Heat it in a rich *béchamel* sauce, and serve it in a *vol-au-vent*, or in a deep dish with a border of fried bread cut in elegant form, and made with one dark and one light sippet, placed alternately. The surface may be covered with a half-inch layer of delicately fried bread-crumbs, perfectly well drained and dried; or they may be spread over the fish without being fried, then moistened with clarified butter, and browned with a salamander. [*See Vocabulary.*]

John Dory

SMALL JOHN DORIES† BAKED
(*Author's Receipt – Good*)

We have found these fish when they were too small to be worth cooking in the usual way, excellent when quite simply baked in the following manner, the flesh being remarkably sweet and tender, much more so than it becomes by frying or broiling. After they've been cleaned, dry them in a cloth, season the insides slightly with fine salt, dredge a little flour on the fish, and stick a few very small bits of butter on them, but only just sufficient to prevent their becoming dry in the oven; lay them singly on a flat dish, and bake them very gently from fourteen to sixteen minutes. Serve them with the same sauce as baked soles.

When extremely fresh, as it usually is in the markets of the coast, fish thus simply dressed *au four* is preferable to that more elaborately prepared by adding various condiments to it after it is placed in a deep dish, and covering it with a thick layer of bread crumbs, moistened with clarified butter.

The appearance of the John Dories is improved by taking off

the heads, and cutting away not only the fins but the filaments of the back.

† [*Nowadays this fish is not always easy to find – as they are ugly they do not tempt the timid customer, but some fishmongers do keep them.*]

TO BOIL A BRILL†

A fresh and full-sized brill always ranks high in the list of fish, as it is of good appearance, and the flesh is sweet and delicate. It requires less cooking than the turbot, even when it is of equal size; but otherwise may be dressed and served in a similar manner. It has not the same rich glutinous skin as that fish, nor are the fins esteemed. They must be cut off when the brill is cleaned; and it may be put into nearly boiling water, unless it be very large. Simmer it gently, and drain it well upon the fish-plate when it is lifted out; dish it on a napkin, and send lobster, anchovy, crab, or shrimp sauce to table with it. Lobster coral, rubbed through a sieve, is commonly sprinkled over it for a formal dinner. The most usual garnish for boiled flat fish is curled parsley placed round it in light tufts; how far it is *appropriate*, individual taste must decide.

Brill, moderate-sized, about 20 minutes; large, 30 minutes.

Obs. The *precise* time which a fish will require to be boiled cannot be given: it must be watched, and not allowed to remain in the water after it begins to crack.

† [*An under-rated fish, similar to turbot (but cheaper and not so fine). A great standby of railway restaurant cars – but if your fishmonger has it, try it.*]

TO BOIL SALMON

(In full season from May to August: may be had much earlier, but is scarce and dear)

To preserve the fine colour of this fish, and to *set the curd* when it is quite freshly caught, it is usual to put it into *boiling*, instead of into cold water. Scale, empty, and wash it with the greatest nicety, and be especially careful to cleanse all the blood from the inside. Stir into the fish-kettle eight ounces of common salt to the gallon of water, let it boil quickly for a minute or two, take off all the scum, put in the salmon and boil it moderately fast, if it be small, but more gently should it be very thick; and assure yourself that it is quite sufficiently done before it is sent to table, for nothing can be more distasteful, even to the eye, than fish which is under dressed.

From two to three pounds of the thick part of a fine salmon will require half an hour to boil it, but eight or ten pounds will be done enough in little more than double that time; less in proportion to its weight should be allowed for a small fish, or for the thin end of a large one. Do not allow the salmon to remain in the water after it is ready to serve, or both its flavour and appearance will be injured. Dish it on a hot napkin, and send dressed cucumber, and anchovy, shrimp, or lobster sauce, and a tureen of plain melted butter to table with it.

To each gallon water, 8 oz salt. Salmon, 2 to 3 lb (thick), ½ hour; 8 to 10 lb, 1¼ hour; small, or thin fish, less time.

CRIMPED SALMON

Cut into slices an inch and a half, or two inches thick, the body of a salmon *quite newly caught* ['*crimp*']; throw them into strong salt and water as they are done, but do not let them soak in it; wash them well, lay them on a fish-plate, and put them into fast boiling water, salted and well-skimmed. In from ten to fifteen minutes they will be done. Dish them on a napkin, and send them very hot to table with lobster sauce, and plain melted butter; or with the caper fish-sauce of Chapter 5. The water should be salted as for salmon boiled in the ordinary way, and the scum should be cleared off with great care after the fish is in.

Separate some cold boiled salmon into flakes, and free them entirely from the skin; break the bones, and boil them in a pint of water for half an hour. Strain off the liquor, put it into a clean saucepan and stir into it by degrees when it begins to boil quickly, two ounces of butter mixed with a large teaspoonful of flour, and when the whole has boiled for two or three minutes add a teaspoonful of essence of anchovies, one of good mushroom catsup, half as much lemon-juice or chili vinegar, a half salt-spoonful of pounded mace, some cayenne, and a very little salt. Shell from half to a whole pint of shrimps, add them to the salmon, and heat the fish very slowly in the sauce by the side of the fire, but do not allow it to boil. When it is very hot, dish and send it quickly to table. French cooks, when they re-dress fish or meat of any kind, prepare the flesh with great nicety, and then put it into a stewpan, and pour the sauce upon it, which is, we think, better than the more usual English mode of laying it into the boiling sauce. The cold salmon may also be reheated in the cream sauce of Chapter 5, or in the *Maître d'Hôtel* sauce which follows it; and will be found excellent with either. This receipt is for a moderate sized dish.

SALMON PUDDING, TO BE SERVED HOT OR COLD
(*A Scotch Receipt – Good*)

Pound or chop small, or rub through a sieve one pound of cold boiled salmon freed entirely from bone and skin; and blend it lightly but thoroughly with half a pound of fine bread-crumbs, a teaspoonful of essence of anchovies, a quarter-pint of cream, a seasoning of fine salt and cayenne, and four well whisked eggs. Press the mixture closely and evenly into a deep dish or mould, buttered in every part, and bake it for one hour in a moderate oven.

Salmon, 1 lb; bread-crumbs, ½ lb; essence of anchovies, 1 teaspoonful; cream, ¼ pint; eggs, 4; salt and cayenne: baked 1 hour.

SLICES OF COD FISH FRIED

Cut the middle or tail of the fish into slices nearly an inch thick, season them with salt and white pepper or cayenne, flour them well, and fry them of a clear equal brown on both sides; drain them on a sieve before the fire, and serve them on a well-heated napkin, with plenty of crisped parsley round them. Or, dip them into beaten egg, and then into fine crumbs mixed with a season-ing of salt and pepper (some cooks add one of minced herbs also), before they are fried. Send melted butter and anchovy sauce to table with them.

8 to 12 minutes.

Obs. This is a much better way of dressing the thin part of the fish than boiling it, and as it is generally cheap, it makes thus an economical, as well as a very good dish: if the slices are lifted from the frying-pan into a good curried gravy, and left in it by the side of the fire for a few minutes before they are sent to table, they will be found excellent.

STEWED COD

Put into boiling water, salted as usual, about three pounds of fresh cod fish cut into slices an inch and a half thick, and boil them gently for five minutes; lift them out, and let them drain. Have ready heated in a wide stewpan nearly a pint of veal gravy or of very good broth, lay in the fish, and stew it for five minutes, then add four tablespoonsful of extremely fine bread-crumbs, and simmer it for three minutes longer. Stir well into the sauce a large teaspoonful of arrowroot quite free from lumps, a fourth part as much of mace, something less of cayenne, and a table-spoonful of essence of anchovies, mixed with a glass of white wine and a dessertspoonful of lemon juice. Boil the whole for a couple of minutes, lift out the fish carefully with a slice, pour the sauce over, and serve it quickly.

Cod fish, 3 lb: boiled 5 minutes. Gravy, or strong broth, nearly 1 pint: 5 minutes. Bread-crumbs, 4 tablespoonsful: 3 minutes. Arrowroot, 1 large teaspoonful; mace, $\frac{1}{4}$ teaspoonful; less of cayenne; essence of anchovies, 1 tablespoonful; lemon-juice, 1 dessertspoonful; sherry or Madeira, 1 wineglassful, 2 minutes.

Obs. A dozen or two of oysters, bearded,† and added with their strained liquor to this dish two or three minutes before it is served, will to many tastes vary it very agreeably.

† [*'Bearded' is cleaned and trimmed of the rather slimy frill round the fish inside the shell.*]

FILLETS OF SOLES

The word *fillet*, whether applied to fish, poultry, game, or butcher's meat, means simply the flesh of either (or of certain portions of it), raised clear from the bones in a handsome form, and divided or not, as the manner in which it is to be served may require. It is an elegant mode of dressing various kinds of fish, and even those which are not the most highly esteemed, afford an excellent dish when thus prepared. Soles to be filleted with advantage should be large; the flesh may then be divided down the middle of the back, next, separated from the fins, and with a very sharp knife raised clear from the bones. A celebrated French cook gives the following instructions for raising these fillets: 'Take them up by running your knife first between the bones and the flesh, then between the skin and the fillet; by leaning pretty hard on the table they will come off very neatly.'

SOLES AU PLAT

Clarify from two or three ounces of fresh butter, and pour it into the dish in which the fish are to be served; add to it a little salt, some cayenne, a teaspoonful of essence of anchovies, and from

35

one to two glasses of sherry, or of any other dry white wine; lay in a couple of fine soles which have been well cleaned and wiped very dry, strew over them a thick layer of fine bread-crumbs, moisten them with clarified butter, set the dish into a moderate oven, and bake the fish for a quarter of an hour. A layer of shrimps placed between the soles is a great improvement; and we would also recommend a little lemon-juice to be mixed with the sauce.

Baked, 15 minutes.

Obs. The soles are, we think, better without the wine in this receipt. They require but a small portion of liquid, which might be supplied by a little additional butter, a spoonful of water or pale gravy, the lemon-juice, and store-sauce. Minced parsley may be mixed with the bread-crumbs when it is liked.

SOLES STEWED IN CREAM

Prepare some very fresh middling sized soles with exceeding nicety, put them into boiling water slightly salted, and simmer them for two minutes only; lift them out, and let them drain; lay them into a wide stewpan with as much sweet rich cream as will nearly cover them; add a good seasoning of pounded mace, cayenne, and salt; stew the fish softly from six to ten minutes, or until the flesh parts readily from the bones; dish them, stir the juice of half a lemon to the sauce, pour it over the soles, and send them immediately to table. Some lemon-rind may be boiled in the cream, if approved; and a small teaspoonful of arrowroot, very smoothly mixed with a little milk, may be stirred to the sauce (should it require thickening) before the lemon-juice is added. Turbot and brill also may be dressed by this receipt, time proportioned to their size being of course allowed for them.

Soles, 3 or 4: boiled in water 2 minutes. Cream, ½ to whole pint; salt, mace, cayenne: fish stewed, 6 to 10 minutes. Juice of half a lemon.

Empty and wash thoroughly, but do not skin the fish. Take off the flesh on both sides close to the bones, passing the knife from the tail to the head; divide each side in two, trim the fillets into good shape, and fold them in a cloth, that the moisture may be well absorbed from them; dip them into, or draw them through, some beaten egg, then dip them into fine crumbs mixed with a small portion of flour, and fry them a fine light brown in lard or clarified butter; drain them well, press them in white blotting-paper, dish them one over the other in a circle, and send the usual sauce to table with them. The fillets may also be broiled after being dipped into eggs seasoned with salt and pepper, then into crumbs of bread, next into clarified butter, and a second time into the bread-crumbs (or, to shorten the process, a portion of clarified butter, may be mixed with the eggs at first), and served with good melted butter, or thickened veal gravy seasoned with cayenne, lemon-juice, and chopped parsley.

Five minutes will fry the fillets, even when very large; rather more time will be required to broil them.

BAKED WHITINGS À LA FRANÇAISE

Proceed with these exactly as with the soles au plat of this chapter; or, pour a little clarified butter into a deep dish, and strew it rather thickly with finely-minced mushrooms mixed with a tea-spoonful of parsley, and (when the flavour is liked and considered appropriate) with an eschalot or two, or the white part of a few green onions, also chopped very small. On these place the fish after they have been scaled, emptied, thoroughly washed, and wiped dry: season them well with salt and white pepper, or cayenne; sprinkle more of the herbs upon them; pour gently from one to two glasses of light white wine into the dish, cover the whitings with a thick layer of fine crumbs of bread, sprinkle these plentifully with clarified butter, and bake the fish from fifteen to twenty minutes. Send a cut lemon only to table with them. When the wine is not liked, a few spoonsful of pale veal gravy can be used instead; or a larger quantity of clarified butter, with a tablespoonful of water, a teaspoonful of lemon-pickle and of mushroom catsup, and a few drops of soy.

15 to 20 minutes.

Mackerel

TO BAKE MACKEREL

After they have been cleaned and well washed, wipe them very dry, fill the insides with the forcemeat of Chapter 8, sew them up, arrange them, with the roes, closely together in a coarse baking-dish, flour them lightly, strew a little fine salt over, and stick bits of butter upon them or pour some equally over them, after having just dissolved it in a small saucepan. Half an hour in a moderate oven will bake them. Oyster forcemeat is always appropriate for any kind of fish which is in season while oysters are so; but the mackerel are commonly served, and are very good with that which we have named. Lift them carefully into a hot dish after they are taken from the oven, and send melted butter and a cut lemon to table with them.

½ hour.

BAKED MACKEREL, OR WHITINGS
(*Cinderella's Receipt – Good*)

The fish for this receipt should be opened only so much as will permit of their being emptied and perfectly cleansed. Wash and wipe them dry, then fold them in a soft cloth, and let them remain in it awhile. Replace the roes, and put the fish into a baking-dish of suitable size, with a tablespoonful of wine, a few drops of chili vinegar, a little salt and cayenne, and about half an ounce of butter, well-blended with a saltspoonful of flour, for each fish. They must be turned round with the heads and tails towards each other, that they may lie compactly in the dish, and the backs should be placed downwards, that the sauce may surround the thickest part of the flesh. Lay two buttered papers over, and press them down upon them; set the dish into a gentle oven for twenty minutes, take off the papers, and send the fish to table in their sauce.

A few minutes more of time must be allowed for mackerel when it is large, should the oven be *very* slow.

Full-sized whitings are excellent thus dressed if carefully managed, and many eaters would infinitely prefer mackerel so prepared, to boiled ones. The writer has port wine always used for the sauce, to which a rather full seasoning of chili vinegar, cayenne, and pounded mace, is added; but sherry, Bucellas, or any other dry wine, can be used instead; and the various condiments added to it, can be varied to the taste. This receipt is a very convenient one, as it is prepared with little trouble, and a stove-oven, if the heat be properly moderated, will answer for the baking. It is an advantage to take off the heads of the fish before they are dressed, and they may then be entirely emptied without being opened. When preferred so, they can be re-dished for table, and the sauce poured over them.

Obs. The dish in which they are baked, should be buttered before they are laid in.

MACKEREL BROILED WHOLE
(*An excellent Receipt*)

Empty and cleanse perfectly a fine and very fresh mackerel, but without opening it more than is needful; dry it well, either in a cloth or by hanging it in a cool air until it is stiff; make with a sharp knife a deep incision the whole length of the fish on either side of the back bone, and about half an inch from it, and with a feather put in a little cayenne and fine salt, mixed with a few drops of good salad oil or clarified butter. Lay the mackerel over a moderate fire upon a well-heated gridiron which has been rubbed with suet; loosen it gently should it stick, which it will do unless often moved; and when it is equally done on both sides, turn the back to the fire. About half an hour will broil it well. If a sheet of thickly-buttered writing-paper be folded round it, and just twisted at the ends before it is laid on the gridiron, it will be finer eaten than if exposed to the fire; but sometimes when this is done, the skin will adhere to the paper, and be drawn off with it, which injures its appearance. A cold *Maître d'Hôtel* sauce may be put into the back before it is sent to table. This is one of the very best modes of dressing a mackerel, which in flavour is quite a different fish when thus prepared to one which is simply boiled. A drop of oil is sometimes passed over the skin to prevent it sticking to the iron. It may be laid to the fire after having been merely cut as we have directed, when it is preferred so.

30 minutes; 25 if *small*.

MACKEREL STEWED WITH WINE
(*Very Good*)

Work very smoothly together a large teaspoonful of flour with two ounces of butter, put them into a stewpan, and stir or shake them round over the fire until the butter is dissolved; add a quarter of a teaspoonful of mace, twice as much salt, and some cayenne; pour in by slow degrees three glasses of claret; and when the sauce boils, lay in a couple of fine mackerel well cleaned, and wiped quite dry; stew them very softly from fifteen to twenty minutes, and turn them when half done; lift them out, and dish them carefully; stir a teaspoonful of made mustard to the sauce, give it a boil, and pour it over the fish. When more convenient, substitute port wine [*or any other red wine*] and a little lemon-juice for the claret.

Mackerel, 2; flour, 1 teaspoonful; butter, 2 oz; seasoning of salt, mace, and cayenne; claret, 3 wine-glassesful; made mustard, 1 teaspoonful: 15 to 20 minutes.

TO DRESS FINNAN HADDOCKS†

These are slightly salted and dried. They are excellent eating, if gently heated through upon the gridiron without being hardened; and are served usually at the breakfast or supper table; a feather dipped in oil may be passed over them before they are laid to the fire.

† [*In Grimsby, where the best Finnan Haddocks are called 'London Haddocks', the recommended method of cooking is to take out the large backbone and cook the fish gently in butter.*]

FRESH HERRINGS
(*Farleigh Receipt*)
(In season from May to October)

Scale and clean the fish with the utmost nicety, split them quite open, and wash the insides with particular care; dry them well in a cloth, take off the heads and tails, and remove the backbones; rub the insides with pepper, salt, and a little pounded mace; stick small bits of butter on them, and skewer two of the fish together as flat as possible, with the skin of both outside; flour, and broil or fry them of a fine brown, and serve them with melted butter mixed with a teaspoonful or more of mustard, some salt, and a little vinegar or lemon-juice.

To broil from 20 to 25 minutes; to fry about 10 minutes.

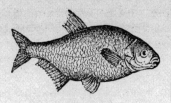

Sea Bream

TO DRESS THE SEA BREAM†

The sea bream, which is common in many of our markets, is not
considered a fish of first-rate quality; but if well broiled or baked,
it will afford a good, and generally a *cheap*, dish of excellent
appearance, the bream being of handsome size and form. Open
and cleanse it perfectly, but do not remove the scales; fold it in a
dry cloth to absorb the moisture which hangs about it; lay it over
a gentle fire, and broil it slowly, that the heat may gradually
penetrate the flesh, which is thick. Should any cracks appear on
the surface, dredge a little flour upon them. If of ordinary
weight, the bream will require quite half an hour's broiling; it
should be turned, of course, when partially done. Send plain
melted butter and anchovy sauce to table with it. In carving it,
remove the skin and scales, and serve only the flesh which lies
beneath them, and which will be very white and succulent. A
more usual and less troublesome mode of dressing the bream is to
season the inside slightly with salt and pepper or cayenne, to dust
a little more salt on the outside, spread a few bits of butter upon
it, and send it to a gentle oven. It is sometimes filled with
common veal-stuffing, and then requires to be rather longer
baked; and it is often merely wrapped in a buttered paper, and
placed in a moderate oven for twenty-five or thirty minutes.

   † [*A sea bream is a fat, rather coarsely-textured fish with very large
scales. Usually quite cheap, and when stuffed as above, can be very good
eating.*]

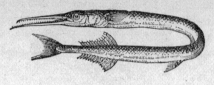

Gar-Fish

THE GAR-FISH†

This is a fish of very singular appearance, elongated in form, and with a mouth which resembles the bill of the snipe, from which circumstance it is often called the snipe-fish. Its bones are all of a *bright green* colour. It is not to be recommended for the table, as the skin contains an oil of exceedingly strong rank flavour; when entirely divested of this, the flesh is tolerably sweet and palatable. Persons who may be disposed from curiosity to taste it will find either broiling or baking in a gentle oven the best mode of cooking it. It should be curled round, and the tail fastened into the bill. As it is not of large size, from fifteen to twenty minutes will dress it sufficiently. Anchovy sauce, parsley and butter, or plain melted butter, may be eaten with it.

† [*I am sure no fishmonger keeps this, but I included it for the information of anyone who does find one.*]

TO FRY SMELTS
(In season from beginning of November to May)

Smelts when quite fresh have a perfume resembling that of a cucumber, and a peculiarly delicate and agreeable flavour when dressed. Draw them at the gills,† as they must not be opened; wash and dry them thoroughly in a cloth; dip them into beaten egg-yolk, and then into the finest bread-crumbs, mixed with a very small quantity of flour; fry them of a clear golden brown, and serve them crisp and dry, with good melted butter in a tureen. They are sometimes dipped into batter and then fried;

43

when this is done, we would recommend for them the French batter of Chapter 5.

3 to 4 minutes.

† [*That is to remove the inside of the fish through the gills, thus leaving the fish whole.*]

TO DRESS WHITE BAIT
(*Greenwich Receipt*)
(In season in July, August and September)

This delicate little fish requires great care to dress it well. Do not touch it with the hands, but throw it from your dish or basket into a cloth, with three or four handsful of flour, and shake it well; then put it into a bait sieve, to separate it from the superfluous flour. Have ready a very deep frying-pan, nearly full of boiling fat, throw in the fish, which will be done in an instant: they must not be allowed to take any colour, for if browned, they are spoiled. Lift them out, and dish them upon a silver or earthenware drainer, without a napkin, piling them very high in the centre. Send them to table with a cut lemon, and slices of brown bread and butter.

WATER SOUCHY
(*Greenwich Receipt*)

This is a very simple and inexpensive dish, much served at the regular fish-dinners for which Greenwich is celebrated, as well as at private tables. It is excellent if well prepared; and as it may be made with fish of various kinds when they are too small to present a good appearance or to be palatable dressed in any other way, it is also very economical. Flounders, perch, tench, and eels, are said to answer best for water souchy; but very delicate soles, and several other varieties of small white fish are often used for it with good effect: it is often made also with slices of salmon, or of salmon-peel, freed from the skin.

Throw into rather more than sufficient water to just cover the quantity of fish required for table, from half to three-quarters of an ounce of salt to the quart, a dozen corns of white pepper, a small bunch of green parsley, and two or three tender parsley roots, first cut into inch lengths, and then split to the size of straw. Simmer the mixture until these last are tender, which will be in from half to a whole hour; then lay in the fish delicately cleaned, cleared from every morsel of brown skin, and divided into equal portions of about two inches in width. Take off all the scum as it rises, and stew the fish softly from eight to twelve minutes, watching it that it may not break from being over-done.

Two minutes before it is dished, strew in a large tablespoonful or more of minced parsley, or some small branches of the herb boiled very green in a separate saucepan (we prefer the latter mode); lift out the fish carefully with a slice, and the parsley roots with it; pour over it the liquor in which it has been boiled, but leave out the peppercorns. For a superior water souchy, take all the bones out of the fish, and stew down the inferior portions of it to a strong broth; about an hour will be sufficient for this. Salt, parsley, and a little cayenne may be added to it. Strain it off clear through a sieve, and use it instead of water for the souchy. The juice of half a good lemon may be thrown into the stew before it is served. A deep dish will of course be required for it. The parsley-roots can be boiled apart when more convenient, but they give an agreeable flavour when added to the liquor at first. Slices of brown or white bread and butter must be sent to table always with water souchy: the first is usually preferred, but to suit all tastes some of each may be served with it.

STEWED TROUT

(Good common Receipt)

(In season from May to August)

Melt three ounces of butter in a broad stewpan, or well tinned iron saucepan, stir to it a tablespoonful of flour, some mace, cayenne, and nutmeg: lay in the fish after it has been emptied, washed very clean, and wiped perfectly dry; shake it in the pan, that it may not stick, and when lightly browned on both sides, pour in three-quarters of a pint of good veal stock, add a small faggot of parsley, one bay leaf, a roll of lemon-peel, and a little salt: stew the fish *very gently* from half to three-quarters of an hour, or more, should it be unusually fine. Dish the trout, skim the fat from the gravy, and pass it through a hot strainer over the fish, which should be served immediately. A little acid can be added to the sauce at pleasure, and a glass of wine when it is considered an improvement. This receipt is for one large or for two middling-sized fish. We can recommend it as a good one from our own experience.

Butter, 3 oz; flour, 1 tablespoonful; seasoning of mace, cayenne, and nutmeg; trout, 1 large, or 2 moderate-sized; veal stock, 3/4 pint; parsley, *small faggot*; 1 bay leaf; roll of lemon-rind; little salt: 1/2 to 3/4 hour.

Obs. Trout may be stewed in equal parts of strong veal gravy, and of red or white wine, without having been previously browned; the sauce should then be thickened, and agreeably flavoured with lemon-juice, and the usual store-sauces, before it is poured over the fish. They are also good when wrapped in buttered paper, and baked or broiled: if very small, the better mode of cooking them is to fry them whole. They should never be plain boiled, as, though naturally a delicious fish, they are then very insipid.

RED HERRINGS,† À LA DAUPHIN

Take off the heads, open the backs of the fish, and remove the backbones: soak the herrings, should they be very dry, for two or three hours in warm milk and water, drain and wipe them. Dissolve a slice of fresh butter, and mix it with the beaten yolks of a couple of eggs and some savoury herbs minced small: dip the fish into these, and spread them thickly with fine bread crumbs; broil them of a light brown, over a moderate fire, and serve them on hot buttered toasts, sprinkled with a little cayenne.

† [*Red Herrings are similar to bloaters, but more salted.*]

3

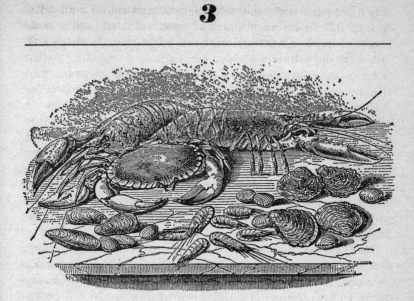

DISHES OF SHELL-FISH

TO SCALLOP OYSTERS

Large coarse oysters should never be dressed in this way. Select
small plump ones for the purpose, let them be opened carefully,
give them a scald in their own liquor, wash them in it free from
grit, and beard them neatly. Butter the scallop shells and shake
some fine bread-crumbs over them; fill them with alternate
layers of oysters, crumbs of bread, and fresh butter cut into small
bits; pour in the oyster-liquor, after it has been strained, put a
thick, smooth layer of bread-crumbs on the top, moisten them
with clarified butter,* place the shells in a Dutch oven before a
clear fire, and turn them often until the tops are equally and
lightly browned: send them immediately to table.

Some persons like a little white pepper or cayenne, and a flavouring of nutmeg added to the oysters; others prefer pounded

47

mace. French cooks recommend with them a mixture of minced mushrooms stewed in butter till quite tender, and sweet herbs finely chopped. The fish is sometimes laid into the shells after having been bearded only.

* *Common cooks merely stick small bits of butter on them.*

TO STEW OYSTERS

A pint of small plump oysters will be sufficient for a quite moderate-sized dish, but twice as many will be required for a large one. Let them be very carefully opened, and not mangled in the slightest degree; wash them free from grit in their own *strained* liquor, lay them into a very clean stewpan or well-tinned saucepan, strain the liquor a second time, pour it on them, and heat them slowly in it. When they are just beginning to simmer, lift them out with a slice or a bored wooden spoon, and take off the beards; add to the liquor a quarter of a pint of good cream, a seasoning of pounded mace, and cayenne, and a little salt, and when it boils, stir in from one to two ounces of good butter, smoothly mixed with a large teaspoonful of flour; continue to stir the sauce until these are perfectly blended with it, then put in the oysters, and let them remain by the side of the fire until they are very hot: they require so little cooking that, if kept for four or five minutes nearly simmering, they will be ready for table, and they are quickly hardened by being allowed to boil, or by too much stewing. Serve them garnished with pale fried sippets.

Small plump oysters, 1 pint; their own liquor: brought slowly to the point of simmering. Cream, ¼ pint; seasoning of pounded mace and cayenne; salt as needed; butter, 1 to 2 oz; flour, 1 large teaspoonful.

Obs. A little lemon-juice should be stirred quickly into the stew just as it is taken from the fire. Another mode of preparing this dish, is to add the strained liquor of the oysters to about an equal quantity of rich *béchamel*, with a little additional thickening; then to heat them in it, after having prepared and plumped them properly. Or, the beards of the fish may be stewed for half an hour in a little pale gravy, or good broth, and this, when strained and mixed with the oyster-liquor, may be brought to the consistency of cream with the French thickening of Chapter 5, or, with flour and butter, then seasoned with spice as above: the process should be quite the same in all of these receipts, though the composition of the sauce is varied. Essence of anchovies, chili vinegar, or yolks of eggs can be added to the taste.

COLD DRESSED CRAB

The flesh of two crabs can be served in one shell when a dish of handsome appearance is required, and the sauce can be mixed with it the instant before it is sent to table, though it will be whiter, and of better appearance without it. The centre may be filled with a red *Mayonnaise*, when a good effect is wanted. For other appropriate sauces see Chapter 6.

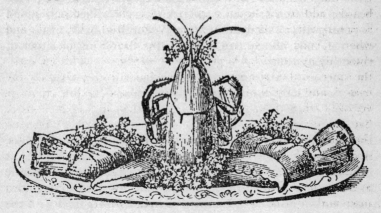

Dressed Lobster

LOBSTERS, FRICASSEED, OR AU BÉCHAMEL
(*Entrée*)

Take the flesh from the claws and tails of two moderate-sized lobsters, cut it into small scallops or dice; heat it slowly quite through in about three-quarters of a pint of good white sauce or *béchamel*; and serve it when it is at the point of boiling, after having stirred briskly to it a little lemon-juice just as it is taken from the fire. The coral, pounded and mixed gradually with a few spoonsful of the sauce, should be added previously. Good shin of beef stock made without vegetables and somewhat reduced by quick boiling, if mixed with an equal proportion of cream, and thickened with arrowroot, will answer extremely well in a general way for this dish, which is most excellent if well made. The sauce should never be thin; nor more than sufficient in quantity to just cover the fish. For a second course fish, only as much must be used as will adhere to the fish, which after being heated should be laid evenly into the shells, which ought to be split quite through the centre of the backs in their entire length, without being broken or divided at the joint, and nicely cleaned. When thus arranged, the lobster may be thickly covered with well dried, fine, pale fried crumbs of bread, or with unfried ones, which must then be equally moistened with clarified butter, and browned with a salamander. A small quantity of salt, mace, and cayenne, may be required to finish the flavouring of either of these preparations.

HOT CRAB, OR LOBSTER
(In season during the same time as Lobsters)

Slice quite small, or pull into light flakes with a couple of forks, the flesh of either fish; put it into a saucepan with a few bits of good butter lightly rolled in flour, and heat it slowly over a gentle fire; then pour over and thoroughly mix with it, from one to two teaspoonsful or more of common or of chili vinegar; if with the former, add to it a tolerable seasoning of cayenne. Grate in a little nutmeg, and when the whole is well heated serve it immediately, either in the shell of the crab or lobster, or in scallop-shells, and serve it plain, or with bread-crumbs over, as in the preceding receipt. A spoonful or so of good meat jelly is, we think, a great improvement to this dish, for which an ounce and a half of butter will be quite sufficient.

This is sometimes called *Buttered Crab*.

Separate carefully the flesh of fresh-boiled lobsters from the shells, and from the tough red skin of the tails, mince the fish up quickly with a very sharp knife, turn it immediately into a large mortar, and strew over it a mixed seasoning of fine cayenne, pounded mace, lightly grated nutmeg, and salt: this last should be sparingly used in the first instance, and it should be reduced to powder before it is added. Pound the lobsters to a perfect paste with from two to three ounces of firm new butter to each fish if of large size, but with less should it be small; and the lobster-coral previously rubbed through a sieve, or with a portion of it only, should any part of it be required for other purposes. When there is no coral, a fine colour may be given to the mixture by stewing the red skin of the tails VERY softly for ten or twelve minutes in part of the butter which is used for it, but which must be strained and left to become perfectly cold before it is mingled with the fish. The degree of seasoning given to the mixture can be regulated by the taste: but no flavour should predominate over that of the lobster itself; and for all delicate preparations, over-spicing should be particularly avoided. A quart or more of fine brown shrimps, if very fresh and quickly shelled at the instant of using, may be chopped up and pounded with the lobsters with excellent effect. Before the mixture is taken from the mortar it should be placed in a cool larder, or set over ice for a short time, to render it firm before it is pressed into the potting-pans or moulds. In putting it into these, be careful to press it into a compact, even mass; smooth the surface, run a little clarified butter over, when it is only *just liquid*, for if hot it would prevent the fish from keeping – and send the lobster to table, neatly garnished with light green foliage; or with ornamentally-cut paper fastened round the mould; or with a small damask napkin tastefully arranged about it.

Obs. By pounding separately part of the white flesh of the fish, freed from every particle of the skin, and by colouring the remainder highly with the coral of the lobster, and then pressing the two in alternate and regular layers into a mould, a dish of pretty appearance is produced, which should be turned out of the mould for table. Ham and turkey (or any other white meat) are often potted in this way.

TO SHELL SHRIMPS AND PRAWNS QUICKLY AND EASILY

This, though a most simple process, would appear, from the manner in which it is performed by many people, to be a very difficult one; indeed it is not unusual for persons of the lower classes, who, from lack of a little skill, find it slow and irksome, to have resource to the dangerous plan of eating the fish entire. It need scarcely be remarked that very serious consequences may accrue from the shells being swallowed with them, particularly when they are taken in large quantities. Unless the fish be stale, when they are apt to break, they will quit the shells easily if the head be held firmly in the right hand and the tail in the other, and the shell of the tail broken by a slight vibratory motion of the right hand, when it will be drawn off with the head adhering to it: a small portion, only will then remain on the other end, which can be removed in an instant.

Gravy Kettle

GRAVIES

When is a gravy not a sauce? At the present time 'gravy' is either the plain meat juice or something from a cube or bottle, and anything more elaborate becomes a 'sauce'. In which case, the 'gravy' receipts belong with the sauces.

I have included a number of the sauce receipts as they are constantly referred to on other pages.

Harvey's sauce, of which much is made, is a dark, sharp sauce, not unlike the soy sauce of the Chinese kitchen, and is still obtainable today. It must be one of the earliest of the bottled sauces and the firm of Harvey was later taken over by that of Lazenby, but by then probably the sauce was manufactured by other firms in the same way that Worcester Sauce is today.

BARON LIEBIG'S BEEF GRAVY

(Most excellent for hashes, minces, and other dishes made of cold meat)

For particulars of this most useful receipt, for extracting all its juices from fresh meat of every kind in the best manner, the cook is referred to the first part of the chapter on soups. The preparation, for which minute directions are given there [*page 4*] if poured on a few bits of lean ham lightly browned, with the other ingredients indicated above, will be converted into gravy of fine flavour and superior quality.

With no addition, beyond that of a little thickening and spice, it will serve admirably for dressing cold meat, in all the usual forms of hashes, minces, *blanquettes*, etc., and convert it into dishes as nourishing as those of meat freshly cooked, and it may be economically made in small quantities with any trimmings of *undressed* beef, mutton, or veal, mixed together, which are free from fat, and not sinewy: flavour may be given to it at once by chopping up with them the lean part only of a slice or two of ham, or of highly-cured beef.

SWEET SAUCE, OR GRAVY FOR VENISON

Add to a quarter-pint of common venison gravy a couple of glasses of port wine or claret, and half an ounce of sugar in lumps. Christopher North's sauce, mixed with three times its measure of gravy, would be an excellent substitute for this.

ESPAGNOLE (SPANISH SAUCE)
(*A highly-flavoured Gravy*)

Dissolve a couple of ounces of good butter in a thick stewpan or saucepan, throw in from four to six sliced eschalots, four ounces of the lean of an undressed ham, three ounces of carrot, cut in small dice, one bay leaf, two or three branches of parsley, and one or two of thyme, but these last must be small; three cloves, a blade of mace, and a dozen corns of pepper; add part of a root of parsley, if it be at hand, and keep the whole stirred or shaken over a moderate fire for twenty minutes, then add by degrees one pint of very strong veal stock or gravy, and stew the whole gently from thirty to forty minutes; strain it, skim off the fat, and it will be ready to serve.

Butter, 2 oz; eschalots, 4 to 6; lean of undressed ham 4 oz; carrots, 3 oz; bay leaf, 1; little thyme and parsley, in branches; cloves, 3; mace, 1 blade; peppercorns, 12; little parsley root: fried gently, 20 minutes. Strong veal stock, or gravy, 1 pint: stewed very softly, 30 to 40 minutes.

Strip the skin and take the fat from three fresh mutton kidneys, slice and flour them; melt two ounces of butter in a deep saucepan, and put in the kidneys, with an onion cut small, and a teaspoonful of fine herbs stripped from the stalks. Keep these well shaken over a clear fire until nearly all the moisture is dried up; then pour in a pint of boiling water, add half a teaspoonful of salt, and a little cayenne or common pepper, and let the gravy boil gently for an hour and a half, or longer, if it be not thick and rich. Strain it through a fine sieve, and take off the fat. Spice or catsup may be added at pleasure.

Mutton kidneys, 3; butter, 2 oz; onion, 1; fine herbs, 1 teaspoonful: ½ hour. Water, 1 pint; salt, ½ teaspoonful; little cayenne, or black pepper: 1½ hour.

Obs. This is an excellent cheap gravy for haricots,† curries, or hashes of mutton; it may be much improved by the addition of two or three eschalots, and a small bit or two of lean meat.

† [*'Haricots', sometimes spelt 'harrico' is a kind of stew. Nothing to do with the haricot bean in this instance. See receipt for Norman Harrico p. 127.*]

GRAVY IN HASTE

Chop fine a few bits of lean meat, a small onion, a few slices of carrot and turnip, and a little thyme and parsley; put these with half an ounce of butter into a thick saucepan, and keep them stirred until they are slightly browned; add a little spice, and water in the proportion of a pint to a pound of meat; clear the gravy from scum, let it boil half an hour, then strain it for use.

Meat, 1 lb; 1 small onion; little carrot, turnip, thyme, and parsley; butter, ½ oz; cloves, 6; corns of pepper, 12; water, 1 pint: ½ hour.

ORANGE GRAVY FOR WILD FOWL

Boil for about ten minutes, in half-pint of rich and highly-flavoured brown gravy, or *Espagnole*, half the rind of a Seville orange, pared as thin as possible, and a small strip of lemon-rind, with a bit of sugar the size of a hazel-nut. Strain it off, add to it a quarter-pint of port or claret, the juice of half a lemon, and a tablespoonful of Seville orange-juice: season it with cayenne, and serve it as hot as possible.

Gravy, ½ pint; ½ the rind of a Seville orange; lemon-peel, 1 small strip; sugar, size of hazel-nut: 10 minutes. Juice of ½ lemon; Seville orange-juice, 1 tablespoonful; cayenne. See also Christopher North's own sauce.

ASPIC, OR CLEAR SAVOURY-JELLY

Boil a couple of calf's feet, with three or four pounds of knuckle of veal, three-quarters of a pound of lean ham, two large onions, three whole carrots, and a large bunch of herbs, in a gallon of water, till it is reduced more than half. Strain it off; when perfectly cold, remove every particle of fat and sediment, and put the jelly into a very clean stewpan, with four whites of eggs, well beaten; keep it stirred until it is nearly boiling; then place it by the side of the fire to simmer for a quarter of an hour. Let it settle, and pour it through a jelly-bag until it is quite clear. Add, when it first begins to simmer, three blades of mace, a teaspoonful of white peppercorns, and sufficient salt to flavour it properly, allowing for the ham, and the reduction. French cooks flavour this jelly with tarragon vinegar when it is clarified; cold poultry, game, fish, plovers' eggs, truffles, and various dressed vegetables, with many other things often elaborately prepared, and highly ornamental, are moulded and served in it, especially at large *déjeuners* and similar repasts. It is also much used to decorate raised pies, and hams; and for many other purposes of the table.

Calf's feet, 2; veal, 4 lb; ham, ¾ lb; onions, 2; carrots, 3; herbs, large bunch; mace, 3 blades; white whole pepper, 1 teaspoonful; water, 1 gallon: 5 to 6 hours. Whites of eggs, 4: 15 minutes.

5

SAUCES

TO THICKEN SAUCES

When this is done with the yolks of eggs, they should first be well beaten, and then mixed with a spoonful of cold stock should it be at hand, and with one or two of the boiling sauce, which should be stirred very quickly to them, and they must in turn be stirred briskly to the sauce, which may be held over the fire, and well shaken for an instant afterwards, but never placed upon it, nor allowed to boil.

To the *roux* or French thickening, the gravy or other liquid which is to be mixed with it should be poured boiling and in small quantities, the saucepan being often well shaken round, and the sauce made to boil up after each portion is added. If this precaution be observed, the butter will never float upon the surface, but the whole will be well and smoothly blended: it will otherwise be difficult to clear the sauce from it perfectly.

For invalids, or persons who object to butter in their soups or sauces, flour only mixed to a smooth batter, and stirred into the boiling liquid may be substituted for other thickening: arrowroot also used in the same way, will answer even better than flour.

SAUCE TOURNÉE, OR PALE THICKENED GRAVY

Sauce tournée is nothing more than rich pale gravy made with veal or poultry and thickened with delicate white *roux*. The French give it a flavouring of mushrooms and green onions, by boiling some of each in it for about half an hour before the sauce is served: it must then be strained, previously to being dished. Either first dissolve an ounce of butter, and then dredge gradually to it three-quarters of an ounce of flour, and proceed as for the preceding receipt; or blend the flour and butter perfectly with a knife before they are thrown into the stewpan, and keep them stirred without ceasing over a clear and gentle fire until they have simmered for some minutes, then place the stewpan high over the fire, and shake it constantly until the *roux* has lost the raw taste of the flour; next, stir very gradually to it a pint of the gravy, which should be boiling. Set it by the side of the stove for a few minutes, skim it thoroughly, and serve it without delay.

Butter, 1 oz; flour, 3/4 oz; strong pale gravy, seasoned with mushrooms and green onions, 1 pint.

Obs. With the addition of three or four yolks of very fresh eggs, mixed with a seasoning of mace, cayenne, and lemon-juice, this becomes *German sauce*, now much used for fricassees, and other dishes; and minced parsley (boiled) and chili vinegar, each in sufficient quantity to flavour it agreeably, convert it into a good fish sauce.

BÉCHAMEL

This is a fine French white sauce, now very much served at good English tables. It may be made in various ways, and more or less expensively; but it should always be thick, smooth, and rich, though delicate in flavour. The most ready mode of preparing it is to take an equal portion of very strong, pale veal gravy, and of good cream (a pint of each for example), and then, by rapid boiling over a very clear fire, to reduce the gravy nearly half; next, to mix with part of the cream a tablespoonful of fine dry flour, to pour it to the remainder, when it boils, and to keep the whole stirred for five minutes or more over a slow fire, for if placed upon a fierce one it would be liable to burn; then to add the gravy, to stir and mix the sauce perfectly, and to simmer it for a few minutes longer. All the flavour should be given by the gravy, in which French cooks boil a handful of mushrooms, a *few* green onions, and some branches of parsley before it is reduced: but a good *béchamel* may be made without them, with a strong *consommé* well reduced.

Strong pale veal gravy (flavoured with mushrooms or not), 1

pint: reduced half. Rich cream, 1 pint; flour, 1 tablespoonful: 5 minutes. With gravy, 4 or 5 minutes.

Obs. Velouté, which is a rather thinner sauce or gravy, is made by simply well reducing the cream and stock separately, and then mixing them together without any thickening.

BÉCHAMEL MAIGRE
(A cheap White Sauce)

A good *béchamel* may be made entirely without meat, when economy is an object, or when no gravy is at hand. Put into a stewpan, with from two to three ounces of butter, a carrot, and a couple of small onions, cut in slices, with a handful of nicely-cleaned mushroom buttons, when these last can be easily procured; and when they have stewed slowly for half an hour, or until the butter is nearly dried up, stir in two tablespoonsful of flour, and pour in a pint of new milk, a little at a time, shaking the stewpan well round, that the sauce may be smooth. Boil the *béchamel* gently for half an hour; add a little salt, and cayenne; strain, and reduce it, if not quite thick, or pour in boiling to the yolks of two fresh eggs.

FRENCH MELTED BUTTER

Pour half-pint of good but not very thick, boiling melted butter to the well-beaten yolks of two or three fresh eggs, and stir them briskly as it is added; put the sauce again into the saucepan, and shake it high over the fire for an instant, but do not allow it to boil or it will curdle. Add a little lemon-juice or vinegar, and serve it immediately.

NORFOLK SAUCE, OR RICH MELTED BUTTER
WITHOUT FLOUR

Put three tablespoonsful of water into a small saucepan, and when it boils add four ounces of fresh butter; as soon as this is quite dissolved, take the saucepan from the fire, and shake it round until the sauce looks thick and smooth. It must not be allowed to boil after the butter is added.

Water, 3 tablespoonsful; butter, 4 oz.

BURNT OR BROWNED BUTTER

Melt in a frying-pan three ounces of fresh butter, and keep it stirred slowly over a gentle fire until it is of a dark brown colour; then pour to it a couple of tablespoonsful of good *hot* vinegar, and season it with black pepper and a little salt. In France this is a favourite sauce with boiled skate, which is served with plenty of crisped parsley, in addition, strewed over it. It is also often poured over poached eggs there: it is called *beurre noir*.

Butter, 3 oz: vinegar, 2 tablespoonsful; pepper; salt.

CLARIFIED BUTTER

Put the butter into a very clean and well-tinned saucepan or enamelled stewpan, and melt it gently over a clear fire; when it just begins to simmer, skim it thoroughly, draw it from the fire, and let it stand a few minutes that the butter-milk may sink to the bottom; then pour it clear of the sediment through a muslin strainer or a fine hair-sieve; put it into jars, and store them in a cool place. Butter thus prepared will answer for all the ordinary purposes of cookery, and remain good for a great length of time. In France, large quantities are melted down in autumn for winter use. The clarified butter ordered for the various receipts in this volume, is merely dissolved with a gentle degree of heat in a small saucepan, skimmed, and poured out for use, leaving the thick sediment behind.

Boil four fresh eggs for quite fifteen minutes, then lay them into plenty of fresh water, and let them remain until they are perfectly cold. Break the shells by rolling them on a table, take them off, separate the white from the yolks, and divide all of the latter into quarter-inch dice; mince two of the white tolerably small, mix them lightly, and stir them into the third of a pint of rich melted butter or of white sauce: serve the whole as hot as possible.

Eggs, 4: boiled 15 minutes, left till cold. The yolks of all, whites of 2; third of pint of good melted butter or white sauce. Salt as needed.

COMMON LOBSTER SAUCE

Add to half a pint of good melted butter a tablespoonful of essence of anchovies, a small half-saltspoonful of freshly pounded mace, and less than a quarter one of cayenne. If a couple of spoonsful of cream should be at hand, stir them to the sauce when it boils; then put in the flesh of the tail and claws of a small lobster cut into dice (or any other form) of equal size. Keep the saucepan by the side of the fire until the fish is quite heated through, but do not let the sauce boil again: serve it very hot. A small quantity can be made on occasion with the remains of a lobster which has been served at table.

Melted butter, ½ pint; essence of anchovies, 1 tablespoonful; pounded mace, small ½ saltspoonful; less than ¼ one of cayenne; cream (if added), 2 tablespoonsful; flesh of small lobster.

CRAB SAUCE

The flesh of a fresh well-conditioned crab of moderate size is more tender and delicate than that of a lobster, and may be converted into an excellent fish sauce. Divide it into small flakes, and add it to some good melted butter, which has been flavoured as for the sauce above. A portion of the cream contained in the fish may first be smoothly mingled with the sauce.

ANCHOVY SAUCE

To half a pint of good melted butter add three dessertspoonsful of essence of anchovies, a quarter of a teaspoonful of mace, and a rather high seasoning of cayenne; or pound the flesh of two or three fine mellow anchovies very smooth, mix it with the boiling butter, simmer these for a minute or two, strain the sauce if needful, add the spices, give it a boil, and serve it.

Melted butter, ½ pint; essence of anchovies, 3 dessertspoonsful; mace, ¼ teaspoonful; cayenne, to taste. Or, 3 large anchovies finely pounded, and the same proportions of butter and spice.

CREAM SAUCE FOR FISH

Knead very smoothly together with a strong-bladed knife, a *large* teaspoonful of flour with three ounces of good butter; stir them in a very clean saucepan or stewpan over a gentle fire until the butter is dissolved, then throw in a little salt and some cayenne, give the whole one minute's simmer, and add, very gradually, half a pint of good cream; keep the sauce constantly stirred, until it boils, then mix with it a dessertspoonful of essence of anchovies, and half as much chili vinegar or lemon-juice. The addition of shelled shrimps or lobsters cut in dice, will convert this at once into a most excellent sauce of either. Pounded mace may be added to it with the cayenne: and it may be thinned with a few spoonsful of milk should it be too thick. Omit the essence of anchovies, and mix with it some parsley boiled very green and minced, and it becomes a good sauce for poultry.

Butter, 3 oz; flour, 1 *large* teaspoonful: 2 to 3 minutes. Cream,

½ pint; essence of anchovies, 1 large dessertspoonful (more if liked); chili vinegar or lemon juice, 1 teaspoonful; salt, ¼ saltspoonful.

FRENCH MAÎTRE D'HÔTEL,* OR
STEWARD'S SAUCE†

Add to half a pint of rich, pale veal gravy, well thickened with white *roux*, a good seasoning of pepper, salt, minced parsley, and lemon-juice; or make the thickening with a small tablespoonful of flour, and a couple of ounces of butter; keep these stirred constantly over a very gentle fire from ten to fifteen minutes, then pour the gravy to them boiling, in small portions, mixing the whole well as it is added, and letting it boil up between each, for unless this be done the butter will be likely to float upon the surface. Simmer the sauce for a few minutes, and skim it well, then add salt should it be needed, a tolerable seasoning of pepper or of cayenne in fine powder, from two or three teaspoonsful of minced parsley, and the strained juice of a small lemon. For some dishes, this sauce is thickened with the yolks of eggs, about four to the pint. The French work into their sauces generally a small bit of fresh butter just before they are taken from the fire, to give them mellowness: this is done usually for the *Maître d'Hôtel Sauce*.

* The Maître d'Hôtel is, properly, the *House Steward*.
† [*If butter is substituted for the gravy the sauce becomes Maître d'Hôtel Sauce Maigre*.]

SAUCE ROBERT

Cut four or five large onions into small dice, and brown them in a stewpan, with three ounces of butter and a dessertspoonful of flour. When of a deep yellow brown, pour to them half a pint of beef or of veal gravy, and let them simmer for fifteen minutes; skim the sauce, add a dessertspoonful of made mustard with it.

Large onions, 4 or 5; butter, 3 oz; flour, dessertspoonful: 10 to

15 minutes. Gravy, ½ pint: 15 minutes. Mustard, dessert-spoonful.

EXCELLENT HORSERADISH SAUCE
(*To serve hot or cold with roast beef*)

Wash and wipe a stick of *young* horseradish, scrape off the outer skin, grate it as small as possible on a fine grater, then with two ounces (or a couple of large tablespoonsful) of it mix a small teaspoonful of salt and four tablespoonsful of good cream; stir in briskly, and by degrees, three dessertspoonsful of vinegar, one of which should be chili vinegar when the horseradish is mild. To heat the sauce, put it into a small and delicately clean saucepan, hold it over, but do not place it *upon* the fire, and stir it without intermission until it is near the point of simmering; but do not allow it to boil, or it will curdle instantly.

Horseradish pulp, 2 oz (or 2 *large* tablespoonsful); salt, 1 teaspoonful; good cream, 4 tablespoonsful; vinegar, 3 dessertspoonsful (of which one should be chili when the root is mild).

Obs. Common English salad-mixture is often added to the grated horseradish when the sauce is to be served cold.

CHRISTOPHER NORTH'S OWN SAUCE FOR MANY MEATS†

Throw into a small basin a heaped saltspoonful of *good* cayenne pepper, in very fine powder, and half quantity of salt;* add a small dessertspoonful of well-refined, pounded, and sifted sugar; mix these thoroughly; then pour in a tablespoonful of the strained juice of a fresh lemon, two of Harvey's sauce, a teaspoonful of the very best mushroom catsup (or of cavice), and a small wineglassful of port wine. Heat the sauce by placing the basin in a saucepan of boiling water, or turn it into a jar, and place this in the water. Serve it directly it is ready with geese or ducks, tame or wild; roast pork, venison, fawn, a grilled blade-bone, or any other broil. A slight flavour of garlic or eschalot vinegar may be given to it at pleasure. Some persons eat it with fish. It is good cold; and, if bottled directly it is made, may be stored for several days. It is better for being mixed some hours before it is served. *The proportions of cayenne may be doubled when a very pungent sauce is desired.*

* *Characteristically, the salt* of this sauce ought, perhaps, to prevail more strongly over the *sugar*, but it will be found for most tastes sufficiently *piquant* as it is.

† ['*Christopher North' was the pseudonym of John Wilson, Professor of Moral Philosophy at Edinburgh, who died in 1854. He was the author of a number of the 'Noctes Ambrosianae' that appeared under his pseudonym in* Blackwoods Magazine.]

GOOSEBERRY SAUCE FOR MACKEREL

Cut the stalks and tops from half to a whole pint of quite young gooseberries, wash them well, just cover them with cold water, and boil them very gently indeed, until they are tender; drain and mix them with a small quantity of melted butter, made with rather less flour than usual. Some eaters prefer the mashed gooseberries without any addition; others like that of a little ginger. The best way of making this sauce is to turn the gooseberries into a hair-sieve to drain, then to press them through it with a wooden spoon, and to stir them in a clean stewpan or saucepan over the fire with from half to a whole teaspoonful of sugar, just to soften their extreme acidity, and a bit of fresh butter about the size of a walnut. When the fruit is not passed through the sieve it is an improvement to seed it.

COMMON SORREL SAUCE

Strip from the stalks and the large fibres, from one to a couple of quarts of freshly-gathered sorrel; wash it very clean, and put it into a well-tinned stewpan or saucepan (or into an enamelled one, which would be far better), without any water; add to it a small slice of good butter, some pepper and salt, and stew it gently, keeping it well stirred until it is exceedingly tender, that it may not burn; then drain it on a sieve, or press the liquid well from it; chop it as fine as possible, and boil it again for a few minutes with a spoonful or two of gravy, or the same quantity of cream or milk, mixed with a half-teaspoonful of flour, or with only a fresh slice of good butter. The beaten yolk of an egg or two stirred in just as the sorrel is taken from the fire will soften the sauce greatly, and a saltspoonful of pounded sugar will also be an improvement.

ASPARAGUS SAUCE, FOR LAMB CUTLETS

Green cut the tender points of some young asparagus into half-inch lengths, or into the size of peas only; wash them well, then drain and throw them into plenty of boiling salt and water. When they are quite tender, which may be in from ten to fifteen minutes, turn them into a hot strainer and drain the water thoroughly from them: put them, at the instant of serving, into half a pint of thickened veal gravy (see *sauce tournée*), mixed with the yolks of a couple of eggs, and well seasoned with salt and cayenne, or white pepper, or into an equal quantity of good melted butter: add to this last a squeeze of lemon-juice. The asparagus will become yellow if reboiled, or if left long in the sauce before it is served.

Asparagus points, ½ pint: boiled 10 to 15 minutes, longer if not quite tender. Thickened veal gravy, ½ pint; lemon-juice, small dessertspoonful, seasoning of salt and white pepper.

CAPER SAUCE

Stir into the third of a pint of good melted butter from three to four dessertspoonsful of capers; add a little of the vinegar, and dish the sauce as soon as it boils. Keep it stirred after the berries are added: part of them may be minced and a little chili vinegar substituted for their own. Pickled nasturtiums† make a very good sauce, and their flavour is sometimes preferred to that of the capers. For a large joint, increase the quantity of butter to half a pint.

Melted butter, third of pint; capers, 3 to 4 dessertspoonsful.

† [*Nasturtium seeds were often used instead of capers. They were first kept in salted cold water for three days, then pickled in a mixture of vinegar, horseradish, pepper, salt, and spices such as cloves and mace.*]

CAPER SAUCE FOR FISH

To nearly half a pint of very rich melted butter add six spoonsful of *strong* veal gravy or jelly, a tablespoonful of essence of anchovies, and some chili vinegar or cayenne, and from two to three tablespoonsful of capers. When there is no gravy at hand substitute a half wineglassful of mushroom catsup, or of Harvey's sauce; though these deepen the colour more than is desirable.

COMMON SAUCE OF CUCUMBERS

Cucumbers which have the fewest seeds are best for this sauce. Pare and slice *two* or *three*, should they be small, and put them into a saucepan, in which two ounces, or rather more, of butter have been dissolved, and are beginning to boil; place them high over the fire, that they may stew as softly as possible, without taking colour, for three-quarters of an hour, or longer should they require it; add to them a good seasoning of white pepper and some salt, when they are half done; and just before they are served stir to them half a teaspoonful of flour, mixed with a morsel of butter; strew in some minced parsley, give it a boil, and finish with a spoonful of good vinegar.

COMMON TOMATA SAUCE

Tomatas are so juicy when ripe that they require little or no liquid to reduce them to a proper consistence for sauce; and they vary so exceedingly in size and quality that it is difficult to give precise directions for the exact quantity which in their unripe state is needed for them. Take off the stalks, halve the tomatas, and gently squeeze out the seeds and watery pulp; then stew them softly with a few spoonsful of gravy or of strong broth until they are quite melted. Press the whole through a hair-sieve, and heat it afresh with a little additional gravy should it be too thick, and some cayenne, and salt. Serve it very hot.

Fine ripe tomatas, 6 or 8; gravy or strong broth, 4 table-spoonsful: ½ to ¾ hour, or longer if needed. Salt and cayenne sufficient to season the sauce, and two or three spoonsful more of gravy if required.

Obs. For a large tureen of this sauce, increase the proportions; and should it be at first too liquid, reduce it by quick boiling. When neither gravy nor broth is at hand, the tomatas may be stewed perfectly tender, but very gently, in a couple of ounces of butter, with some cayenne and salt only, or with the addition of a very little finely minced onion; then rubbed through a sieve, and heated, and served without any addition, or with only that of a teaspoonful of chili vinegar; or, when the colour is not a principal consideration, with a few spoonsful of rich cream, smoothly mixed with a little flour to prevent its curdling. The sauce must be stirred without ceasing should the last be added, and boiled for four to five minutes.

BAKED APPLE SAUCE
(*Good*)

Put a tablespoonful of water into a quart basin, and fill it with good boiling apples, pared, quartered, and *carefully* cored: put a plate over, and set them into a moderate oven for about an hour, or until they are reduced quite to a pulp; beat them smooth with a clean wooden spoon, adding to them a little sugar and a morsel of fresh butter, when these are liked, though they will scarcely be required.

The sauce made thus is far superior to that which is boiled.

When no other oven is at hand, a Dutch or an American one would probably answer for it; but we cannot assert this on our own experience.

Good boiling apples, 1 quart: baked 1 hour (more or less according to the quality of the fruit, and temperature of the oven); sugar, 1 oz; butter, ½ oz.

BROWN APPLE SAUCE

Stew gently down to a thick and perfectly smooth marmalade, a pound of pearmains, or of any other well-flavoured boiling apples, in about the third of a pint of rich brown gravy: season the sauce rather highly with black pepper or cayenne, and serve it very hot. Curry sauce will make an excellent substitute for the gravy when a very piquant accompaniment is wanted for pork or other rich meat.

Apples pared and cored, 1 lb; good brown gravy, third of pint: ¾ to 1¼ hours. Pepper or cayenne as needed.

SOUBISE
(French Receipt)

Peel some fine white onions, and trim away all tough and discoloured parts; mince them small, and throw them into plenty of boiling water; when they have boiled quickly for five minutes drain them well in a sieve, then stew them very softly indeed in an ounce or two of fresh butter until they are dry and perfectly tender; stir to them as much *béchamel* as will bring them to the consistence of very thick pea-soup, pass the whole through a strainer, pressing the onion strongly that none may remain behind, and heat the sauce afresh, without allowing it to boil. A small half-teaspoonful of pounded sugar is sometimes added to this *soubise*.

White part of onions, 2 lb; blanched 5 minutes. Butter, 2 oz: 30 to 50 minutes. *Béchamel*, ¾ to 1 pint, or more.

Obs. These sauces are served more frequently with lamb or mutton cutlets than with any other dishes; but they would probably find many approvers if sent to table with roast mutton, or boiled veal. Half the quantity given above will be sufficient for a moderate-sized dish.

MILD RAGOUT OF GARLIC, OR L'AIL À LA BORDELAISE

Divide some fine cloves of garlic, strip off the skin, and when all are ready throw them into plenty of boiling water slightly salted; in five minutes drain this from them, and pour in as much more, which should also be quite boiling; continue to change it every five or six minutes until the garlic is quite tender: throw in a moderate proportion of salt the last time to give it the proper flavour. Drain it thoroughly, and serve it in the dish with roast mutton, or put it into good brown gravy or white sauce for table. By changing very frequently the water in which it is boiled, the root will be deprived of its naturally pungent flavour and smell, and rendered extremely mild: when it is not wished to be quite so much so, change the water every ten minutes only.

Garlic, 1 pint: 15 to 25 minutes, or more. Water to be changed every 5 to 6 minutes; or every 10 minutes when not wished so *very* mild. Gravy or sauce, 1 pint.

OLIVE SAUCE

Remove the stones from some fine French or Italian olives by paring the fruit close to them, round and round in the form of a corkscrew: they will then resume their original shape when done.† Weigh six ounces thus prepared, throw them into boiling water, let them blanch for five minutes; then drain, and throw them into cold water, and leave them in it from half an hour to an hour, proportioning the time to their saltiness; drain them well, and stew them gently from fifteen to twenty-five minutes in a pint of very rich brown gravy or *Espagnole* (see Chapter 4); add the juice of half a lemon, and serve the sauce very hot. Half this quantity will be sufficient for a small party.

Olives, stoned, 6 oz; rich gravy, 1 pint: 15 to 25 minutes. Juice, ½ lemon.

Obs. In France this sauce is served very commonly with ducks, and sometimes with beef-steaks, and with stewed fowl.

† [*There is a gadget on the market that presses the stones out of olives (or of cherries) which saves much time and trouble.*]

PARSLEY-GREEN, FOR COLOURING SAUCES

Gather a quantity of young parsley, strip it from the stalks, wash it very clean, shake it as dry as possible in a cloth, pound it in a mortar, press all the juice closely from it through a hair-sieve reversed, and put it into a clean jar; set it into a pan of boiling water, and in about three minutes, if *gently* simmered, the juice will be poached sufficiently; lay it then upon a clean sieve to drain, and it will be ready for use.

Spinach-green is prepared in the same manner. The juice of various herbs pounded together may be pressed from them through a sieve and added to cold sauces.

FRENCH BATTER
(For frying vegetables, and for apple, peach, or orange fritters)

Cut a couple of ounces of good butter into small bits, pour on it less than a quarter of a pint of boiling water, and when it is dissolved add three-quarters of a pint of cold water, so that the whole shall not be quite milk warm; mix it then by degrees and very smoothly with twelve ounces of fine dry flour and a *small* pinch of salt if the batter be for fruit fritters, but with more if for meat or vegetables. Just before it is used, stir into it the white of two eggs beaten to a solid froth; but previously to this, add a little water should it appear too thick, as some flour requires more liquid than others to bring it to the proper consistence; this is an exceedingly light crisp batter, excellent for the purposes for which it is named.

Butter, 2 oz; water, from 3/4 to nearly 1 pint; little salt; flour, 3/4 lb; whites of 2 eggs, beaten to snow.

BROWNED FLOUR FOR THICKENING SOUPS AND GRAVIES

Spread it on a tin or dish and colour it, without burning, in a gentle oven or before the fire in a Dutch or American oven: turn it often, or the edges will be too much browned before the middle is enough so. This, blended with butter, makes a convenient thickening for soups or gravies of which it is desirable to deepen the colour.

6

COLD SAUCES AND SALADS

SUPERIOR MINT-SAUCE
(To serve with lamb)

The mint for this sauce should be fresh and young, for when old
it is tough and indigestible. Strip the leaves from the stems, wash
them with great nicety, and drain them on a sieve, or dry them in
a cloth; chop them very fine, put them into a sauce-tureen, and to
three heaped tablespoonsful of the mint add two of pounded
sugar; let them remain a short time well mixed together, then
pour to them gradually six tablespoonsful of good vinegar. The
sauce thus made is excellent, and far more wholesome than when
a larger proportion of vinegar and a smaller one of sugar is used
for it; but, after the first trial, the proportions can easily be adapted to the taste of the eaters.

STRAINED MINT-SAUCE

Persons with whom the mint in substance disagrees can have the
flavour of the herb without it, by mixing the ingredients of the
preceding receipt, and straining the sauce after it has stood for
two or three hours; the mint should be well pressed when this is
done. The flavour will be the more readily extracted if the mint
and sugar are well mixed, and left for a time before the vinegar is
added.

COLD DUTCH OR AMERICAN SAUCE, FOR SALADS OF
DRESSED VEGETABLES, SALT FISH, OR HARD EGGS

Put into a saucepan three ounces of good butter very smoothly blended with a quite small teaspoonful of flour, and add to them a large wineglassful of cold water, half as much sharp vinegar (or very fresh, strained, lemon-juice) a saltspoonful of salt, and half as much cayenne in fine powder. Keep these shaken briskly round, or stirred over a clear fire, until they form a smooth sauce and boil rapidly; then stir them very quickly to the beaten yolks of four fresh eggs, which will immediately give the sauce the consistence of custard; pour it hot over the salad, and place it on ice, or in a very cool larder until it is quite cold: if properly made, it will be very thick and smooth, and slightly *set*, as if it contained a small portion of isinglass. A dessertspoonful of parsley – or of tarragon – can be mingled with it at *pleasure*, or any flavour given to it with store-sauces which is liked. It converts flakes of salf-fish, sliced potatoes (new or old), and hard eggs, into excellent salads.

ENGLISH SAUCE FOR SALAD, COLD MEAT,
OR COLD FISH†

The first essential for a smooth, well-made English salad dressing is to have the yolks of the eggs used for it sufficiently hard to be reduced easily to a perfect paste. They should be boiled at least fifteen minutes, and should have become *quite* cold before they are taken from the shells; they should also be well covered with water when they are cooked, or some parts of them will be tough, and will spoil the appearance of the sauce by rendering it lumpy, unless they be worked through a sieve, a process which is always better avoided if possible. To a couple of yolks broken up and mashed to a paste with the back of a wooden spoon, add a small saltspoonful of salt, a large one of pounded sugar, a few grains of fine cayenne, and a teaspoonful of cold water; mix these well, and stir to them by degrees a quarter of a pint of sweet cream; throw in next, stirring the sauce briskly, a tablespoonful of strong chili vinegar, and add as much common or French vinegar as will acidulate the mixture agreeably. A tablespoonful of either will be sufficient for many tastes, but it is easy to increase the proportion when more is liked. Six tablespoonsful of olive oil, of the purest quality, may be substituted for the cream: it should be added in very small portions to the other ingredients and stirred briskly as each is added until the sauce resembles custard. When this is used, the water should be omitted. The piquancy of this preparation – which is very delicate, made by the directions just given – may be heightened by the addition of a little eschalot vinegar, Harvey's sauce, essence of anchovies, French mustard, or tarragon vinegar: or by bruising with the eggs a morsel of garlic, half the size of a hazel-nut: it should always, however, be rendered as appropriate as may be to the dish with which it is to be served.

Obs. As we have before had occasion to remark, garlic, when very sparingly and judiciously used, imparts a remarkably fine savour to a sauce or gravy, and neither a strong nor a coarse one, as it does when used in larger quantities. The veriest morsel (or, as the French call it, a mere *soupçon*) of the root, is sufficient to give this agreeable piquancy, but unless the proportion be extremely small, the effect will be quite different. The Italians dress their salads upon a round of delicately toasted bread, which is rubbed with garlic, saturated with oil, and sprinkled with cayenne, before it is laid into the bowl: they also eat the bread thus prepared, but with less of oil, and untoasted often, before their meals as a digester.

†[*This is very much the same as Remoulade Sauce.*]

THE POET'S RECEIPT FOR SALAD*

'Two large potatoes, passed through kitchen sieve
Unwonted softness to the salad give;
Of mordent mustard, add a single spoon,
Distrust the condiment which bites so soon;

75

But deem it not, thou man of herbs, a fault,
To add a double quantity of salt;
Three times the spoon with oil of Lucca crown,
And once with vinegar, procured from town;
True flavour needs it, and your poet begs
The pounded yellow of two well-boiled eggs;
Let onion atoms lurk within the bowl,
And, scarce suspected, animate the whole;
And lastly, in the flavoured compound toss
A magic teaspoon of anchovy sauce:
Then, though green turtle fail, though venison's tough,
And ham and turkey are not boiled enough,
Serenely full, the epicure may say –
Fate cannot harm me – I have dined today.'

Two well-boiled potatoes, passed through a sieve; a teaspoonful of mustard; two teaspoonsful of salt; one of essence of anchovy; about a quarter of a teaspoonful of very finely-chopped onions, well bruised into the mixture; three tablespoonsful of oil; one of vinegar; the yolks of two eggs, hard boiled. Stir up the salad immediately before dinner, and stir it up thoroughly.

N.B. As this salad is the result of great experience and reflection, it is hoped young salad makers will not attempt to make any improvements upon it.

* This receipt, though long privately circulated amongst the friends and acquaintance of its distinguished and regretted author,† now (with permission) appears for the first time in print. We could not venture to deviate by a word from the original, but we would suggest, that the mixture forms almost a substitute for salad, instead of a mere dressing. It is, however, an admirable compound for those to whom the slight flavouring of onion is not an objection.

† [*The 'distinguished and regretted author' was Sidney Smith.*]

SAUCE MAYONNAISE
(*For salads, cold meat, poultry, fish, or vegetables*)

This is a very fine sauce when all the ingredients used for it are good; but it will prove an uneatable compound to a delicate taste unless it be made with oil of the purest quality.

Put into a large basin the yolks only of two very fresh eggs, carefully freed from specks, with a little salt and cayenne; stir these well together, then add about a teaspoonful of the purest salad oil, and work the mixture round with a wooden spoon until it appears like cream. Pour in by slow degrees nearly half a pint of oil, continuing at each interval to work the sauce as at first until it resumes the smoothness of cream, and not a particle of the oil remains visible; then add a couple of tablespoonsful of plain French or of tarragon vinegar, and one of cold water to whiten the sauce; a bit of clear veal jelly the size of an egg will improve it greatly. The reader who may have a prejudice against the unboiled eggs which enter into the composition of the Mayonnaise, will find that the most fastidious taste would not detect their being raw, if the sauce be well made; and persons who dislike oil may partake of it in this form, without being aware of its presence, provided always that it be perfectly fresh, and pure in flavour, for otherwise it will be easily perceptible.

Yolks of fresh unboiled eggs, 2; salt, ½ saltspoonful, or rather more; cayenne; oil, full third of pint; French or tarragon vinegar, 2 tablespoonsful; cold water, 1 tablespoonful; meat jelly (if at hand), size of an egg.

RED OR GREEN MAYONNAISE SAUCE

Colour may be given to the preceding *Sauce Mayonnaise* by mingling with it some hard lobster-coral reduced to powder by rubbing it through a very fine hair-sieve: the red hue of this is one of the most brilliant and beautiful that can be seen, but the sauce for which it is used can only be appropriately served with fish or fish-salads. Spinach-green will impart a fine tint to any preparation, but its flavour is objectionable: that of parsley-green† is more agreeable.

† [*See receipt on p. 71.*]

77

Mingle thoroughly a tablespoonful of brown sugar with a tea-spoonful of made mustard, a third as much of salt, some pepper, from three to four tablespoonsful of very fine salad-oil, and two of strong vinegar: or apportion the same ingredients otherwise to the taste.

FORCED† EGGS FOR GARNISHING SALAD

Pound and press through the back of a hair-sieve the flesh of three very fine, or of four moderate-sized anchovies, freed from the bones and skin. Boil six fresh eggs for twelve minutes, and when they are perfectly cold halve them lengthwise, take out the yolks, pound them to a paste with a third of their volume of fresh butter, then add the anchovies, a quarter of a teaspoonful of mace, and as much cayenne as will season the mixture well; beat these together thoroughly, and fill the whites of egg neatly with them. A *morsel* of garlic, perfectly blended with the other in-gredients, would to some tastes improve this preparation: a portion of anchovy-butter, or of potted ham, will supply the place of fish in it very advantageously.

Eggs, 6; anchovies, 4; butter, size of 2 yolks; mace, ¼ tea-spoonful; cayenne, third as much.

† [*Stuffed, as in forcemeat.*]

TRUFFLED BUTTER (AND TRUFFLES POTTED IN BUTTER)
(*For the breakfast or luncheon table*)

Cut up a pound of sweet fresh butter, and dissolve it gently over a clear fire; take off the scum which will gather thickly upon it, and when it has simmered for three or four minutes, draw it from the fire, and let it stand until all the butter-milk has sub-sided; pour it softly from this upon six ounces of ready-pared sound French truffles, cut into small, but rather thick, slices, and laid into a delicately clean enamelled saucepan; add a full seasoning of freshly pounded mace and fine cayenne, a small saltspoonful of salt, and half a not large nutmeg. [*Removed after the truffles are cooked.*] When the butter has become quite cold, proceed to heat the truffles slowly, shaking the saucepan often briskly round, and stew them as gently as possible for twenty minutes, or longer should they not then be very tender. If allowed to heat, and to boil quickly, they will become *hard*, and the preparation, as regards the *truffles*, will be a comparative failure. Lift them with a spoon into quite dry earthen or china pans, and pour the butter on them; or add to them sufficient of it only to cover them well and to exclude the air, and pot the remainder of the butter apart: it will be finely flavoured, and may be eaten by delicate persons to whom the truffle itself would be injurious. It may also be used in compounding savoury sauces, and for moistening small *croustades* before they are fried or baked. The truffles themselves will remain good for months when thus prepared, if kept free from damp; and in flavour they will be found excellent. The parings taken from them will also impart a very agreeable savour to the butter, and will serve extremely well for it for immediate use. They will also be valuable as additions to gravies or to soups.

We should observe, that the juice which will have exuded from the truffles in the stewing will cause the preparation to become mouldy, or otherwise injure it, if it be put into the pans either with them or with the butter. The truffles must be well drained from it when they are taken from the saucepan, and the butter must remain undisturbed for a few minutes, when it can be poured clear from the juice, which will have subsided to the bottom of the pan. We have given here the result of our first experiment, which we found on further trial to answer perfectly.

The herbs and vegetables for a salad cannot be too freshly gathered: they should be carefully cleared from insects and washed with scrupulous nicety; they are better when not prepared until near the time of sending them to table, and should not be sauced until the instant before they are served. Tender lettuces, of which the stems should be cut off, and the outer leaves be stripped away, mustard and cress, young radishes, and occasionally chives or small green onions (when the taste of a party is in favour of these last) are the usual ingredients of summer salads. (In early spring, as we have stated in another chapter, the young white leaves of the dandelion will supply a very wholesome and excellent salad, of which the slight bitterness is to many persons as agreeable as that of the endive.) Half-grown cucumbers sliced thin, and mixed with them, are a favourite addition with many persons. In England it is customary to cut the lettuces extremely fine; the French, who object to the *flavour of the knife*, which they fancy this mode imparts, break them small instead. Young celery alone, sliced, and dressed with a rich salad mixture, is excellent: it is still in some families served thus always with roast pheasants.

Beetroot, baked or boiled, blanched endive, small salad-herbs which are easily raised at any time of the year, celery, and hardy lettuces, with any ready-dressed vegetable, will supply salads through the winter. Cucumber vinegar is an agreeable addition to these.

FRENCH SALAD

In winter this is made principally of beautifully-blanched endive, washed delicately clean and broken into small branches with the fingers, then taken from the water and shaken dry in a basket of peculiar form, appropriated to the purpose,* or in a fine cloth; then arranged in the salad bowl, and strewed with herbs (tarragon generally, when in season) minced small: the dressing is not added until just before the salad is eaten. In summer, young lettuces are substituted for the endive, and intermixed with a variety of herbs, some of which are not generally cultivated in England.

* Salad-baskets are also to be found in many good English kitchens, but they are not in such general use here as on the Continent.

FRENCH SALAD DRESSING

Stir a saltspoonful of salt and half as much pepper into a large spoonful of oil, and when the salt is dissolved, mix with them four additional spoonsful of oil, and pour the whole over the salad; let it be *well* turned, and then add a couple of spoonsful of tarragon vinegar; mix the whole thoroughly, and serve it without delay. The salad should not be dressed in this way until the instant before it is wanted for table: the proportions of salt and pepper can be increased at pleasure, and common or cucumber vinegar may be substituted for the tarragon, which, however, is more frequently used in France than any other.

Salt, 1 spoonful: pepper, ½ as much; oil, 5 saladspoonsful; tarragon, or other vinegar, 2 spoonsful.

AN EXCELLENT HERRING SALAD

(Swedish Receipt)

Soak, skin, split, and bone a large Norway herring; lay the two sides along a dish, and slice them slopingly (or substitute for this one or two fine Dutch herring). Arrange in symmetrical order over the fish slices of cooked beetroot, cold boiled potatoes, and pickled gherkins; then add one or two sharp apples chopped small, and the yolks and whites, separately minced, of some hardboiled eggs, with any thing else which may be at hand, and may serve to vary tastefully the decoration of the dish. Place these ingredients in small heaps of well-contrasting colours on the surface of the salad, and lay a border of curled celery leaves or parsley round the bowl.

For sauce, rub the yolk of one hard-boiled egg quite smooth with some salt; to this add oil and vinegar as for an ordinary salad, and dilute the whole with some thick sour cream.

Obs. 'Sour cream' is an ingredient not much approved by English taste, but it enters largely into German cookery, and into that of Sweden, and of other northern countries also. About half a pound of cold beef cut into small thin shavings or collops, is often added to a herring salad abroad: it may be either of simply roasted or boiled, or of salted and smoked meat.

TARTAR SAUCE
(*Sauce à la Tartare*)

Add to *remoulade,* or to any other sauce of the same nature [*such as English sauce: see p. 74*]; a teaspoonful or more of made mustard, one of finely-minced eschalots, one of parsley or tarragon, and one of capers or of pickled gherkins, with a rather high seasoning of cayenne, and some salt if needed. The tartar-mustard of this chapter, or good French mustard, is to be preferred to English for this sauce, which is usually made very pungent, and for which any ingredients can be used to the taste which will serve to render it so. Tarragon vinegar, *minced tarragon* and eschalots, and plenty of oil, are used for it in France, in conjunction with the yolks of one or two eggs, and chopped capers, or gherkins, to which olives are sometimes added.

SHRIMP CHATNEY
(*Mauritian Receipt*)

Shell with care a quart of fresh shrimps (for the mode of doing this see Chapter 3), mince them quickly upon a dish with a large sharp knife, then turn them into a mortar and pound them to a perfectly smooth paste. Next, mix with them very gradually two or three spoonsful of salad oil of the best quality, some young green chilies chopped small (or when these cannot be procured, some *good* cayenne pepper as a substitute), some young onions finely minced, a little salt if required, and as much vinegar or strained lemon-juice as will render the sauce pleasantly acid. Half a saltspoonful or more of powdered ginger is sometimes in addition to the above ingredients.

When they are preferred, two or three small shalots minced and well bruised with the shrimps may be substituted for the onions. The proportion of oil should be double that of the vinegar used; but in this preparation, as in all others of the same nature, individual taste must regulate the proportion of the most powerful condiments which enter into its composition. All Chatneys should be *quite thick*, almost of the consistence of mashed turnips or stewed tomatas, or stiff bread sauce. They are served with curries; and also with steaks, cutlets, cold meat, and fish. In the East the native cooks crush to a pulp upon a stone slab, and with a stone roller, the ingredients which we direct to be pounded. On occasion the fish might be merely minced. When beaten to a paste, they should be well separated with a fork as the chilies, etc., are added.

7

Mushrooms, Eschalots, and Tomatas

STORE SAUCES

By Store Sauces Eliza Acton means those made for the store cupboard, not those bought in a shop.

CHATNEY SAUCE
(Bengal Receipt)

Stone four ounces of good raisins, and chop them small, with half a pound of crabs, sour apples, unripe bullaces, or of any other hard acid fruit. Take four ounces of coarse brown sugar, two of powdered ginger, and the same quantity of salt and cayenne pepper; grind these ingredients separately in a mortar, as fine as possible; then pound the fruits well, and mix the spices with them, one by one; beat them together until they are perfectly blended, and add gradually as much vinegar as will make the sauce of the consistency of thick cream. Put it into bottles with an ounce of garlic, divided into cloves, and cork it tightly.

Stoned raisins, 4 oz; crabs, or other acid fruit, ½ lb; coarse sugar, 4 oz; salt, 2 oz; cayenne pepper, 2 oz; garlic, 1 oz; vinegar, enough to dilute it properly.

Hard acid fruit in a crude state is, we think, an ingredient not much to be recommended; and it is always better to deviate a little from 'an approved receipt' than to endanger health by the use of ingredients of a questionable character. Gooseberries or tomatas, after being subjected to a moderate degree of heat, might be eaten with far less hazard.

MUSHROOM CATSUP

Break a peck of large mushrooms into a deep earthen pan; strew three-quarters of a pound of salt amongst them, and set them into a very cool oven for one night, with a fold of cloth or paper over them. The following day strain off the liquor, measure, and boil it for fifteen minutes; then, for each quart, add an ounce of black pepper, a quarter of an ounce of allspice, half an ounce of ginger, and two large blades of mace, and let it boil fast for twenty minutes longer. When thoroughly cold, put it into bottles, cork them well, and dip the necks into melted bottle-cement, or seal them so as to secure the catsup from the air.

Mushrooms, 1 peck; salt, ¾ lb. Liquor to boil, 15 minutes. To each quart, 1 oz black pepper; ¼ oz allspice; ½ oz ginger; 2 blades mace: 20 minutes.

DOUBLE MUSHROOM CATSUP

On a gallon of fresh mushrooms strew three ounces of salt, and pour to them a quart of ready-made catsup (that which is a year old will do if it be perfectly good); keep these stirred occasionally for four days, then drain the liquor very dry from the mushrooms, and boil it for fifteen minutes with an ounce of whole black pepper, a drachm [*very small pinch*] of mace, an ounce of ginger, and three or four grains only of cayenne.

Mushrooms, 1 gallon; salt, 3 oz; mushroom catsup, 1 quart; pepper-corns, 1 oz; mace, 1 drachm; ginger, 1 oz; cayenne, 3 to 4 grains: 15 minutes.

COMPOUND, OR COOK'S CATSUP

Take a pint and a half of mushroom catsup when it is first made and ready boiled (the double is best for the purpose), simmer in it for five minutes an ounce of small eschalots nicely peeled; add to these half a pint of walnut catsup, and a wineglassful of cayenne vinegar, or of chili vinegar; give the whole one boil, pour it out, and when cold, bottle it with the eschalots in it.

Mushroom catsup, 1½ pints; eschalots, 1 oz; walnut catsup or pickle, ½ pint; cayenne or chili vinegar, 1 wineglassful.

PONTAC CATSUP FOR FISH

On one pint of ripe elderberries stripped from the stalks, pour three quarters of a pint of boiling vinegar, and let it stand in a cool oven all night; the next day strain off the liquid without pressure, and boil it for five minutes with a half-teaspoonful of salt, a small race [*piece*] of ginger, a blade of mace, forty corns of pepper, twelve cloves and four eschalots. Bottle it with the spice when it is quite cold.

BOTTLED TOMATAS, OR TOMATA CATSUP

Cut half a peck of ripe tomatas into quarters; lay them on dishes and sprinkle over them half a pound of salt. The next day drain the juice from them through a hair-sieve into a stewpan, and boil it for half an hour with three dozens of small capsicums and half a pound of eschalots; then add the tomatas, which should be ready pulped through a strainer. Boil the whole for thirty minutes longer; have some clean wide-necked bottles, kept warm by the fire, fill them with the catsup while it is quite hot; cork, and dip the necks into melted bottle-resin or cement.

Tomatas, ½ peck; salt, ½ lb; capsicums, 3 doz; eschalots, ½ lb: ½ hour. After pulp is added, ½ hour.

Obs. This receipt has been kindly contributed by a person who makes by it every year large quantities of the catsup, which is considered excellent: for sauce it must be mixed with gravy or melted butter. We have not ourselves been able to make trial of it.

TARRAGON VINEGAR

Gather the tarragon just before it blossoms, which will be late in July, or early in August; strip it from the larger stalks, and put it into small stone jars or wide-necked bottles, and in doing this twist some of the branches so as to bruise the leaves and wring them asunder; then pour in sufficient distilled or very pale vinegar to cover the tarragon; let it infuse for two months, or more: it will take no harm even by standing all the winter. When it is poured off, strain it very clear, put it into small dry bottles, and cork them well. Sweet basil vinegar is made in exactly the same way, but it should not be left on the leaves more than three weeks. The jars or bottles should be filled to the neck with the tarragon before the vinegar is added: its flavour is strong and peculiar, but to many tastes very agreeable. It imparts quite a foreign character to the dishes for which it is used.

GREEN MINT VINEGAR

Slightly chop, or bruise, freshly-gathered mint, and put it into bottles; fill them nearly to the necks, and add vinegar as for tarragon: in forty days, strain it off and bottle it for use.

The mint itself, ready minced for sauce, will keep well in vinegar, though the colour will not be very good. The young leaves stripped from the stems, should be used for this preparation.

Throw into a pint and a half of ready boiling vinegar a few grains
of cayenne, or half an ounce of peppercorns, a large saltspoonful
of salt, and a pint of the white part of the roots and stems of some
fine fresh celery sliced up thin: let it boil for two or three minutes,
turn it into a stone jar, and secure it well from the air as soon as it
is cold. It may be strained off and bottled in three or four weeks
but may remain as many months in the jar without injury.

ESCHALOT WINE

This is a useful preparation, since it can be used to impart the
flavour of the eschalot to dishes for which acid is not required.
Peel and slice, or bruise, four ounces of eschalots, put them into a
bottle, and add to them a pint of sherry; in a fortnight pour off
the wine, and should it not be strongly flavoured with the eschalots, steep in it two ounces more, for another fortnight; a half-
teaspoonful of cayenne may be added at first. The bottle should
be shaken occasionally, while the eschalots are infusing, but
should remain undisturbed for the last two or three days, that
the wine may be clear when it is poured off to bottle for keeping.
Sweet-basil wine is made by steeping the fresh leaves of the herb
in wine, from ten to fifteen days.

Eschalots, 4 oz; sherry, 1 pint: 15 days, or more.

LEMON BRANDY
(For flavouring sweet dishes)

Fill any sized wide-necked bottle lightly with the very thin rinds
of fresh lemons, and cover them with good brandy; let them
remain for a fortnight or three weeks only, then strain off the
spirit and keep it well corked for use: a few apricot-kernels
blanched and infused with the lemon-rind will give it an agreeable flavour.

Peel small, sound, freshly-gathered flaps, cut off the stems, and scrape out the fur entirely; then arrange the mushrooms singly on tins or dishes, and dry them as gradually as possible in a gentle oven. Put them, when they are done, into tin canisters, and store them where they will be secure from damp. French cooks give them a single boil in water, from which they are then well drained, and dried, as usual. When wanted for table, they should be put into cold gravy, slowly heated, and gently simmered, until they are tender.

MUSHROOM POWDER

When the mushrooms have been prepared with great nicety, and dried, as in the foregoing receipt, pound them to a very fine powder; sift it, and put it immediately into small and *perfectly dry* bottles; cork and seal them without delay, for if the powder be long exposed to the air, so as to imbibe any humidity, or if it be not well secured from it in the bottles, it will be likely to become putrid: much of that which is purchased, even at the best Italian warehouses, is found to be so, and, as it is sold at a very high price, it is a great economy, as well as a surer plan, to have it carefully prepared at home. It is an exceedingly useful store, and an excellent addition to many dishes and sauces. To insure its being good, the mushrooms should be gathered in dry weather, and if any addition of spices be made to the powder (some persons mix with it a seasoning of mace and cayenne), they should be put into the oven for a while before they are used: but even these precautions will not be sufficient, unless the powder be stored in a very dry place after it is bottled. A teaspoonful of it, with a quarter-pint of strong veal gravy, as much cream, and a small dessertspoonful of flour, will make a good *béchamel* or white sauce.

Rub four ounces of the best Durham mustard very smooth with a full teaspoonful of salt, and wet it by degrees with strong horseradish vinegar, a dessertspoonful of cayenne, or of chili vinegar, and one or two of tarragon vinegar when its flavour is not disliked. A quarter-pint of vinegar poured boiling upon an ounce of scraped horseradish, and left for one night, closely covered, will be ready to use for this mustard, but it will be better for standing two or three days.

Durham mustard, 4 oz; salt, large teaspoonful; cayenne, or chili vinegar, 1 dessertspoonful; horseradish vinegar, quarter-pint.

Obs. This is an exceedingly pungent compound, but has many approvers.

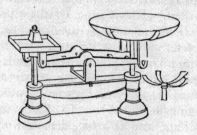

8

Weighing Machine

FORCEMEATS†

GENERAL REMARKS

The coarse and unpalatable compounds so constantly met with under the denomination of forcemeat, even at tables otherwise tolerably well served, show with how little attention they are commonly prepared.

Many very indifferent cooks pique themselves on never doing anything by rule, and the consequence of their throwing together at random (or 'by guess' as they call it) the ingredients which ought to be proportioned with exceeding exactness is repeated failure in all they attempt to do. Long experience, and a very correct eye may, it is true, enable a person to dispense with weights and measures without hazarding the success of their operations; but it is an experiment which the learner will do better to avoid.

A large marble or Wedgwood mortar is indispensable in making all the finer kinds of forcemeat; and equally so indeed for many other purposes in cookery; no kitchen, therefore, should be without one;* and for whatever preparation it may be used, the pounding should be continued with patience and perseverance until not a single lump of fibre be perceptible in the mass of the articles beaten together. This particularly applies to potted meats, which should resemble the smoothest paste; as well as to several varieties of forcemeat. Of these last it should be observed, that such as are made by the French method (see *quenelles*) are the most appropriate for an elegant dinner, either to serve in soups or to fill boned poultry of any kind; but when their exceeding lightness, which to foreigners constitutes one of their great excellences, is objected to, it may be remedied by substituting dry crumbs of bread for the panada, and pounding a small quantity of the lean of a boiled ham, with the other ingredients: however, this should be done only for the balls.

No particular herb or spice should be allowed to predominate powerfully in these compositions; but the whole of the seasonings should be taken in such quantity only as will produce an agreeable savour when they are blended together.

† [*'Forcemeat' means stuffing, having been Anglicized from the French word 'Farcé'.*]

* Two or three mortars, varying in size, should be in every household where it is expected that the cookery should be well conducted: they are often required also for many other domestic purposes, yet it is not unusual to find both these and scales, weights, and measures of every kind, altogether wanting in English kitchens.

A GOOD COMMON FORCEMEAT

Add to four ounces of bread-crumbs two of the lean of a boiled ham, quite free from sinew, and *very* finely minced; two of good butter, a dessertspoonful of herbs, chopped small, some lemon-grate, nutmeg, a little salt, a good seasoning of pepper or cayenne and one whole egg, or the yolks of two. This may be fried in balls of moderate size, for five minutes, to serve with roast veal, or it may be put into the joint in the usual way.

Bread-crumbs, 3 oz; lean of ham, 2 oz; butter, 2 oz; minced herbs, 1 dessertspoonful; lemon-grate, 1 teaspoonful; nutmeg, mace, and cayenne, together, 1 small teaspoonful; little salt; 1 whole egg, or yolks of 2.

Mix well together six ounces of fine stale crumbs, with an equal weight of beef-kidney suet, chopped extremely small, a large dessertspoonful of parsley, mixed with a little lemon-thyme, a teaspoonful of salt, a quarter one of cayenne, and a saltspoonful or rather more of mace and nutmeg together; work these up with three unbeaten egg-yolks, and three teaspoonsful of milk; then put the forcemeat into a large mortar, and pound it perfectly smooth. Take it out, and let it remain in a cool place for half an hour at least before it is used; then roll it into balls, if it be wanted to serve in that form; flour and fry them gently from seven to eight minutes and dry them well before they are dished.

Beef suet finely minced, 6 oz; bread-crumbs, 6 oz; parsley, mixed with little thyme, 1 large dessertspoonful; salt, 1 teaspoonful; mace, large saltspoonful, and one fourth as much cayenne; unbeaten egg-yolks, 3; milk, 3 teaspoonsful; well pounded. Fried in balls, 7 to 8 minutes, or poached, 6 to 7.

Obs. The finely grated rind of half a lemon can be added to this forcemeat at pleasure; and for some purposes a *morsel* of garlic, or three or four minced eschalots, may be mixed with it before it is put into the mortar.

MUSHROOM FORCEMEAT

Cut closely off the stems of some small, just-opened mushrooms, peel them, and take out the fur. Dissolve an ounce and a half of good butter in a saucepan, throw them into it with a little cayenne and a slight sprinkling of mace, and stew them softly, keeping them well shaken, from five to seven minutes; then turn them into a dish, spread them over it, and raise one end, that the liquid may drain from them. When they are quite cold, mince, and then mix them with four ounces of fine bread-crumbs, an ounce and a half of good butter, and *part* of that in which they were stewed, should the forcemeat appear too moist to admit of the whole, as the yolk of one egg, at the least, must be added, to bind the ingredients together; strew in a saltspoonful of salt, a third as much of cayenne, and about the same quantity of mace and nutmeg, with a teaspoonful of grated lemon-rind. The seasonings must be rather sparingly used, that the flavour of the mushrooms may not be overpowered by them. Mix the whole thoroughly with the unbeaten yolk of one egg, or of two, and use the forcemeat poached in small balls for soup, or fried and served in the dish with roast fowls, or round minced veal; or to fill boiled fowls, partridges, or turkeys.

Small mushrooms, peeled and trimmed, 4 oz; butter, 1½ oz; slight sprinkling mace and cayenne: 5 to 7 minutes. Mushrooms minced; bread-crumbs, 4 oz; butter, 1½ oz (with part of that used in the stewing); salt, 1 saltspoonful; third as much of cayenne, of mace, and of nutmeg; grated lemon-rind, 1 teaspoonful; yolk of 1 or 2 eggs. In balls, poached, 5 to 6 minutes; fried, 6 to 8 minutes.

Obs. This, like most other forcemeats, is improved by being well beaten in a large mortar after it is entirely mixed.

ONION AND SAGE STUFFING, FOR PORK, GEESE, OR DUCKS

Boil three large onions from ten to fifteen minutes, press the water from them, chop them small, and mix with them an equal quantity of bread-crumbs, a heaped tablespoonful of minced sage, an ounce of butter, a half saltspoonful of pepper, and twice as much of salt, and put them into the body of the goose; part of the liver boiled for two or three minutes and shred fine, is sometimes added to these, and the whole is bound together with the yolk of one egg or two; but they are quite as frequently served without. The onions can be used raw, when their very strong flavour is not objected to, but the odour of the whole dish will then be somewhat overpowering.

Large onions, 3: boiled 10 to 15 minutes. Sage, 2 to 3 dessertspoonsful (or ½ to ¾ oz); butter, 1 oz; pepper, ½ saltspoonful; salt, 1 saltspoonful.

The body of a goose is sometimes entirely filled with mashed potatoes, seasoned with salt and pepper only; or mixed with a small quantity of eschalot, onion, or herb-seasonings.

MR COOKE'S FORCEMEAT FOR DUCKS OR GEESE

Two parts of chopped onion, two parts of bread-crumbs, three of butter, one of pounded sage, and a seasoning of pepper and salt.

This receipt we have not proved.

BRAIN CAKES

Wash and soak the brains well in cold water, and afterwards in hot; free them from the skin and large fibres, and boil them in water, slightly salted, from two to three minutes; beat them up with a teaspoonful of sage very finely chopped, or with equal parts of sage and parsley, half a teaspoonful or rather more of salt, half as much mace, a little white pepper or cayenne, and one egg; drop them in small cakes into the pan, and fry them in butter, a fine light brown: two yolks of eggs will make the cakes more delicate than the white and yolk of one. A teaspoonful of flour and a little lemon-grate are sometimes added.

CHESTNUT FORCEMEAT

Strip the outer skin from some fine sound chestnuts, then throw them into a saucepan of hot water, and set them over the fire for a minute or two, when they may easily be blanched like almonds. Put them into cold water as they are peeled. Dry them in a cloth, and weigh them. Stew six ounces of them very gently from fifteen to twenty minutes in just sufficient strong veal gravy to cover them. Take them up, drain them on a sieve, and when cold pound them perfectly smooth with half their weight of the nicest bacon rasped clear from all rust or fibre, or with an equal quantity of fresh butter, two ounces of dry bread-crumbs, a small teaspoonful of grated lemon-rind, one of salt, half as much mace or nutmeg, a moderate quantity of cayenne, and the unbeaten yolks of two or of three eggs. This mixture makes most excellent forcemeat cakes, which must be moulded with a knife, a spoon, or the fingers, dipped in flour; more should be dredged over, and pressed upon them, and they should be slowly fried from ten to fifteen minutes.

Chestnuts, 6 oz; veal gravy, ⅓ of a pint: 15 to 20 minutes. Bacon or butter, 3 oz; bread-crumbs, 2 oz; lemon-peel and salt, 1 teaspoonful each; mace or nutmeg, ½ teaspoonful; cayenne; yolks 2 or 3 eggs: fried 10 to 15 minutes.

FRENCH FORCEMEAT CALLED QUENELLES

This is a peculiarly light and delicate kind of forcemeat, which by good French cooks is compounded with exceeding care. It is served abroad in a variety of forms, and is made of very finely-grained white veal, or of the undressed flesh of poultry, or of rabbits, rasped quite free from sinew, then chopped and pounded to the finest paste, first by itself, and afterwards with an equal quantity of boiled calf's udder or of butter, and of *panada*, which is but another name for bread soaked in cream or gravy and then dried over the fire until it forms a sort of paste. As the three ingredients should be equal in *volume*, not in weight, they are each rolled into a separate ball before they are mixed, that their size may be determined by the eye. When the fat of the fillet of veal (which in England is not often divided for sale, as it is in France) is not to be procured, a rather less proportion of butter will serve in its stead. The following will be found a very good, and not a troublesome receipt for veal forcemeat of this kind.

Rasp quite clear from sinew, after the fat and skin have been entirely cleared from it, four ounces of the finest veal; chop, and pound it well: if it be carefully prepared there will be no necessity for passing it through a sieve, but this should otherwise be done. Soak in a small saucepan two ounces of the crumb of a stale loaf in a little rich but pale veal gravy or white sauce; then press and drain as much as possible of the moisture from it, and stir it over a gentle fire until it is as dry as it will become without burning: it will adhere in a ball to the spoon, and leave the saucepan quite dry when it is sufficiently done. Mix with it, while it is still hot, the yolk of one egg, and when it is quite cold, add it to the veal with three ounces of very fresh butter, a quarter of a teaspoonful of mace, half as much cayenne, a little nutmeg, and a saltspoonful of salt. When these are perfectly beaten and well blended together, add another whole egg after having merely taken out the specks: the mixture will then be ready for use, and may be moulded into balls, or small thick oval shapes a little flattened, and poached in soup or gravy from ten to fifteen minutes. These *quenelles* may be served by themselves in a rich sauce as a corner dish, or in conjunction with other things. They may likewise be first poached for three or four minutes, and left on a drainer to become cold; then dipped into egg and the finest bread-crumbs and fried, and served as *croquettes*.

PANADA

This is the name given to the soaked bread which is mixed with the French forcemeats, and which renders them so peculiarly delicate. Pour on the crumb of two or three rolls, or on that of any other very light bread, as much good boiling broth, milk, or cream, as will cover and moisten it well; put a plate over to keep in the steam, and let it remain for half an hour, or more; then drain off the superfluous liquid, and squeeze the panada dry by wringing it in a thin cloth into a ball; put it into a small stewpan or enamelled saucepan, and pour to it as much only of rich white sauce or of gravy as it can easily absorb, and stir it constantly with a wooden spoon over a clear and gentle fire, until it forms a very dry paste and adheres in a mass to the spoon; when it is in this state, mix with it thoroughly the unbeaten yolks of two fresh eggs, which will give it firmness, and set it aside to become quite cold before it is put into the mortar. The best French cooks give the highest degree of savour that they can to this panada, and add no other seasoning to the forcemeats of which it forms a part: it is used in an equal proportion with the meat, and with the calf's udder or butter of which they are composed, as we have shown in the preceding receipt for *quenelles*. They stew slowly for the purpose, a small bit of lean ham, two or three minced eschalots, a bay leaf, a few mushrooms, a little parsley, a clove or two, and a small blade of mace in a little good butter, and when they are sufficiently browned, pour to them as much broth or gravy as will be needed for the panada; and when this has simmered from twenty to thirty minutes, so as to have acquired the proper flavour without being much reduced, they strain it over, and boil it into the bread. The common course of cookery in an English kitchen does not often require the practice of the greater niceties and refinements of the art: and *trouble* (of which the French appear to be perfectly regardless when the excellence of their preparations is concerned) is there in general so much thought of, and exclaimed against, that a more summary process would probably meet with a better chance of success.

A quicker and rougher mode of making the panada, and indeed the forcemeat altogether, is to pour strong veal broth or gravy upon it, and after it has soaked, to boil it dry, without any addition except that of a little fine spice, lemon-grate, or any other favourite English seasoning. Minced herbs, salt, cayenne, and mace, may be beaten with the meat, to which a small portion of well pounded ham may likewise be added at pleasure.

9

BOILING, ROASTING, ETC.

The first thing that has to be remembered when reading these receipts in relation to the present day is that 'Roasting' in the mid-nineteenth century was roasting on a spit, and required 'unremitting attention on the part of the cook rather than any great exertion or skill'.

'Baking, or oven cookery' is much nearer to our idea of roasting, and is recommended as being convenient for the small establishment, 'as many and great disadvantages attend the sending to a public oven', which was still a common practice then and even later.

'Broiling' is grilling, a word that has journeyed across the Atlantic and is now coming back into use in England.

'Braising' is said to be a 'more expensive mode of stewing meat', and as Eliza Acton sensibly remarks, 'no attempt should be made to braise a joint in any vessel that is not nearly of its own size'. Also that, 'Common cooks sometimes stew meat in a mixture of butter and water, and call it braising'.

The other point that must be remembered by anyone using these receipts for present day eating, is that the amounts suggested are enormously larger than anyone wants now, and that the stoves used in those days burned solid fuel, and so were less predictable and slower than the modern cookers. Adjustment in proportions and timing must be made.

A thorough practical knowledge of the processes described in the present chapter will form a really good cook far sooner and more completely than any array of mere receipts can do, however minutely they may be explained; they should, therefore, be well studied and comprehended, before any attempt is made to compound difficult dishes: and the principles of roasting, boiling, stewing, and baking, at least, ought to be clearly understood by every servant who undertakes the duties of what is called *plain cookery*, which is, in fact, of more importance than any other, because it is in almost universal request in this country for families of moderate fortune; and any person who excels in it will easily become expert in what are considered the higher branches of the art.

In a vast number of English kitchens the cookery fails from the hurried manner in which it is conducted, and from the excess of heat produced by the enormous coal-fires constantly kept burning there at all seasons, without which ignorant servants imagine no dinner can be properly cooked; a mistake which cannot fail quickly to become apparent to the most inexperienced reader who will give a patient trial to the slow methods of cooking recommended in the following pages. These will be found to combine exceeding economy in the consumption of fuel, with a degree of superiority in the food prepared by them, which would scarcely be credited unless it were put to the test. In stewing, and baking in closely covered vessels, this superiority is more particularly remarkable; and we would willingly give a far larger space to so useful a subject than our limits will permit: we are, however, compelled, though with regret, to restrict ourselves to such details as we have now supplied in various parts of this volume.

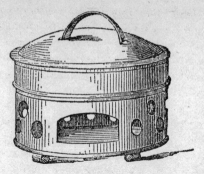

A Conjuror

BROILING

Steaks or cutlets may be quickly cooked with a sheet or two of lighted paper only, in the apparatus shown above, and called a conjuror. Lift off the cover and lay in the meat properly seasoned, with a small slice of butter under it, and insert the lighted paper in the aperture shown in the place; in from eight to ten minutes the meat will be done, and found to be remarkably tender, and very palatable: it must be turned and moved occasionally during the process. This is an especially convenient mode of cooking for persons whose hours of dining are rendered uncertain by their avocations. For medical men engaged in extensive country practice it has often proved so; and we would especially recommend it to the notice of emigrants, to whom it would often prove invaluable. The part in which the meat is placed is of block tin, and fits closed into the stand, which is of sheet iron. The conjuror from which our design was drawn, was purchased in a country town in Essex, and was exceedingly well made, and very cheap. We find on inquiry that the maker has quitted the place, or we would insert his address.

Nottingham Jar

BAKING, OR OVEN COOKERY

The improved construction of the ovens connected with all modern cooking stoves, gives great facility at the present day for *home baking* even in very small establishments; and without this convenience it is impossible for justice to be done to the person who conducts the cookery; and many and great disadvantages attend the sending to a public oven; and it is very discouraging to a servant who has prepared her dishes with nicety and skill, to have them injured by the negligence of other persons. One of the best modes of cooking with which we are acquainted is by means of a jar, resembling in form that shown above, well pasted down, and covered with a fold of thick paper, and then placed in a gentle oven. Rice is most excellent when thus slowly baked with a certain proportion of liquid, either by itself, or mingled with meat, fish, or fruit; but we must reserve for another volume particulars of this little system of *slow oven-cookery* in which for some years past we have had numberless experiments made with almost uniform success: it is especially suited to invalids, from preserving the *entire* amount of nourishment contained in the articles of food dressed by it; and it is to their use that we hope to appropriate it.

The oven may be used with advantage for many purposes for which it is not commonly put into requisition. Calves' feet, covered with a proper proportion of water, may be reduced to a strong jelly if left in it for some hours; the half-head, boned and rolled, will be found excellent eating, if laid, with the bones, into a deep pan and baked quite tender in sufficient broth or water, to keep it covered in every part until done; good soup also may be made in the same way, the usual ingredients being at once added to the meat, with the exception of the vegetables, which will not become tender if put into a cold liquid, and should therefore be thrown in after it begins to simmer. Baking is likewise one of the best modes of dressing various kinds of fish: pike and red mullet amongst others. Salmon cut into thick slices, freed from the skin, well seasoned with spice, mixed with salt (and with minced herbs, at pleasure), then arranged evenly in a dish, and covered thickly with crumbs of bread, moistened with clarified butter, as directed in Chapter 2, for baked soles, and placed in the oven for about half an hour, will be found very rich and highly flavoured. Part of the middle of the salmon left entire, well cleaned, and thoroughly dried, then seasoned, and securely wrapped in two or three folds of thickly buttered paper, will also prove excellent eating, if gently baked. (This may likewise be roasted in a Dutch oven, either folded in the paper, or left without it, and basted with butter.)†

Hams, when freshly cured, and not over salted, if neatly trimmed, and covered with a coarse paste, are both more juicy, and of finer flavour baked than boiled. Savoury or pickled beef too, put into a deep pan with a little gravy, and plenty of butter or chopped suet on the top, to prevent the outside from becoming dry; then covered with paste, or with several folds of thick paper, and set into a moderate oven for four or five hours or even longer, if it be of large weight, is an excellent dish. A goose, a leg of pork, and a sucking pig, if properly attended to while in the oven, are said to be nearly, or quite as good as if roasted; but baking is both an unpalatable and an unprofitable mode of cooking joints of meat in general, though its great convenience to many persons who have but few other facilities for obtaining the luxury of a hot dinner renders it a very common one.

† [*Aluminium foil, buttered, can be used the same way as buttered paper, and salmon baked like this is delicious.*]

Braising is but a more expensive mode of stewing meat. The following French recipe will explain the process. We would observe, however, that the layers of beef or veal, in which the joint to be braised is imbedded, can afterwards be converted into excellent soup, gravy, or glaze; and that there need, in consequence, be no waste nor any unreasonable degree of expense attending it; but it is a troublesome process, and quite as good a result may be obtained by simmering the meat in very strong gravy. Should the flavour of the bacon be considered an advantage, slices of it can be laid over the article braised, and secured to it with a fillet of tape.

'*To braise the inside* (or *small fillet*, as it is called in France) *of a sirloin of beef*: Raise the fillet clean from the joint; and with a sharp knife strip off all the skin, leaving the surface of the meat as smooth as possible; have ready some strips of unsmoked bacon, half as thick as your little finger, roll them in a mixture of thyme finely minced, spices in powder, and a little pepper and salt. Lard the fillet quite through with these, and tie it round with tape in any shape you choose. Line the bottom of a stewpan (or braising-pan) with slices of bacon; next put in a layer of beef or veal, four onions, two bay leaves, two carrots, and a bunch of sweet herbs, and place the fillet on them. Cover it with slices of bacon, put some trimmings of meat all round it, and pour on to it half a pint of good beef broth or gravy. Let it stew as gently as possible for two hours and a half; take it up, and keep it very hot; strain, and reduce the gravy by quick boiling until it is thick enough to glaze with; brush the meat over with it, put the rest in the dish with the fillet, after the tape has been removed from it, and send it directly to table.'

Equal parts of Madeira and gravy are sometimes used to moisten the meat.

Common cooks sometimes stew meat in a mixture of butter and water, and *call it braising*.

TO BROWN THE SURFACE OF A DISH WITHOUT BAKING
OR PLACING IT AT THE FIRE

This is done with a salamander [*see Vocabulary*], as it is called; it is heated in the fire, and held over the dish sufficiently near to give it colour. It is very much used in a superior order of cookery. A kitchen shovel is sometimes substituted for it in an emergency.

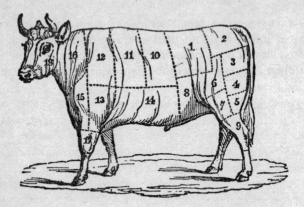

No.
1. *Sirloin.*
2. *Rump.*
3. *Edge-bone.*
4. *Buttocks, or Round.*
5. *Mouse Buttock.*
6. *Veiny Piece.*
7. *Thick Flank.*
8. *Thin Flank.*
9. *Leg.*
10. *Fore Rib. (Five Ribs.)*

No.
11. *Middle Rib. (Four Ribs.)*
12. *Chuck Rib. (Three Ribs.)*
13. *Shoulder, or Leg of*
    Mutton Piece.
14. *Brisket.*
15. *Clod.*
16. *Neck.*
17. *Shin.*
18. *Cheek.*

BEEF

BEEF STEAKS À LA FRANÇAISE
(*Entrée*)

Cut the beef into small thin steaks, season them with fine salt and pepper, dredge them slightly with flour, and fry them in butter over a brisk fire; arrange them in a chain round a very hot dish, and pour into the centre the olive sauce of Chapter 5.

STEWED BEEF STEAK
(*Entrée*)

This may be cut from one to two inches thick, and the time of stewing it must be proportioned to its size. Dissolve a slice of butter in a large saucepan or stewpan, and brown the steak on both sides, moving it often that it may not burn; then shake in a little flour, and when it is coloured pour in by degrees rather more than sufficient broth or water to cover the meat. When it boils, season it with salt, take off the scum, slice in one onion, a carrot or two, and half a turnip; add a small bunch of sweet herbs, and stew the steak very softly from two hours and a half to three hours. A quarter of an hour before it is served, stir well into the gravy three teaspoonsful of rice-flour smoothly mixed with a little cayenne, half a wineglassful of mushroom catsup, and a slight seasoning of spice. A teaspoonful of currie powder, in addition, will improve both the flavour and the appearance of the sauce. The onion is sometimes browned with the meat; and the quantity is considerably increased. Eschalots may be used instead, where their strong flavour is approved. A few button-mushrooms stewed from twenty to thirty minutes with the meat, will render the catsup unnecessary. Wine, or any favourite store sauce, can be added at will.

2½ to 3 hours.

BEEF STEAK STEWED IN ITS OWN GRAVY
(*Good and wholesome*)

Trim all the fat and skin from a rump steak of nearly an inch thick, and divide it once or twice; just dip it into cold water, let it drain for an instant, sprinkle it on both sides with pepper, and then flour it rather thickly; lay it quite flat into a well-tinned iron saucepan or stewpan, which has been rinsed with cold water, of which three or four tablespoonsful should be left in it. Place it over (not upon) a *very* gentle fire, and keep it just simmering from an hour and a half to an hour and three-quarters, when, if the meat be good, it will have become perfectly tender. Add salt to it when it first begins to boil, and turn it when rather more than half done. A couple of spoonsful of gravy, half as much catsup, and a slight seasoning of spice, would, to many tastes, improve the dish, of which, however, the great recommendation is its wholesome simplicity, which renders it suitable to the most delicate stomach. A thick mutton cutlet from the middle of the leg is excellent dressed thus.

1½ to 1¾ hour.

BEEF OR MUTTON CAKE
(*Very good*)

Chop two pounds of lean and very tender beef or mutton, with three-quarters of a pound of beef suet, mix them well, and season them with a dessertspoonful of salt, nearly as much pounded cloves, a teaspoonful of pounded mace, and half a teaspoonful of cayenne. Line a round baking dish with thin slices of fat bacon, press the meat closely into it, smooth the top, and cover it with bacon, set a plate on it with a weight, and bake it two hours and a quarter. Take off the bacon, and serve the meat hot, with a little rich brown gravy, or set it by until cold, when it will be equally good. The fat of the meat which is used for this dish can be chopped up with it instead of suet, where it is liked as well; and onion, or eschalot, shred fine, minced savoury herbs, grated lemon-peel, rasped [*shredded finely*] bacon, or mushrooms cut small, may in turn be added to vary it in flavour.

Lean beef or mutton, 2 lb; suet, ¾ lb; salt and cloves in powder, each a dessertspoonful; mace, 1 teaspoonful; half as much cayenne: baked 2¼ hours.

Obs. A larger portion of suet or of fat will render these cakes lighter, but will not otherwise improve them: they may be made of veal or of venison, but one-third of mutton suet or of fat bacon should be mixed with this last.

FRENCH BEEF À LA MODE
(*A common Receipt*)

Take seven or eight pounds of a rump of beef (or of any other tender joint), free from bone, and skewer it firmly into a good shape. Put two ounces of butter into a thick saucepan or stewpan, and when it boils stir to it a tablespoonful of flour; keep these well shaken over a gentle fire until they are of a fine amber colour; then lay in the beef, and brown it on both sides, taking care that it shall not stick to the pan. Pour to it by slow degrees, letting each portion boil before the next is added or the butter will float upon the surface and be difficult to clear off afterwards, three-quarters of a pint of hot water or gravy; add a bunch of savoury herbs, one large or two small carrots cut in thick slices, two or three moderate-sized onions, two bay leaves, and sufficient pepper and salt to season the gravy. Let the meat simmer gently from four to five hours, and turn it when it is half done. When ready to serve, lift the beef into a hot dish, lay the vegetables round, and pour the gravy over it, after having taken out the herbs and skimmed away the fat. In France, half or the whole of a calf's foot is stewed with the beef, which is there generally larded with thick lardoons of fat bacon. Veal dressed in this way is even better than beef. The stewpan used for either should be as nearly of the size of the meat as possible.

Beef, 7 to 8 lb: 4 to 5 hours.

TO STEW A RUMP OF BEEF

This joint is more easily carved, and is of better appearance when the bones are removed before it is dressed. Roll and bind it firmly with a fillet of tape, cover it with strong cold beef broth or gravy, and stew it very gently indeed from six hours to between seven and eight; add to it, after the scum has been well cleared off, one large or two moderate-sized onions stuck with thirty cloves, a head of celery, two carrots, two turnips, and a large faggot of savoury herbs. When the beef is perfectly tender quite through, which may be known by probing it with a sharp thin skewer, remove the fillets of tape, dish it neatly, and serve it with a rich *Espagnole*, and garnish of forced tomatas, or with a highly-flavoured brown English gravy, and stewed carrots in the dish: for these last the preparation of eschalots, of page 88 may be substituted with good effect. They should be well drained, laid round the meat, and a little brown gravy should be poured over the whole.

This is the most simple and economical manner of stewing the beef; but should a richer one be desired, half roast the joint, and stew it afterwards in strong gravy to which a pint of mushrooms, and a pint of sherry or Madeira, should be added an hour before it is ready for table. Keep it hot while a portion of the gravy is thickened with a well-made brown roux, and seasoned with salt, cayenne, and any other spice it may require. Garnish it with large balls of forcemeat highly seasoned with minced eschalots, rolled in egg and bread-crumbs, and fried a fine golden brown.

Plainly stewed from 6 to 7 or 8 hours. Or: half roasted then stewed from 4 to 5 hours.

Obs. Grated horse-radish, mixed with some well-thickened brown gravy, a teaspoonful of mustard, and a little lemon-juice or vinegar, is a good sauce for stewed beef.

BEEF PALATES†
(*Entrée*)

First rub them well with salt, to cleanse them well; then wash them thoroughly in several waters, and leave them to soak for half an hour before they are dressed. Set them over the fire in cold water, and boil them gently until the skin will peel off, and the palates are tolerably tender. It is difficult to state the exact time required for this, as some will be done in two hours and a half, and others in not less than from four to five hours. When thus prepared, the palates may be cut into various forms, and simmered until fit to serve in rich brown gravy, highly flavoured with ham, cayenne, wine, and lemon-peel; or they will make an excellent currie. As they are very insipid of themselves, they require a sauce of some piquancy, in which, after they have been peeled and trimmed, they should be stewed from twenty to thirty minutes, or until they are perfectly tender. The black parts of them must be cut away, when the skin is taken off. An onion, stuck with a few cloves, a carrot sliced, a teaspoonful of whole white pepper, a slice of butter, and a teaspoonful of salt, may be boiled with the palates in the first instance; and they will be found very good, if sent to table in curried gravy or in the Soubise of Chapter 5, made thinner than the receipts direct.

Boiled from 2½ to 4 or 5 hours. Stewed from 20 to 30 minutes.

Obs. A French cook of some celebrity orders the palates to be laid on the gridiron until the skin can be easily peeled or scraped off; the plan seems a good one, but we have not tried it.

† [*I doubt if palates are obtainable nowadays, but tongues are, and might well be substituted, but will not need to cook for so long.*]

BROILED OX-TAIL
(*Entrée – Very good*)

When the ox-tail is ready for the stewpan, throw it into plenty of boiling water slightly salted, and simmer it for fifteen minutes; then take it up and put it into fresh water to cool; wipe it, and lay it round in a small stewpan without dividing it, just cover it with good beef gravy, and stew it gently until very tender: drain it a little, sprinkle over it a small quantity of salt and cayenne, dip it into clarified butter and then into some fine bread-crumbs, with which it should be thickly covered, lay it on the gridiron and when equally browned all over serve it immediately. If more convenient the ox-tail may be set into the oven or before the fire, until properly coloured: it may likewise be sent to table without broiling, dished upon stewed cabbage or in its own gravy thickened, and with tomata sauce, in a tureen.

Let the meat hang a couple of days in mild weather, and four or five in winter, before it is salted or pickled. During the heat of summer it is better to immerse it entirely in brine, that it may be secured alike from the flies, and from the danger of becoming putrid. Trim it, and take out the kernels from the fat; then rub a little fine dry salt over it, and leave it until the following day; drain it well from the blood, which will be found to have flowed from it, and it will be ready for any of the following modes of curing, which are all excellent of their kind, and have been well proved.

In very cold weather, the salt may be applied quite warm to the meat: it should always be perfectly dry, and reduced to powder.

Saltpetre hardens and renders the meat indigestible; sugar, on the contrary, mellows and improves it much; and it is more tender when cured with bay salt than when common salt is used for it.

HAMBURGH PICKLE FOR BEEF, HAMS, AND TONGUE

Boil together, for twenty minutes, two gallons of water, three pounds of bay salt, two pounds of coarse sugar, two ounces of saltpetre, and two of black pepper, bruised, and tied in a fold of muslin; clear off the scum thoroughly, as it rises, pour the pickle into a deep earthen pan, and when it is quite cold lay in the meat, of which every part must be perfectly covered with it. A moderate-sized round of beef will be ready for table in a fortnight; it should be turned occasionally in the brine. Five pounds of common salt may be substituted for the quantity of bay salt given above; but the meat will not be so finely flavoured.

Water, 2 gallons; bay salt, 3 lb; saltpetre, 2 oz; black pepper, 2 oz; sugar, 2 lb: 20 minutes.

To three gallons of spring water add six pounds of common salt, two pounds of bay salt, two pounds of common loaf sugar, and two ounces of saltpetre. Boil these over a gentle fire, and be careful to take off all the scum as it rises: when quite cold it will be fit for use. Rub the meat to be cured, with fine salt, and let it drain for a day in order to free it from the blood; then immerse it in the brine, taking care that every part of it shall be covered. Young pork should not remain more than from three to five days in the pickle; but hams for drying may be left in it for a fortnight at least: tongues will be ready in rather less time. Beef may remain from one week to two, according to its size, and the degree of saltiness desired for it. A little experience will soon teach the exact time required for the different kinds of meat. When the pickle has been in use for about three months, boil it up again gently, and take the scum carefully off. Add to it three pounds of common salt, four ounces of sugar, and one of saltpetre: it will remain good for many months.

Water, 3 gallons; common salt, 6 lb; bay salt, 2 lb; loaf sugar, 2 lb; saltpetre, 2 oz: boil 20 to 30 minutes.

A COMMON RECEIPT FOR SALTING BEEF

One ounce of saltpetre, and a pound of common salt, will be sufficient for sixteen pounds of beef. Both should be well dried, and finely powdered; the saltpetre rubbed first equally over the meat, and the salt next applied in every part. It should be rubbed thoroughly with the pickle and turned daily, from a week to ten days. An ounce or two of sugar mixed with the saltpetre will render the beef more tender and palatable.

Beef, 16 lb; saltpetre, 1 oz; salt, 1 lb: 7 to 10 days.

(*Good and wholesome*)

For twelve pounds of the round, rump, or thick flank of beef, take a large teaspoonful of freshly-pounded mace, and of ground black pepper, twice as much of cloves, one small nutmeg, and a quarter of a teaspoonful of cayenne, all in the finest powder. Mix them *well* with seven ounces of brown sugar, rub the beef with them and let it lie three days; add to it then half a pound of fine salt, and rub and turn it once in twenty-four hours for twelve days. Just wash, but do not soak it; skewer, or bind it into good form, put it into a stewpan or saucepan nearly of its size, pour to it a pint and a half of good beef broth, and when it begins to boil, take off the scum, and throw in one small onion, a moderate-sized faggot of thyme and parsley, and two large, or four small carrots. Let it simmer quite softly for four hours and a half, and if not wanted to serve hot, leave it in its own liquor until it is nearly cold. This is an excellent and far more wholesome dish than the hard bright-coloured beef which is cured with large quantities of salt and saltpetre; two or three ounces of juniper-berries may be added to it with the spice, to heighten its flavour.

Beef, 12 lb; sugar, 7 oz; mace and black pepper, each, 1 large teaspoonful; cloves, in powder, 1 large dessertspoonful; nutmeg, 1; cayenne, ¼ teaspoonful: 3 days. Fine salt, ½ lb: 12 days. Beef broth (or bouillon), 1½ pint; onion, 1 small; bunch of herbs; carrots, 2 large, or 4 small: stewed 4½ hours.

Obs. We give this receipt *exactly* as we have often had it used, but celery and turnips might be added to the gravy; and when the appearance of the meat is much considered, three-quarters of an ounce of saltpetre may be mixed with the spices; the beef may also be plainly boiled in water only, with a few vegetables, or baked in a deep pan with a little gravy. No meat must ever be left to cool in the stewpan or saucepan in which it is cooked; it must be lifted into a pan of its own depth, and the liquor poured upon it.

'Select a fine rib of beef, and have it cut small or large in width, according to your taste; it may thus be made to weigh from five to twelve pounds, or more. Take out the bone, and wrap the meat round like a fillet of veal, securing it with two or three wooden skewers; place it in a strong pickle for four or five days, and then cook it, taking care that it does not boil, but only simmers, from forty minutes, or more according to its size. It is best to put it on in hot water, as it will not draw the gravy so much as cold. Many persons adjust a rib of beef in this way for roasting: let them try it salted, and they need not envy the possessor of the finest round of beef.' We give the receipt to our readers in its original form, and we can assure them, from our own experience, that it is a good one; but we would recommend that, in dressing the meat, quite the usual time for each pound of it should be allowed. When boned and rolled at the butcher's, the skewers should be removed when it is first brought in; it should be well wiped with a dry cloth, or washed with a little fresh brine, and a small quantity of salt and saltpetre should be rubbed over the inside, it may then be firmly bound with tape, and will be quite ready to boil when taken from the pickle. The sirloin, after the inside fillet is removed, may be cured and dressed in the same way, and will be found super-excellent if the beef be well fatted and properly kept. The Hamburgh pickle (see page 112) is perhaps the best for these joints. Part of the rump, taken clear of bones, answers admirably when prepared by this receipt.

BEEF ROLL, OR CANELLON DE BŒUF
(Entrée)

Chop and mix thoroughly two pounds of lean and very tender beef with one pound of slightly striped bacon; season them with a large teaspoonful of pepper, a little salt, a small nutmeg, or two-thirds as much mace, the grated rind of a lemon, or a teaspoonful of thyme and parsley finely minced. Form the whole into a thick rouleau, wrap a buttered paper round it, enclose it in a paste made of flour and water, and send it to a moderate oven for a couple of hours.† Remove the paper and the crust and serve the meat with a little brown gravy. Lamb and veal are excellent dressed in this way, particularly when mixed with plenty of mushrooms. Brown cucumber sauce should be served with the lamb; and currie, or oyster sauce, when there are no mushrooms, with the veal. A flavouring of onion or of eschalot, where it is liked, can be added at pleasure to the beef; suet, or the fat of the meat, may be substituted for the bacon.

Beef, 2 lb; bacon, 1 lb; pepper ¼ oz; little salt; small nutmeg; rind of 1 lemon, or savoury herbs, 1 teaspoonful: baked 2 hours.

† [*Nowadays very good results can be obtained by wrapping meat in foil instead of paste as it serves the same function.*]

SCOTCH MINCED COLLOPS

Chop the beef small, season it with salt and pepper, put it, in its raw state, into small jars, and pour on the top some clarified butter. When wanted for use put the clarified butter into a frying-pan, and slice some onions into the pan and fry them. Add a little water to them, and put in the minced meat. Stew it well, and in a few minutes it will be fit to serve.

TO ROAST A BEEF HEART

Wash and soak the heart very thoroughly, cut away the lobes, fill the cavities with a veal forcemeat, secure it well with a needle and twine, or very coarse thread, and roast it at a good fire for an hour and a half, keeping it basted plentifully with butter. Pour melted butter over it, after it is dished, and send it to table as hot as possible. Many persons boil the heart for three-quarters of an hour before it is put to the fire, and this is said to render it more delicate eating; the time of roasting must of course be proportionately diminished. Good brown gravy may be substituted for the melted butter, and currant jelly also may be served with it.

1½ hour, or more.

Slice the kidney rather thin after having stripped off the skin and removed the fat; season it with pepper, salt, and grated nutmeg, and sprinkle over it plenty of minced parsley, or equal parts of parsley and eschalots chopped very small. Fry the slices over a brisk fire, and when nicely browned on both sides, stir amongst them a teaspoonful of flour, and pour in by degrees a cup of gravy and a glass of white wine; bring the sauce to the point of boiling, add a morsel of fresh butter and a tablespoonful of lemon-juice, and pour the whole into a hot dish garnished with fried bread. This is a French receipt, and a very excellent one.

AN EXCELLENT HASH OF COLD BEEF

Put a slice of butter into a thick saucepan, and when it boils throw in a dessertspoonful of minced herbs, and an onion (or two or three eschalots) shred small; shake them over the fire until they are lightly browned, then stir in a tablespoonful of flour, a little cayenne, some mace or nutmeg, and half a teaspoonful of salt. When the whole is well coloured, pour to it three-quarters of a pint or more of broth or gravy, according to the quantity of meat to be served in it. Let this boil gently for fifteen minutes; then strain it, add half a wineglassful of mushroom or of compound catsup, lay in the meat, and keep it by the side of the fire until it is heated through and is on the point of simmering, but be sure not to let it boil. Serve it up in a very hot dish, and garnish it with fried or toasted sippets of bread.

Obs. The cook should be reminded that if the meat in a hash or mince be allowed to boil, it will immediately become hard, and can then only be rendered eatable by very *long stewing*, which is by no means desirable for meat which is already sufficiently cooked.

BRESLAW OF BEEF
(*Good*)

Trim the brown edges from half a pound of undressed roast beef, shred it small, and mix it with four ounces of fine bread-crumbs, a teaspoonful of minced parsley, and two-thirds as much of thyme, two ounces of butter broken small, half a cupful of gravy or cream, a high seasoning of pepper and cayenne and mace or nutmeg, a small teaspoonful of salt, and three large eggs well whisked. Melt a little butter in a deep dish, pour in the beef, and bake it half an hour; turn it out, and send it to table with brown gravy in a tureen. When cream or gravy is not at hand, an additional egg or two and rather more butter must be used. We think that grated lemon-rind improves the breslaw. A portion of fat from the joint can be added where it is liked. The mixture is sometimes baked in buttered cups.

Beef, ½ lb; bread-crumbs, 4 oz; butter, 2 oz; gravy or cream, ½ cupful; parsley, 1 teaspoonful; thyme, two-thirds of teaspoonful; eggs, 3 or 4, if small; salt, 1 teaspoonful; pepper and nutmeg, ½ teaspoonful each: bake ½ hour.

NORMAN HASH

Peel and fry two dozens of button onions in butter until they are lightly browned, then stir to them a tablespoonful of flour, and when the whole is of a deep amber shade, pour in a wineglassful and a half of red wine, and a large cup of boiling broth or water; add a seasoning of salt and common pepper or cayenne, and a little lemon-pickle catsup or lemon-juice, and boil the whole until the onions are quite tender; cut and trim into small handsome slices the remains of either a roast or boiled joint of beef, and arrange them in a clean saucepan; pour the gravy and onions on them, and let them stand for a while to imbibe the flavour of the sauce; then place the hash near the fire, and when it is thoroughly hot serve it immediately, without allowing it to boil.

FRENCH RECEIPT FOR HASHED BOUILLI

Shake over a slow fire a bit of butter the size of an egg, and a tablespoonful of flour; when they have simmered for a minute, stir to them a little finely-chopped onion, and a dessertspoonful of minced parsley; so soon as the whole is equally browned, add sufficient pepper, salt, and nutmeg to season the hash properly, and from half to three-quarters of a pint of boiling water or of bouillon. Put in the beef cut into small but thick slices; let it stand by the fire and heat gradually; and when near the point of boiling thicken the sauce with the yolks of three eggs, mixed with a tablespoonful of lemon-juice. For change, omit the eggs, and substitute a tablespoonful of catsup, and another of pickled gherkins minced or sliced.

BAKED MINCED BEEF

Mince tolerably fine, with a moderate proportion of its own fat, as much of the inside of a cold roast joint as will suffice for a dish: that which is least done is best for the purpose. Season it rather highly with cayenne and mace or nutmeg, and moderately with salt; add, when they are liked, one or two eschalots minced small, with a few chopped mushrooms either fresh or pickled, or two tablespoonsful of mushroom catsup. Mix the whole well with a cupful of *good* gravy, and put it into a deep dish. Place on the top an inch-thick layer of bread-crumbs, moisten these plentifully with clarified butter passed through a small strainer over them, and send the mince to a slow oven for twenty minutes, or brown it in a Dutch oven.

Spread on the dish in which the saunders are to be served, a layer of smoothly mashed potatoes, which have been seasoned with salt and mixed with about an ounce of butter to the pound. On these spread equally and thickly some underdressed beef or mutton minced and mixed with a little of the gravy that has run from the joint, or with a few spoonsful of any other; and season it with salt, pepper, and a small quantity of nutmeg. Place evenly over this another layer of potatoes, and send the dish to a moderate oven for half an hour. A very superior kind of saunders is made by substituting fresh meat for roasted; but this requires to be baked an hour or something more. Sausage-meat highly seasoned may be served in this way, instead of beef or mutton.

No.
1. Loin, Best End.
2. Loin, Chump End.
3. Fillet.
4. Hind Knuckle.
5. Fore Knuckle.
6. Neck, Best End.

No.
7. Neck, Scrag End.
8. Blade Bone.
9. Breast, Best End.
10. Breast, Brisket End.
11. Cheek.

In season all the year, but scarce and expensive in mid-winter, and very early spring.

VEAL

CALF'S HEAD, THE WARDER'S WAY

Boil the half-head until tolerably tender; let it cool, and bone it entirely; replace the brain, lay the head into a stewpan, and simmer it gently for an hour in rich gravy. From five-and-twenty to thirty minutes before it is dished, add half a pint of mushroom-buttons. Thicken the gravy, if needful, with rice flour or with flour and butter, and serve plenty of forcemeat-balls round the head. For dishes of this kind, a little sweet-basil wine, or a few sprigs of the herb itself, impart a very agreeable flavour. When neither these nor mushrooms are within reach, the very thin rind of a small but fresh lemon may be boiled in the gravy, and the strained juice added at the instant of serving.

Boiled from 1 to 2 hours; stewed 1 hour.

Obs. The skin, *with the ear*, may be left on the head for this receipt, and the latter slit into narrow strips from the tip to within an inch and a half of the base; which will give it a feathery and ornamental appearance, the head may then be glazed or not at pleasure.

BURLINGTON WHIMSEY†
(*An excellent Receipt*)

Set aside until quite cold half a dressed calf's head. If, on cutting it, the gelatinous part should not appear perfectly tender, pare it off closely from the head, weigh, and mince it; put it into a pint of good gravy, and stew it gently from ten to fifteen minutes. Mince as much more of the head as will make up a pound of weight after the edges are trimmed off, and part of the fat is taken away; add to this three ounces of the lean of a boiled ham finely chopped, the grated rind of a large lemon, three teaspoonsful of parsley and one of thyme shred very small, three-quarters of a teaspoonful of mace, half a small nutmeg grated, a teaspoonful of salt, and a half-quarter one of cayenne; stir the whole well together, and put it, with half a pint more of gravy, to the portion which has been already simmered. When the whimsey has boiled *softly* from four to five minutes, pour it into moulds or pans, in which slices of the tongue have been evenly arranged, and when quite cold it will turn out very firmly. It may be garnished, before it is sent to table, with branches of parsley, which should, however, be perfectly dry: and when served for supper or luncheon, it may be accompanied by a salad dressing.

Calf's head, 1 lb; lean of ham, 3 oz; gravy, 1½ pint; rind of 1 large lemon; parsley, 3 teaspoonsful; thyme and salt, each 1 teaspoonful; mace, ¾ teaspoonful; ½ nutmeg; cayenne, ⅛ part of a teaspoonful: 5 minutes.

Obs. The remains of a plain boiled head may be made to serve for this dish, provided the gravy used with it be well jellied and of high flavour. Slices from the small end of a boiled and smoked ox-tongue, from their bright colour, improve greatly its appearance. It should be tasted before it is poured out, that salt or any other seasoning may be added if needful. After three or four days' keeping, should any mould appear upon the surface, take it off, re-melt the whimsey, and give it two minutes' boil. For change, the herbs may be omitted, and the quantity of ham increased, or some minced tongue substituted for it.

† [*I fear this is too elaborate a receipt for common use, but the charming name made me include it.*]

ROAST LOIN OF VEAL

It is not usual to stuff a loin of veal, but we greatly recommend the practice, as an infinite improvement to the joint. Make some good common forcemeat and insert it between the skin and the flesh just over the ends of the bones. Skewer down the flap, place the joint at a moderate distance from a sound fire, keep it constantly basted, and be especially careful not to allow the kidney fat to burn: to prevent this, and to ensure the good appearance of the joint, a buttered paper is often fastened round the loin, and removed about half an hour before it is taken from the fire. It is the fashion in some counties to serve *egg-sauce* and brown gravy with the roast loin, or breast of veal.

The cook will scarcely need to be told that she must separate the skin from the flank, with a sharp knife, quite from the end, to the place where the forcemeat is to be put, and then skewer the whole very securely. When the veal is not papered, dredge it well with flour soon after it is laid to the fire.

2 to 2½ hours.

TO BONE A SHOULDER OF VEAL, MUTTON, OR LAMB

Spread a clean cloth upon a table or dresser, and lay the joint flat upon in, with the skin downwards; with a sharp knife cut off the flesh from the inner side nearly down to the blade bone, of which detach the edges first, then work the knife *under* it, keeping it always *close to the bone*, and using all possible precaution not to pierce the outer skin; when it is in every part separated from the flesh, loosen it from the socket with the point of the knife, and remove it; or, without dividing the two bones, cut round the joint until it is freed entirely from the meat, and proceed to detach the second bone. That of the knuckle is frequently left in, but for some dishes it is necessary to take it out; in doing this, be careful not to tear the skin. A most excellent grill may be made by leaving sufficient meat for it upon the bones of a shoulder of mutton, when they are removed from the joint: it will be found very superior to the broiled blade-bone of a *roast* shoulder, which is so much liked by many people.

STEWED SHOULDER OF VEAL
(*English Receipt*)

Bone a shoulder of veal, and strew the inside thickly with savoury herbs, minced small; season it well with salt, cayenne, and pounded mace; and place on these a layer of ham cut in thin slices and freed from rind and rust. Roll up the veal, and bind it tightly with a fillet [*a piece of tape or string*]; roast it for an hour and a half, then simmer it gently in good brown gravy for five hours; add forcemeat balls before it is dished; skim the fat from the gravy, and serve it with the meat. This receipt, for which we are indebted to a correspondent on whom we can depend, and which we have not therefore considered it necessary to test ourselves, is for a joint which weighs ten pounds before it is boned.

ROAST NECK OF VEAL

The best end of the neck will make an excellent roast. A forcemeat may be inserted between the skin and the flesh, by first separating them with a sharp knife; or the dish may be garnished with the forcemeat in balls. From an hour and a half to two hours will roast it. Pour melted butter over it when it is dished, and serve it like other joints. Let it be floured when first laid to the fire, kept constantly basted, and always at a sufficient distance to prevent its being scorched.

1½ to 2 hours.

For the forcemeat, see Chapter 8. From 8 to 10 minutes will fry the balls.

NECK OF VEAL À LA CRÊME
(Or au Béchamel)

Take the best end of a neck of white and well-fed veal, detach the flesh from the ends of the bones, cut them sufficiently short to give the joint a good square form, fold and skewer the skin over them, wrap a buttered paper round the meat, lay it at a moderate distance from a clear fire, and keep it well basted with butter for an hour and a quarter; then remove the paper and continue the basting with a pint, or more, of *béchamel* or of rich white sauce, until the veal is sufficiently roasted, and well encrusted with it. Serve some *béchamel* under it in the dish, and send it very hot to table. For variety, give the *béchamel* in making it a high flavour of mushrooms, and add some small buttons stewed very white and tender, to the portion reserved for saucing the joint.

2 to 2¼ hours.

VEAL GOOSE
(City of London Receipt)

'This is made with the upper part of the flank of a loin of veal (or sometimes that of the fillet) covered with a stuffing of sage and onions, then rolled, and roasted or broiled. It is served with brown gravy and apple sauce, is extremely savoury, and has many admirers.' We transcribe the exact receipt for this dish, which was procured for us from a house in the City, which is famed for it. We had it tested with the skin of the best end of a fine *neck* of veal, from which it was pared with something more than an inch depth of the flesh adhering to it. It was roasted one hour, and answered extremely well. It is a convenient mode of dressing the flank of the veal for eaters who do not object to the somewhat coarse savour of the preparation. When the *tendrons* or gristles of a breast, or part of a breast of veal, are required for a separate dish, the remaining portion of the joint may be dressed in this way after the bones have been taken out; or, without removing them, the stuffing may be inserted under the skin.

BORDYKE VEAL CAKE†
(*Good*)

Take a pound and a half of veal perfectly clear of fat and skin, and eight ounces of the nicest striped bacon; chop them separately, then mix them well together with the grated rind of a small lemon, half a teaspoonful of salt, a fourth as much of cayenne, the third part of a nutmeg grated, and a half-teaspoonful of freshly pounded mace. When it is pressed into the dish, let it be somewhat higher in the centre than at the edge; and whether to be served hot or cold, lift it out as soon as it comes from the oven, and place it on a strainer that the fat may drain from it; it will keep many days if the under side be dry. The bacon should be weighed after the rind, and any rust it may exhibit, have been trimmed from it. This cake is excellent cold, but slices, if preferred hot, may be warmed through in a Dutch oven, or on the gridiron, or in a few spoonsful of gravy. The same ingredients made into small cakes, well floured, and slowly fried from twelve to fifteen minutes, then served with gravy made in the pan as for cutlets, will be found extremely good.

Veal, 1½ lb; striped bacon, 8 oz; salt and mace, ½ teaspoonful each: rind of lemon, 1; third of 1 nutmeg; cayenne, 4 grains: baked 1¼ to 1½ hour.

† ['Bordyke', *which occurs in several receipts, was the name of the house in which Miss Acton lived in Tonbridge.*]

Cut two pounds of veal, free from fat, into small half-inch thick cutlets; flour them well, and fry them in butter with two small cucumbers sliced, sprinkled with pepper, and floured, one moderate sized lettuce, and twenty-four green gooseberries cut open lengthwise and seeded. When the whole is nicely browned, lift it into a thick saucepan, and pour gradually into the pan half a pint, or rather more, of boiling water, broth, or gravy. Add as much salt and pepper as it requires. Give it a minute's simmer, and pour it over the meat, shaking it well round the pan as this is done. Let the veal stew gently from three-quarters of an hour to an hour. A bunch of green onions cut small may be added to the other vegetables if liked; and the veal will eat better, if slightly seasoned with salt and pepper before it is floured; a portion of fat can be left on it if preferred.

Veal 2 lb; cucumbers, 2; lettuce, 1; green gooseberries, 24; water or broth, ½ pint or more: ¾ to 1 hour.

NORMAN HARRICO†

Brown in a stewpan or fry lightly, after having sprinkled them with pepper, salt and flour, from two to three pounds of veal cutlets. If taken from the neck or loin, chop the bones very short, and trim away the greater portion of the fat. Arrange them as flat as they can be in a saucepan; give a pint of water a boil in the pan in which they have been browned, and pour it on them; add a small faggot of parsley, and, should the flavour be liked, one of green onions also. Let the meat simmer softly for half an hour; then cover it with small new potatoes which have had a single boil in water, give the saucepan a shake, and let the harrico stew very gently for another half hour, or until the potatoes are quite done, and the veal is tender. When the cutlets are thick and the potatoes approaching their full size, more time will be required for the meat, and the vegetables may be at once divided; if extremely young they will need the previous boil. Before the harrico is served, skim the fat from it, and add salt and pepper should it not be sufficiently seasoned. A few bits of lean ham, or shoulder of bacon browned with veal, will much improve this dish, and for some tastes, a little acid will render it more agreeable [*lemon juice or vinegar*]. Very delicate pork chops may be dressed in the same way. A cutlet taken from the fillet and freed from fat and skin, answers best for this dish. Additional vegetables, cooked apart, can be added to it after it is dished. Peas boiled very green and well drained, or young carrots sliced and stewed tender in butter, are both well suited to it.

Veal, 2 to 3 lb; water (or gravy), 1 pint; new potatoes 1½ to 2 lb; faggot, parsley, and green onions: 1 hour or more.

† [*'Harrico', sometimes spelt 'Haricot' has nothing to do with the beans of the same name, and comes from the French 'halicot', meaning a stew. Oddly, Eliza Acton gives the receipt for veal or pork only, but more usually it was made with lamb or mutton.*]

PLAIN VEAL CUTLETS

Take them if possible free from bone, and after having trimmed them into proper shape, beat them with a cutlet-bat or paste-roller until the fibre of the meat is thoroughly broken; flour them well to prevent the escape of the gravy, and fry them from twelve to fifteen minutes over a fire which is not sufficiently fierce to burn them before they are quite cooked through: they should be of a fine amber brown, and *perfectly done*. Lift them into a hot dish, pour the fat from the pan, throw in a slice of fresh butter, and when it is melted, stir or dredge in a dessertspoonful of flour; keep these shaken until they are well-coloured, then pour gradually to them a cup of gravy or of boiling water; add pepper, salt, a little lemon-pickle or juice, give the whole a boil, and pour it over the cutlets: a few forcemeat balls fried and served with them are usually a very acceptable addition to this dish, even when it is garnished or accompanied with rashers of ham or bacon. A morsel of *glaze*, or of the jelly of roast meat, should when at hand be added to the sauce, which a little mushroom powder would further improve: mushroom sauce, indeed, is considered by many epicures, as indispensible with veal cutlets. We have recommended in this one instance that the meat should be thoroughly *beaten*, because we find that the veal is wonderfully improved by the process, which, however, we still deprecate for other meat.

12 to 15 minutes.

VEAL CUTLETS À L'INDIENNE, OR INDIAN FASHION
(*Entrée*)

Mix well together four ounces of very fine stale bread-crumbs, a teaspoonful of salt, and a tablespoonful of the best currie-powder. Cut down into small well-shaped cutlets or collops, two pounds of veal free from fat, skin, or bone; beat the slices flat, and dip them first into some beaten egg-yolks, and then into the seasoned crumbs; moisten them again with egg, and pass them a second time through bread-crumbs. When all are ready, fry them in three or four ounces of butter over a moderate fire, from twelve to fourteen minutes. For sauce, mix smoothly with a knife, a teaspoonful of flour and an equal quantity of currie-powder, with a small slice of butter; shake these in the pan for about five minutes, pour to them a cup of gravy or boiling water, add salt and cayenne, if required and the strained juice of half a lemon; simmer the whole till well flavoured, and pour it round the cutlets. A better plan is to have some good currie sauce ready prepared to send to table with this dish; which may likewise be served with only well-made common cutlet gravy, from the pan, when much of the pungent flavour of the currie-powder is not desired.

Bread-crumbs, 4 oz; salt, 1 teaspoonful; currie-powder, 1 tablespoonful; veal, 2 lb: 12 to 14 minutes.

Obs. These cutlets may be broiled; they should then be well beaten first, and dipped into clarified butter instead of egg before they are passed through the curried seasoning.

VEAL CUTLETS À LA MODE LONDRES
OR LONDON FASHION
(*Entrée*)

Raise the flesh entire from the upper side of the best end of a neck of veal, free it from the skin, and from the greater portion of the fat, slice it equally into cutlets little more than a quarter of an inch thick, brush them with eggs, strew them with fine bread-crumbs, and fry them of a light brown. Toast, or fry apart as many small slices of bacon as there are cutlets, and let them be trimmed nearly to the same shape; place them alternately on their edges round the inside of a hot dish (so as to form a sort of chain), and pour into the middle some rich gravy made in the pan, and very slightly flavoured with eschalot; or substitute for this some good brown mushroom sauce. Savoury herbs, grated lemon-rind, nutmeg or mace, salt and white pepper or cayenne, should be mixed with the bread-crumbs, or they may be varied at pleasure. A cheek of bacon is best adapted to this dish.

SWEETBREADS SIMPLY DRESSED
(*Entrée*)

In whatever way sweetbreads are dressed, they should first be well soaked in lukewarm water, then thrown into boiling water to *blanch* them, as it is called, and to render them firm. If lifted out after they have boiled from five to ten minutes according to their size, and laid immediately into fresh spring water to cool, their colour will be the better preserved. They may then be gently stewed for three-quarters of an hour in veal gravy, which with the usual additions of cream, lemon, and egg-yolks, may be converted into a fricassee sauce for them when they are done; or they may be lifted from, *glazed*, and served with good Spanish gravy; or, the glazing being omitted, they may be sauced with the sharp *Maître d'Hôtel* sauce of page 63. They may also be simply floured, and roasted in a Dutch oven, being often basted with butter, and frequently turned. A full sized sweetbread, after having been blanched, will require quite three-quarters of an hour to dress it.

Blanched 5 to 10 minutes. Stewed ¾ hour or more.

SWEETBREAD CUTLETS
(*Entrée*)

Boil the sweetbreads for half an hour in water or veal broth, and when they are perfectly cold, cut them into slices of equal thickness, brush them with yolk of egg, and dip them into very fine bread-crumbs seasoned with salt, cayenne, grated lemon-rind, and mace; fry them in butter of a fine light brown, arrange them in a dish placing them high in the centre, and pour *under* them a gravy made in the pan, thickened with mushroom powder and flavoured with lemon-juice; or, in lieu of this, sauce them with some rich brown gravy, to which a glass of sherry or Madeira has been added. When it can be done conveniently, take as many slices of a cold boiled tongue as there are sweetbread cutlets; pare the rind from them, trim them into good shape, and dress them with the sweetbreads, after they have been egged and seasoned in the same way; and place each cutlet upon a slice of tongue when they are dished. For variety, substitute *croûtons* of fried bread stamped out to the size of the cutlets with a round or fluted paste or cake cutter. The crumb of a stale loaf, very evenly sliced, is best for the purpose.

STEWED CALF'S FEET
(*Cheap and Good*)

This is an excellent family dish, highly nutritous, and often very inexpensive, as the feet during the summer are usually sold at a low rate. Wash them with nicety, divide them at the joint, and split the claws; arrange them closely in a thick stewpan or saucepan, and pour in as much cold water as will cover them about half an inch: three pints will be sufficient for a couple of large feet. When broth or stock is at hand, it is good economy to substitute it for the water, as by this means a portion of strong and well-flavoured jellied gravy will be obtained for general use, the full quantity not being needed as sauce for the feet. The whole preparation will be much improved by laying a thick slice of the lean of an unboiled ham, knuckle of bacon, hung beef, or the end of a dried tongue, at the bottom of the pan, before the other ingredients are added; or, when none of these are at hand, by supplying the deficiency with a few bits of lean beef or veal: the feet being of themselves insipid, will be much more palatable with one or the other of these additions. Throw in from half to three-quarters of a teaspoonful of salt when they begin to boil, and after the scum has been all cleared off, add a few branches of parsley, a little celery, one small onion or more, stuck with half a dozen cloves, a carrot or two, a large blade of mace, and twenty corns of whole pepper; stew them softly until the flesh will part entirely from the bones; take it from them, strain part of the gravy, and skim off all the fat, flavour it with catsup or any other store sauce, and thicken it, when it boils, with arrowroot or flour and butter; put in the flesh of the feet, and serve the dish as soon as the whole is very hot. A glass of wine, a little lemon-juice, and a few forcemeat balls, will convert this into a very superior stew; a handful of mushroom-buttons also simmered in it for half an hour before it is dished, will vary it agreeably.

Calf's feet (large), 2; water, 3 pints; salt, ½ to ¾ teaspoonful; onions, 1 to 3; cloves, 6; peppercorns, 20; mace, large blade; little celery and parsley; carrots, 1 or 2: stewed softly, 2½ to 3¼ hours. Mushroom catsup, 1 tablespoonful; flour, or arrowroot, 1 large teaspoonful; butter, 1 to 2 oz. Cayenne, to taste.

BLANQUETTE OF VEAL, OR LAMB WITH MUSHROOMS
(*Entrée*)

Slice very thin the white part of some cold veal, divide and trim it into scallops not larger than a shilling, and lay it into a clean saucepan or stewpan. Wipe with a bit of new flannel and a few grains of salt, from a quarter- to half-pint of mushroom-buttons, and slice them into a little butter which just begins to simmer; stew them in it from twelve to fifteen minutes, without allowing them to take the slightest colour; then lift them out and lay them on the veal. Pour boiling to them a pint of *sauce tournée* (see page 57); let the *blanquette* remain near, but not close to the fire for a while: bring it nearer, heat it slowly, and when it is on the point of boiling mix a spoonful or two of the sauce from it with the well beaten yolks of four fresh eggs; stir them to the remainder; add the strained juice of half a small lemon; shake the saucepan above the fire until the sauce is just set, and serve the *blanquette* instantly.

Cold veal, ¾ lb; mushrooms, ¼ to ½ pint: stewed in 1½ oz butter, 12 to 15 minutes. Sauce *tournée*, or thickened veal gravy, 1 pint; yolks of eggs, 4; lemon-juice, 1 tablespoonful.

Obs. Any white meat may be served *en blanquette*. The mushrooms are not indispensable for it, but they are always a great improvement. White sauce substituted for the thickened veal gravy will at once convert this dish into an inexpensive English fricassee. Mace, salt, and cayenne, must be added to either preparation, should it require seasoning.

MINCED VEAL AND OYSTERS†

The most elegant mode of preparing this dish is to mince about a pound of the whitest part of the inside of a cold roast fillet or loin of veal, to heat it without allowing it to boil, in a pint of rich white sauce, or *béchamel*, and to mix with it at the moment of serving, three dozens of small oysters ready bearded, and plumped in their own strained liquor, which is also to be added to the mince; the requisite quantity of salt, cayenne, and mace should be sprinkled over the veal before it is put into the sauce. Garnish the dish with pale fried sippets of bread, or with *fleuron** of brioche, or of puff paste. Nearly half-pint of mushrooms minced, and stewed white in a little butter, may be mixed with the veal instead of the oysters; or should they be very small they may be added to it whole: from ten to twelve minutes will be sufficient to make them tender. Balls of delicately fried oyster-forcemeat laid round the dish will give another good variety of it.

Veal minced, 1 lb; white sauce, 1 pint; oysters, 3 dozen, with their liquor; or mushrooms, ½ pint, stewed in butter 10 to 12 minutes.

* Fleurons, flowers, or flower-like figures, cut out with tin shapes.

† [*In this, as in many other receipts, there is a mixture of meat and fish, oysters being much used in those days as an ingredient of a dish, rather than the delicacy they are now.*]

VEAL-SYDNEY
(*Good*)

Pour boiling on an ounce and a half of fine bread-crumbs nearly half-pint of good veal stock or gravy, and let them stand till cool; mix with them then, two ounces of beef-suet shred very small, half a pound of cold roast veal carefully trimmed from the brown edges, skin, and fat, and finely minced; the grated rind of half a lemon, nearly a teaspoonful of salt, a little cayenne, the third of a teaspoonful of mace or nutmeg, and four well-beaten eggs. Whisk up the whole well together, put it into a buttered dish, and bake it from three-quarters of an hour to an hour. Cream may be used instead of gravy when more convenient, but this last will give the better flavour. A little clarified butter put into the dish before the other ingredients are poured in will be an improvement.

Bread-crumbs, 1½ oz; gravy or cream, nearly ½ pint; beef-suet, 2 oz; cold veal, ½ lb; rind of ½ lemon; salt, small teaspoonful; third as much mace or nutmeg; little cayenne; eggs, 4 large or 5 small: ¾ to 1 hour.

12

No.
1. Leg.
2. Best End of Loin.
3. Chump End of Loin.
4. Neck, Best End.
5. Neck, Scrag End.

No.
6. Shoulder.
7. Breast.
A Saddle is the Two Loins.
A Chine, the Two Necks.

Mutton is best suited for table in autumn, winter, and early spring. It is not considered quite so good when grass-lamb is in full season, nor during the sultry months of summer.

MUTTON

ROAST SADDLE OF MUTTON†

This is an excellent joint, though not considered a very economical one. It is usual for the butcher to raise the skin from it before it is sent in, and to skewer it on again, that in the roasting the juices of the meat may be better preserved, and the fat prevented from taking too much colour, as this should be but delicately browned. In less than half an hour before the mutton is done, remove the skin, and flour the joint lightly after having basted it well. Our own great objection to frothed meat would lead us to recommend that the skin should be taken off half an hour earlier, and that the joint should be kept at sufficient distance from the fire to prevent the possibility of the fat being burned; and that something more of time should be allowed for the roasting. With constant basting, great care, and good management, the cook may always ensure the proper appearance of this, or of any other joint (except, perhaps, of a haunch of venison) without having recourse to papering or pasting, or even to replacing the skin; but when unremitted attention cannot be given to this one part of the dinner, it is advisable to take all precautions that can secure it from being spoiled.

2½ to 2¾ hours. More if *very* large.

† [*At the present time lamb is easier to find than mutton, though there may be many a case of Mutton dressed as Lamb and the worse for it.*]

A BOILED LEG OF MUTTON, WITH TONGUE AND TURNIPS
(*An excellent Receipt*)

Trim into handsome form a well-kept, but perfectly sweet leg of mutton, of middling weight; wash, but do not soak it; lay it into a vessel as nearly of its size as convenient, and pour in rather more than sufficient cold water* to cover it; set it over a good fire, and when it begins to boil take off the scum, and continue to do so until no more appears; throw in a tablespoonful of salt (after the first skimming), which will assist to bring it to the surface, and as soon as the liquor is clear, add two moderate-sized onions stuck with a dozen cloves, a large faggot of parsley, thyme, and winter savoury, and four or five large carrots, and half an hour afterwards as many turnips. Draw the pan to the side of the fire, and let the mutton be simmered *gently* from two hours to two and a half, from the time of its first beginning to boil. Serve it with caper, brown cucumber, or oyster sauce. If stewed *softly*, as we have directed, the mutton will be found excellent dressed thus; otherwise, it will but resemble the unpalatable and ragged-looking joints of fast-boiled meat, so constantly sent to table by common English cooks. Any undressed bones of veal, mutton, or beef, boiled with the joint will improve it much, and the liquor will then make excellent soup or *bouillon*.

A small smoked ox-tongue boiled very tender will generally be much approved as an accompaniment to the mutton, though it is out of the usual course to serve them together: innovation on established usages is, however, sometimes to be recommended. The tongue should be garnished with well-prepared mashed turnips, moulded with a tablespoon into the form of a half-egg, and sent to table as hot as possible; or the turnips may be dished apart.

2 to 2½ hours.

* We have left this receipt unaltered, instead of applying to it Baron Liebig's directions for his improved method of boiling meat, because his objections to the immersion of the joint in *cold* water are partially obviated, by its being placed immediately over a sound fire, and heated quickly; and the mutton is very good thus dressed.

TO ROAST A LOIN OF MUTTON

The flesh of the loin of mutton is superior to that of the leg, when roasted; but to the frugal housekeeper this consideration is usually overbalanced by the great weight of fat attached to it; this, however, when economy is more considered than appearance, may be pared off and melted down for various kitchen uses. When thus reduced in size, the mutton will be soon roasted. If it is to be dressed in the usual way, the butcher should be desired to take off the skin: and care should be taken to preserve the fat from being ever so lightly burned: it should be managed, indeed, in the same manner as the saddle, in every respect, and carved also in the same way, either in its entire length or in oblique slices.†

Without the fat, 1 to 1½ hour; with 1¼ to 1¾ hour.

† [*Carving a saddle appears to be a matter of choice. In many places – particularly in London clubs where it is still a popular joint – it is carved parallel to the backbone, but if carved in oblique slices a reasonable proportion of fat to lean is obtained, which makes it less wasteful for the smaller household.*]

Skin and bone a loin of mutton, and lay it into a stewpan, or braising-pan, with a pint of water, a large onion stuck with a dozen cloves, half a pint of port wine and a spoonful of vinegar; add, when it boils, a small faggot of thyme and parsley, and some pepper and salt: let it stew three hours, and turn it often. Make some gravy of the bones, and add it at intervals to the mutton when required.

This receipt comes to us so strongly recommended by persons who have partaken frequently of the dish, that we have not thought it needful to prove it ourselves.

3 hours.

ROAST NECK OF MUTTON

This is a very favourite joint in many families [*and contains the cutlets, as opposed to the chops of the loin*], the flesh being more tender and succulent than that even of the loin; and when only a small roast is required, the best end of the neck of mutton, or the middle, if divested of a large portion of the fat and cut into good shape, will furnish one of appropriate size and of excellent quality. Let the ends be cut quite even and the bones short, so as to give a handsome squareness of form to the meat. The butcher, if directed to do so, will chop off the chine bone, and divide the long bones sufficiently at the joints to prevent any difficulty in separating them at table. From four to five pounds weight of the neck will require from an hour to an hour and a quarter of roasting at a clear and brisk, but not *fierce*, fire. It should be placed at a distance until it is heated through, and then moved nearer, and kept *thoroughly basted* until it is done. Tomatas baked or roasted may be sent to table with it; or a little plain gravy and red currant jelly; or it may be served without either.

When the entire joint, with the exception of the scrag-end (which should always be taken off), is cooked, proportionate time must be allowed for it.

Half roast or stew, or parboil, a small, or moderate-sized shoulder of mutton; lift it into a hot dish, score it on both sides down to the bone, season it well with fine salt and cayenne or pepper, and finish cooking it upon the gridiron over a brisk fire. Skim the fat from any gravy that may have flowed from it, and keep the dish which contains it quite hot to receive the joint again. Warm a cupful of pickled mushrooms, let a part of them be minced, and strew them over the broil when it is ready to be served; arrange the remainder round it, and send it instantly to table. The reader will scarcely need to be told that this is an excellent dish.

CHINA CHILO

Mince a pound of an undressed loin or leg of mutton, with or without a portion of its fat; mix with it two or three young lettuces shred small, a pint of young peas, a teaspoonful of salt, half as much pepper, four tablespoonsful of water, from two to three ounces of good butter, and, if the flavour be liked, a few green onions minced. Keep the whole well stirred with a fork over a clear and gentle fire until it is quite hot, then place it closely covered by the side of the stove, or on a high trivet, that it may stew as softly as possible for a couple of hours. One or even two half-grown cucumbers, cut small by scoring the ends deeply as they are sliced, or a quarter-pint of minced mushrooms may be added with good effect; or a dessertspoonful of currie-powder and a large chopped onion. A dish of boiled rice should be sent to table with it.

Mutton, 1 pound; green peas, 1 pint; young lettuces, 2; salt, 1 teaspoonful; pepper, ½ teaspoonful; water, 4 tablespoonsful; butter, 2 to 3 oz: 2 hours. Varieties: cucumbers, 2; or mushrooms minced, ¼ pint; or currie-powder, 1 dessertspoonful, and 1 large onion.

Take two pounds of small thick mutton cutlets with or without fat, according to the taste of the persons to whom the stew is to be served; take also four pounds of good potatoes, weighed after they are pared; slice them thick, and put a portion of them in a flat layer into a large thick saucepan or stewpan; season the mutton well with pepper, and place some of it on the potatoes; cover it with another layer, and proceed in the same manner with all, reserving plenty of the vegetable for the top; pour in three-quarters of a pint of cold water, and add, when the stew begins to boil, an ounce of salt; let it simmer gently for two hours, and serve it very hot. When the addition of onion is liked, strew some minced over the potatoes.

Mutton cutlets, 2 lb; potatoes, 4 lb; pepper, ½ oz; salt, 1 oz; water, ¾ pint: 2 hours.

Obs. For a real Irish stew the potatoes should be boiled to a mash: an additional quarter of an hour may be necessary for the full quantity here, but for half of it two hours are quite sufficient.

A BAKED IRISH STEW

Fill a brown upright Nottingham jar with alternate layers of mutton (or beef), sliced potatoes, and mild onions; and put in water and seasoning as above; cover the top closely with whole potatoes (pared), and send the stew to a moderate oven. The potatoes on the top should be well cooked and *browned* before the stew is served. We have not considered it necessary to try this receipt, which was given to us by some friends who keep an excellent table, and who recommended it much. It is, of course, suited only to a quite plain family dinner. The onions can be omitted when their flavour is not liked.

Skin six or eight fine fresh mutton kidneys, and without opening them, remove the fat; slice them rather thin, strew over them a large dessertspoonful of minced herbs, of which two-thirds should be parsley and the remainder thyme, with a tolerable seasoning of pepper or cayenne, and some fine salt. Melt two ounces of butter in a frying-pan, put in the kidneys and brown them quickly on both sides; when nearly done, stir amongst them a dessertspoonful of flour and shake them well in the pan; pour in the third of a pint of gravy (or of hot water in default of this), the juice of half a lemon, and as much of Harvey's sauce, or of mushroom catsup, as will flavour the whole pleasantly; bring these to the point of boiling, and pour them into a dish garnished with fried sippets, or lift out the kidneys first, give the sauce a boil and pour it on them. In France, a couple of glasses of champagne, or, for variety, of claret, are frequently added to this dish: one of port wine can be substituted for either of these. A dessertspoonful of minced eschalots may be strewed over the kidneys with the herbs; or two dozens of very small ones previously stewed until tender in fresh butter over a gentle fire, may be added after they are dished. This is a very excellent and approved receipt.

Fried 6 minutes.

SADDLE OF LAMB

This is an exceedingly nice joint for a small party. It should be roasted at a brisk fire, and kept constantly basted with its own dripping: it will require from an hour and three-quarters to two hours roasting. Send it to table with mint sauce, brown cucumber sauce, and a salad.

1¾ to 2 hours.

Obs. The following will be found an excellent receipt for mint sauce: With three heaped tablespoonsful of finely-chopped young mint, mix two of pounded and sifted sugar, and six of the best vinegar; stir it until the sugar is dissolved.

LOIN OF LAMB STEWED IN BUTTER
(Entrée)

Wash the joint, and wipe it very dry; skewer down the flap, and lay it into a close-shutting and thick stewpan or saucepan, in which three ounces of good butter have been just dissolved, but not allowed to boil; let it simmer slowly over a very gentle fire for two hours and a quarter, and turn it when it is rather more than half done. Lift it out, skim and pour the gravy over it; send asparagus, cucumber, or *soubise* sauce to table with it; or brown gravy, mint sauce, and a salad.

2¼ hours.

LAMB OR MUTTON CUTLETS, WITH SOUBISE SAUCE
(Entrée)

The best end of two necks of either will be required for a handsome dish. Cut them thin with one bone to each; trim off the fat and all the skin, scrape the bones very clean that they may look white, and season the cutlets with salt and white pepper; brush them with egg, dip them into very fine bread-crumbs, then into clarified butter, and again into the bread-crumbs, which should be flattened evenly upon them, and broil them over a very clear and brisk fire, or fry them in a little good butter of a fine clear brown; press them into two sheets of white blotting paper to extract the grease, and dish them in a circle, and pour into the centre a *soubise* sauce, or a *purée* of cucumbers. Brown cucumber sauce or a rich gravy, may be substituted for either of these in serving a quite simple dinner. Cutlets of the loin may be dressed in the same way after being dipped into crumbs of bread mixed with a full seasoning of minced herbs, and with a small quantity of eschalot when its flavour is liked. The small flat bone at the end of the cutlets should be taken off, to give them a good appearance.

13

No.
1. *The Spare Rib.*
2. *Hand.*
3. *Belly, or Spring.*

No.
4. *Fore Loin.*
5. *Hind Loin.*
6. *Leg.*

In season from Michaelmas to March: should be avoided in very warm weather.

PORK

TO ROAST A SUCKING PIG

After the pig has been scalded and prepared for the spit, wipe it as dry as possible, and put into the body about half a pint of fine bread-crumbs, mixed with three heaped teaspoonsful of sage, minced very small, three ounces of good butter, a large salt-spoonful of salt, and two-thirds as much of pepper or some cayenne. Sew it up with soft, but strong cotton; truss it as a hare, with the fore legs skewered back, and the hind ones forward; lay it to a strong clear fire, but keep it at a moderate distance, as it would quickly blister or scorch if placed too near. So soon as it has become warm, rub it with a bit of butter tied in a fold of muslin or of thin cloth, and repeat this process constantly while it is roasting. When the gravy begins to drop from it, put basins or small deep tureens under, to catch it in.* As soon as the pig is of a fine light amber brown and the steam draws strongly towards the fire, wipe it quite dry with a clean cloth, and rub a bit of cold butter over it. When it is half done, a pig iron, or in lieu of this, a large flat iron should be hung in the centre of the grate, or the middle of the pig will be done long before the ends. When it is ready for table lay it into a very hot dish, and before the spit is withdrawn, take off and open the head and split the body in two; chop together quickly the stuffing and the brains, put them into half-pint of good veal gravy ready thickened, add a glass of Madeira or of sherry and the gravy which has dropped from the pig; pour a small portion of this under the roast and serve the remainder as hot as possible in a tureen: a little pounded mace and cayenne with a squeeze of lemon-juice, may be added, should the flavour require heightening. Fine bread sauce, and plain gravy should likewise be served with it. Some persons still prefer the old-fashioned currant sauce to any other: and many have the brains and stuffing stirred into rich melted butter, instead of gravy; but the receipt which we have given has usually been so much approved, that we can recommend it with some confidence, as it stands. Modern taste would perhaps be rather in favour of rich brown gravy and thick tomata sauce.

In dishing the pig lay the body flat in the middle, and the head and ears at the ends and sides. When very pure oil can be obtained, it is preferable to butter for the basting: it should be laid on with a bunch of feathers. A pig of three weeks old is considered as best suited to the table, and it should always be dressed if possible the day it is killed.

1¼ to 1¾ hour.

* A deep oblong dish of suitable size seems better adapted to this purpose.

BAKED PIG

Prepare the pig exactly as for roasting; truss, and place it in the dish in which it is to be sent to the oven, and anoint it thickly in every part with white of egg which has been slightly beaten; it will require no basting, nor further attention of any kind, and will be well crisped by this process.

TO BROIL OR FRY PORK CUTLETS

Cut them about half an inch thick from a delicate loin of pork, trim them into neat form, and take off part of the fat, or the whole of it when it is not liked; dredge a little pepper or cayenne upon them, and broil them over a clear and moderate fire from fifteen to eighteen minutes: sprinkle a little fine salt upon them just before they are dished. They may be dipped into egg and then into bread-crumbs mixed with minced sage, and finished in the usual way. When fried, flour them well, and season them with salt and pepper first. Serve them with gravy in the pan, or with *sauce Robert*.

TO BOIL A HAM

The degree of soaking which must be given to a ham before it is boiled, must depend both on the manner in which it has been cured, and on its age. If highly salted, hard, and old, a day and night, or even longer, may be requisite to dilate the pores sufficiently, and to extract a portion of the salt. To do either effectually the water must be several times changed during the steeping. After the ham has been scraped, or brushed, as clean as possible, pare away lightly any part which, from being blackened or rusty, would disfigure it; though it is better *not* to cut the flesh at all unless it be really requisite for the good appearance of the joint. Lay it into a ham-kettle, or into any other vessel of a similar form, and cover it plentifully with cold water; bring it *very slowly* to boil, and clear off carefully the scum which will be thrown up in great abundance. So soon as the water has been cleared from this, draw back the pan quite to the edge of the stove, that the ham may be simmered softly but steadily, until it is tender. On no account allow it to boil fast. A bunch of herbs and three or four carrots, thrown in directly after the water has been skimmed, will improve it. When it can be probed very easily with a sharp skewer, or larding-pin, lift it out, strip off the skin, and should there be an oven at hand, set it in for a few minutes after having laid it on a drainer; strew fine raspings over it, or grate a hard-toasted crust, unless it is to be glazed, when neither of these must be used.

Small ham, 3½ to 4 hours; moderate sized, 4 to 4½ hours; very large, 5 to 5½ hours.

Obs. We have seen the following manner of boiling a ham recommended, but we have not tried it: 'Put into the water in which it is to be boiled, a quart of old cider and a pint of vinegar, a large bunch of sweet herbs, and a bay leaf. When it is two-thirds done, skin, cover it with raspings, and set it in an oven until it is done enough: it will prove incomparably superior to a ham boiled in the usual way.'

TO BAKE A HAM

Unless when too salt from not being sufficiently soaked, a ham (particularly a young and fresh one) eats much better baked than boiled, and remains longer good. The safer plan to ensure its being sufficiently steeped, is to lay it into plenty of cold water over night. The following day soak it for an hour or more in warm water, wash it delicately clean, trim smoothly off all rusty parts, and lay it with the rind downwards into a large common pie-dish; press an oiled paper closely over it, and then fasten securely to the edge of the dish a *thick* cover of coarse paste; and send the ham to a moderate oven, of which the heat will be well sustained until it is baked. Or, when more convenient, lay the ham at once – rind downwards – on the paste, of which sufficient should be made, and rolled off to an inch in thickness, to completely envelop it. Press a sheet of oiled foolscap paper upon it; gather up the paste firmly all round, draw and pinch the edges together, and fold them over on the upper side of the ham, taking care to close them so that no gravy can escape. Send it to a well-heated, but not fierce oven. A very small ham will require quite three hours baking, and a large one five. The crust and the skin must be removed while it is hot. When part only of a ham is dressed, this mode is better far than boiling it.

BACON BROILED OR FRIED

Cut it evenly in thin slices or *rashers*, as they are generally called, pare from them all rind and rust, curl them round, fasten them with small slight skewers, then fry, broil, or toast them in a Dutch oven; draw out the skewers before they are sent to table. A few minutes will dress them either way. They may also be cooked without being curled. The rind should always be taken off, and the bacon gently toasted, grilled, or fried, that it may be well done without being too much dried or hardened: it should be cut *thin*.

ITALIAN PORK CHEESE

Chop, not very fine, one pound of lean pork with two pounds of the inside fat; strew over, and mix thoroughly with them three teaspoonful of salt, nearly half as much pepper, a half-tablespoonful of mixed parsley, thyme, and sage (and sweet-basil, if it can be procured), all minced extremely small. Press the meat closely and evenly into shallow tin – such as are used for Yorkshire puddings will answer well – and bake it in a very gentle oven from an hour to an hour and a half: it is served cold in slices. Should the proportion of fat be considered too much, it can be diminished on a second trial.

Minced mushrooms or truffles may be added with very good effect to all meat-cakes, or compositions of this kind.

Lean of pork, 1 lb; fat, 2 lb; salt, 3 teaspoonful; pepper, 1½ teaspoonful; mixed herbs, ½ tablespoonful: 1 to 1½ hour.

To three pounds of lean pork, add two of fat [*pork*], and let both be taken clear of skin [*skin removed*]. As sausages are lighter, though not so delicate, when the meat is somewhat coarsely chopped, this difference should be attended to in making them. When the fat and lean are partially mixed, strew over them two ounces and a half of dry salt, beaten to powder, and mixed with one ounce of ground black pepper, and three large tablespoonsful of sage, very finely minced. Turn the meat with the chopping-knife, until the ingredients are well blended. Test it before it is taken off the block, by frying a small portion, that if more seasoning be desired, it may at once be added. A full-sized nutmeg [*grated*], and a small dessertspoonful of pounded mace, would, to many tastes, improve it. This sausage-meat is usually formed into cakes, which, after being well floured, are roasted in a Dutch oven. They must be watched, and often turned, that no part may be scorched.

Lean of pork, 3 lb; fat 2 lb; salt, 2½ oz; pepper, 1 oz; minced sage, 3 large tablespoonsful.

Chop, first separately, and then together, one pound and a quarter of veal, perfectly free from fat, skin, and sinew, with an equal weight of lean pork, and of the inside fat of the pig. Mix well, and strew over the meat an ounce and a quarter of salt, half an ounce of pepper, one nutmeg grated, and a *large* teaspoonful of pounded mace. Turn, and chop the sausages until they are equally seasoned throughout, and tolerably fine; press them into a clean pan, and keep them in a very cool place. Form them, when wanted for table, into cakes something less than an inch thick; and flour and fry them then for about ten minutes in a little butter, or roast them in a Dutch or American oven.

Lean of veal and pork, of each 1 lb 4 oz; fat of pork, 1 lb 4 oz;

salt, 1¼ oz; pepper, ½oz; nutmeg, 1; mace, 1 *large* teaspoonful:
fried in cakes, 10 minutes.

SAUSAGES AND CHESTNUTS
(*Entrée – An excellent dish – French*)

Roast, and take the husk and skin from forty fine Spanish chestnuts; fry gently, in a morsel of butter, six small flat oval cakes of
fine sausage-meat, and when they are well browned, lift them out
and pour into a saucepan, which should be bright in the inside,
the greater part of the fat in which they have been fried; mix
with it a large teaspoonful of flour, and stir these over the fire till
they are well and equally browned; then pour in by degrees
nearly half-pint of strong beef or veal broth, or gravy, and two
glasses of good white wine; add a *small* bunch of savoury herbs,
and as much salt and pepper, or cayenne, as will season the whole
properly; give it a boil, lay in the sausages round the pan, and the
chestnuts in the centre; stew them *very* softly for nearly an hour;
take out the herbs, dish the sausages neatly and heap the chestnuts in the centre, strain the sauce over them and serve them
very hot. There should be no sage mixed with the pork to dress
thus.

Chestnuts roasted, 40; sausages, 6; gravy, nearly ½ pint;
sherry or Madeira, 2 wineglassesful: stewed together from 50 to
60 minutes.

TRUFFLED SAUSAGES†
(*Saucisses aux Truffes*)

With two pounds of the lean of young tender pork, mix one
pound of fat, a quarter of a pound of truffles, minced very small,
an once and a half of salt, a seasoning of cayenne, or quite half
an ounce of white pepper, a nutmeg, a teaspoonful of freshly
pounded mace, and a dessertspoonful or more of savoury herbs
dried and reduced to powder. Test a morsel of the mixture;

heighten any of the seasonings to the taste; and put the meat into delicately clean skins: if it be for immediate use, and the addition is liked, moisten it, before it is dressed, with one or two glassesful of Madeira. The substitution of a clove of garlic for the truffles, will convert these into *Saucisses à l'Ail*, or garlic sausages.

† [*Truffles (like oysters) are more of a delicacy now than when the receipt first appeared. But it is easy to substitute the garlic as suggested.*]

14

POULTRY

TO BONE A FOWL OR TURKEY WITHOUT OPENING IT

After the fowl has been drawn and singed, wipe it inside and out with a clean cloth, but do not wash it. Take off the head, cut through the skin all round the first joint of the legs, and pull them from the fowl, to draw out the large tendons. Raise the flesh first from the lower part of the back-bone, and a little also from the end of the breast-bone, if necessary; work the knife gradually to the socket of the thigh; with the point of the knife detach the joint from it, take the end of the bone firmly in the fingers, and cut the flesh clean from it down to the next joint, round which pass the point of the knife carefully, and when the skin is loosened from it in every part, cut round the next bone, keeping the edge of the knife close to it, until the whole of the leg is done. Remove the bones of the other leg in the same manner; then detach the flesh from the back and breast-bone sufficiently to enable you to reach the upper joints of the wings; proceed with these as with the legs, but be especially careful not to pierce the skin of the second joint. It is usual to leave the pinions unboned, in order to give more easily its natural form to the fowl when it is dressed. The merrythought [*wishbone*] and neck-bones may now easily be cut away, the back- and side-bones taken out without being divided, and the breast bone separated carefully from the flesh (which, as the work progresses, must be turned back from the bones upon the fowl, until it is completely inside out). After the one remaining bone is removed, draw the wings and legs back to their proper form, and turn the fowl right side outwards.

A turkey is boned exactly in the same manner, but as it requires a very large proportion of forcemeat to fill it entirely, the legs and wings are sometimes drawn into the body, to diminish the expense of this. If very securely trussed, and sewn, the bird may be either boiled, or stewed in rich gravy, as well as roasted, after being boned and forced; but it must be most gently cooked, or it may burst.

ANOTHER MODE OF BONING A FOWL OR TURKEY

Cut through the skin down the centre of the back, and raise the flesh carefully on either side with the point of a sharp knife, until the sockets of the wings and thighs are reached. Till a little practice has been gained, it will perhaps be better to bone these joints before proceeding further; but after they are once detached from it, the whole of the body may easily be separated from the flesh and taken out entire: only the neck-bones and merrythought will then remain to be removed. The bird thus prepared may either be restored to its original form, by filling the legs and wings with forcemeat, and the body with the livers of two or three fowls mixed with alternate layers of parboiled tongue freed from the rind, fine sausage meat, or veal forcemeat, or thin slices of the nicest bacon, or aught else of good flavour, which will give a marbled appearance to the fowl, when it is carved; and then be sewn up and trussed as usual.

TURKEY À LA FLAMANDE, OR DINDE POUDRÉE

Prepare as for boiling a fine well-kept hen turkey; wipe the inside thoroughly with a dry cloth, but do not wash it; throw in a little salt to draw out the blood, let it remain a couple of hours or more, then drain and wipe it again; next, rub the outside in every part with about four ounces of fine dry salt, mixed with a large table-spoonful of pounded sugar; rub the turkey well with these, and turn it every day for four days; then fill it entirely with equal parts of choice sausage-meat, and of the crumb of bread soaked in boiling milk or cream, and wrung dry in a cloth; season these with the grated rind of a large lemon and nutmeg, mace, cayenne, and fine herbs, in the same proportion as for veal force-meat (see Chapter 8). Sew the turkey up very securely, and when trussed, roll it in a cloth, tie it closely at both ends, put it into boiling water, and boil it very gently between three and four hours. When taken up, sprinkle it thickly with fine crumbs of bread, mixed with plenty of parsley, shred extremely small. Serve it cold, with a sauce made of the strained juice and grated rind of two lemons, a teaspoonful of made mustard, and one of pounded sugar, with as much oil as will prevent its being more than pleasantly acid, and a little salt, if needed; work these together until perfectly mixed, and send them to table in a tureen.

This receipt was given to us abroad, by a Flemish lady, who had had the dish often served with great success in Paris. We have inserted it on her authority, not on our own experience; but we think it may be quite depended on.

TO ROAST A FOWL

(Fowls are always in season when they can be procured sufficiently young to be tender. About February they become dear and scarce; and small spring chickens are generally very expensive. As summer advances they decline in price.)

Strip off the feathers, and carefully pick every stump from the skin, as nothing can be more uninviting than the appearance of any kind of poultry where this has been neglected, nor more indicative of slovenliness on the part of the cook. Take off the head and neck close to the body, but leave sufficient of the skin to tie over the part that is cut. In drawing the bird, do not open it more than is needful, and use great precaution to avoid breaking the gall-bladder. Hold the legs in boiling water for two or three minutes that the skin may be peeled from them easily; cut the claws, and then, with a bit of lighted writing-paper, singe off the hairs without blackening the fowl. Wash, and wipe it afterwards very dry, and let the liver and gizzard be made delicately clean, and fastened into the pinions. Truss and spit it firmly; flour it well when first laid to the fire, baste it frequently with butter, and when it is done draw out the skewers, dish it, pour a little good gravy over, and send it to table with bread, mushroom, egg, chestnut, or olive sauce. A common mode of serving roast fowls in France is *aux cressons*, that is laid upon young water-cresses,* which have previously been freed from the outer leaves, thoroughly washed, shaken dry in a clean cloth, and sprinkled with a little fine salt, and sometimes with a small quantity of vinegar: these should cover the dish, and after the fowls are placed on them, gravy should be poured over as usual.

The body of a fowl may be filled with very small mushrooms prepared as for partridges (see partridges with mushrooms), then sewn up, roasted and served with mushroom-sauce: this is an excellent mode of dressing it. A little rasped bacon, or a bit or two of the lean of beef or veal minced, or cut into dice, may be put inside the bird when either is considered an improvement; but its own liver, or that of another fowl, will be found to impart a much finer flavour than any of these last; and so likewise will a tea-spoonful of really good mushroom powder smoothly mixed with a slice of good butter, and a seasoning of fine salt and cayenne.**

Full-sized fowl, 1 hour: young chicken, 25 to 35 minutes.

* This is done with many other roasts which are served in the second course; but the *vinegar* is seldom added in this country.

** We cannot much recommend these *mere superfluities* of the table.

Either of these, when merely split and broiled, is very dry and unsavoury eating; but will be greatly improved if first boiled gently from five to ten minutes and left to become cold, then divided, dipped into egg and well seasoned bread-crumbs, plentifully sprinkled with clarified butter, dipped again into the crumbs, and broiled over a clear and gentle fire from half to three-quarters of an hour. It should be served very hot, with mushroom-sauce or with a little good plain gravy, which may be thickened and flavoured with a teaspoonful of mushroom-powder mixed with half as much flour and a little butter; or with some *Espagnole*. It should be opened at the back, and evenly divided quite through; the legs should be trussed like those of a boiled fowl; the breast-bone, or that of the back may be removed at pleasure, and both sides of the bird should be made as flat as they can be that the fire may penetrate every part equally: the inside should be first laid towards it. The neck, feet and gizzard may be boiled down with a small quantity of onion and carrot, previously browned in a morsel of butter to make the gravy; and the liver, after having been simmered with them for five or six minutes, may be used to thicken it after it is strained. A teaspoonful of lemon-juice, some cayenne, and minced parsley should be added to it, and a little arrowroot, or flour and butter.

½ to ¾ hour.

FRICASSEED FOWLS OR CHICKENS
(*Entrée*)

To make a fricassee of good appearance without great expense, prepare, with exceeding nicety, a couple of plump chickens, strip off the skin, and carve them very neatly. Reserve the wings, breasts, merrythoughts, and thighs; and stew down the inferior joints with a couple of blades of mace, a small bunch of savoury herbs, a few white peppercorns, a pint and a half of water, and a small half-teaspoonful of salt. When something more than a third part reduced, strain the gravy, let it cool, and skim off every particle of fat. Arrange the joints which are to be fricasseed in one layer if it can be done conveniently, and pour to them as much of the gravy as will nearly cover them; add the very thin rind of half a fine fresh lemon, and simmer the fowls gently from half to three-quarters of an hour; throw in sufficient salt, pounded mace, and cayenne, to give the sauce a good flavour, thicken it with a large teaspoonful of arrowroot, and stir to it the third of a pint of rich boiling cream; then lift the stewpan from the fire, and shake it briskly round while the beaten yolks of three fresh eggs, mixed with a spoonful or two of cream, are added; continue to shake the pan gently above the fire till the sauce is just set, but it must not be allowed to boil, or it will curdle in an instant.

½ to ¾ hour.

ENGLISH CHICKEN CUTLETS
(*Entrée*)

Skin and cut into joints one or two young chickens, and remove the bones with care from the breasts, merrythoughts [*wishbones*], and thighs, which are separated from the legs. Mix well together a teaspoonful of salt, nearly a fourth as much of mace, a little grated nutmeg, and some cayenne; flatten and form into good shape, the boned joints of chicken, and the flesh of the wings; rub a little of the seasoning over them in every part, dip them into beaten egg, and then into very fine bread-crumbs, and fry them gently in fresh butter until they are of a delicate brown. Some of the bones and trimmings may be boiled down in half a pint of water, with a roll of lemon-peel, a little salt, and eight or ten white peppercorns, to make the gravy, which, after being strained and cleared from fat, may be poured hot to some thickening made in the pan with a slice of fresh butter and a dessert-spoonful of flour; a teaspoonful of mushroom-powder would improve it greatly, and a small quantity of lemon-juice should be added before it is poured out, with salt and cayenne if required. Pile the cutlets high in the centre of the dish, and serve the sauce under them, or in a tureen.

CUTLETS OF FOWLS, PARTRIDGES, OR PIGEONS
(*Entrée – French Receipt*)

Take closely off the flesh of the breast and wing together, on either side of the bone, and when the *large fillets*, as they are called, are thus raised from three birds, which will give but six cutlets, take the strips of flesh that lie under the wings, and that of the merrythoughts, and flatten two or three of these together, that there may be nine cutlets at least, of equal size. When all are ready, fry to a pale brown as many diamond-shaped sippets of bread as there are fillets of fowl, and let them be quite as large; place these before the fire to dry, and wipe out the pan. Dip the cutlets into some yolks of eggs, mixed with a little clarified butter, and strew them in every part with the finest bread-crumbs, moderately seasoned with salt, cayenne, and pounded mace. Dissolve as much good butter as will be required to dress them, and fry them in it of a light amber-colour: arrange them upon the sippets of bread, pile them high in the dish, and pour a rich brown gravy or *Espagnole* round, but not *over* them.

FRIED CHICKEN À LA MALABAR
(*Entrée*)

This is an Indian dish. Cut up the chicken, wipe it dry, and rub it well with currie-powder mixed with a little salt; fry it in a bit of butter, taking care that it is of a nice light brown. In the mean time cut two or three onions into thin slices, draw them out into rings, and cut the rings into little bits about half an inch long; fry them for a long time gently in a little clarified butter, until they have gradually dried up and are of a delicate yellow-brown. Be careful that they are not burnt, as the burnt taste of a single bit would spoil the flavour of the whole. When they are as dry as chips, without the least grease or moisture upon them, mix a little salt with them, strew them over the fried chicken, and serve up with lemon on a plate.

We have extracted this recipe from a clever little work called the 'Hand-Book of Cookery'.

HASHED FOWL
(*Entrée*)

After having taken off in joints, as much of a cold fowl or *fowls* as will suffice for a dish, bruise the bodies with a paste roller, pour to them a pint of water, and boil them for an hour and a half to two hours, with the addition of a little pepper and salt only, or with a small quantity of onion, carrot, and savoury herbs. Strain, and skim the fat from the gravy, put it into a clean saucepan, and should it require thickening, stir to it, when it boils, half a teaspoonful of flour smoothly mixed with a small bit of butter; add a little mushroom catsup, or other store-sauce, with a slight seasoning of mace or nutmeg. Lay in the fowl, and keep it near the fire until it is heated quite through, and is at the point of boiling: serve it with fried sippets round the dish. For a hash of higher relish, add to the bones when they are first stewed down a large onion minced and browned in butter, and before the fowl is dished, add some cayenne and the juice of half a lemon.

FRITOT OF COLD FOWLS

Cut into joints and take the skin from some cold fowls, lay them into a deep dish, strew over them a little fine salt and cayenne, add the juice of a lemon, and let them remain for an hour, moving them occasionally that they may all absorb a portion of the acid; then dip them one by one into some French batter (see Chapter 5), and fry them a pale brown over a gentle fire. Serve them garnished with very green crisped parsley. A few drops of eschalot vinegar may be mixed with the lemon-juice which is poured to the fowls, or slices of raw onion or eschalot, and small branches of sweet herbs may be laid amongst them, and cleared off before they are dipped into the batter. Gravy made of the trimmings, thickened, and well flavoured, may be sent to table with them in a tureen: and dressed bacon, in a dish apart.

FOWLS À LA MAYONNAISE

Carve with great nicety a couple of cold roast fowls; place the inferior joints, if they are served at all, close together in the middle of a dish, and arrange the others round and over them, piling them high in the centre. Garnish them with the hearts of young lettuces cut in two, and hard-boiled eggs, halved length-wise. At the moment of serving, pour over the fowls a well-made *mayonnaise* sauce (see Chapter 6), or, if preferred, an English salad-dressing, compounded with thick cream, instead of oil.

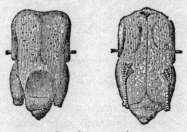

Ducks trussed

TO ROAST DUCKS

(Ducks are in season all the year, but are thought to be in their per-fection about June or early in July. Ducklings (or half-grown ducks) are in the greatest request in spring, when there is no game in the market, and other poultry is somewhat scarce.)

In preparing these for the spit, be careful to clear the skin en-tirely from the stumps of the feathers; take off the heads and necks, but leave the feet on, and hold them for a few minutes in boiling water to loosen the skin, which must be peeled off. Wash the inside of the birds by pouring water through them, but merely wipe the outsides with a dry cloth. Put into the bodies a seasoning of parboiled onions mixed with minced sage, salt, pepper, and a slice of butter when this mode of dressing them is liked; but as the taste of a whole party is seldom in its favour, one, when a couple are roasted, is often served without the stuffing. Cut off the pinions at the first joint from the bodies, truss the feet behind the backs, spit the birds firmly, and roast them at a brisk fire, but do not place them sufficiently near to be scorched; baste them constantly, and when the breasts are well plumped, and the steam from them draws towards the fire, dish, and serve them quickly with a little good brown gravy poured round them, and some also in a tureen; or instead of this, with some which has been made with the necks, gizzards, and livers well stewed down, with a slight seasoning of browned onion, some herbs, and spice.

Young ducks, ½ hour: full sized, from ¾ to 1 hour.

Obs. Olive-sauce may be served with roast as well as with stewed ducks.

STEWED DUCKS
(*Entrée*)

A couple of quite young ducks, or a fine, full-grown, but still tender one, will be required for this dish. Cut either down neatly into joints, and arrange them in a single layer if possible, in a wide stewpan; pour in about three-quarters of a pint of strong cold beef stock or gravy; let it be well cleared from scum when it begins to boil, then throw in a little salt, a rather full seasoning of cayenne, and a few thin strips of lemon-rind. Simmer the ducks very softly for three-quarters of an hour, or somewhat longer should the joints be large; then stir into the gravy a tablespoonful of the finest rice-flour, mixed with a wineglassful or rather more of port wine, and a dessertspoonful of lemon-juice: in ten minutes after, dish the stew and send it to table instantly.

The ducks may be served with a small portion only of their sauce, and dished in a circle, with green peas *à la Française* heaped high in the centre: the lemon-rind and port wine should then be altogether omitted, and a small bunch of green onions and parsley, with two or three young carrots, may be stewed down with the birds, or three or four minced eschalots, delicately fried in butter, may be used to flavour the gravy.

TO ROAST PIGEONS

(In season from March to Michaelmas, and whenever they can be had young.)

These should be dressed while they are very fresh. If extremely young they will be ready in twelve hours for the spit, otherwise, in twenty-four. Take off the heads and necks, and cut off the toes at the first joint; draw them carefully, and pour plenty of water through them: wipe them dry, and put into each bird a small bit of butter lightly dipped into a little cayenne (formerly it was rolled in minced parsley, but this is no longer the fashionable mode of preparing them). Truss the wings over the backs, and roast them at a brisk fire, keeping them well and constantly basted with butter. Serve them with brown gravy, and a tureen of parsley and butter. For the second course, dish them upon young water-cresses, as directed for roast fowl *aux cressons*, page 154. About twenty minutes will roast them.

18 to 20 minutes; five minutes longer, if large; rather less, if *very* young.

GAME

TO ROAST A HAUNCH OF VENISON

To give venison the flavour and the tenderness so much prized by epicures, it must be well kept; and by taking the necessary precautions, it will hang a considerable time without detriment. Wipe it with soft dry cloths, wherever the slightest moisture appears on the surface, and dust it plentifully with freshly-ground pepper or powdered ginger, to preserve it from the flies. The application of the pyroligneous or acetic acid would effectually protect it from these, as well as from the effects of the weather; but the joint must then be, not only well washed, but *soaked* for some considerable time, and this would be very detrimental.

To prepare the venison for the spit, wash it slightly with tepid water or merely wipe it thoroughly with damp cloths, and dry it afterwards with clean ones; then lay over the fat side a large sheet of thickly-buttered paper, and next a paste of flour and water about three-quarters of an inch thick; cover this again with two or three sheets of stout paper, secure the whole well with twine, and lay the haunch to a sound clear fire; baste the paper immediately with butter or clarified dripping, and roast the joint from three hours and a half to four and a half, according to its weight and quality. Doe venison will require half an hour less time than buck venison. Twenty minutes before the joint is done remove the paste and paper, baste the meat in every part with butter, and dredge it very lightly with flour; let it take a pale brown colour, and send it to table as hot as possible with gravy in a tureen, and good currant jelly. It is not now customary to serve any other sauces with it.

3½ to 4½ hours.

Obs. The kind of gravy appropriate to venison is a matter on which individual taste must decide. When preparations of high savour are preferred to the pure flavour of the game, the *Espagnole* (or Spanish sauce) of Chapter 4, can be sent to table with it. When a simple unflavoured one is better liked, some mutton cutlets freed entirely from fat, then very slightly broiled over a quick fire, and stewed gently down in a light extract of mutton prepared by Liebig's directions, Chapter 1, for about an hour, will produce an excellent plain gravy: it should be seasoned with salt and pepper (or fine cayenne) only. When venison abounds, it should be used for the gravy instead of mutton.

TO HASH VENISON*

For superior hash of venison, add to three-quarters of a pint of strong thickened brown gravy, Christopher North's sauce, in the proportion directed for it in the receipt of page 64. Cut the venison in small thin slices of equal size, arrange them in a clean saucepan, pour the gravy on them, let them stand for ten minutes or more, then place them near the fire, and bring the whole very slowly to the *point* of boiling only: serve the hash immediately in a hot-water dish.

For a plain dinner, when no gravy is at hand, break down the bones of the venison small, after the flesh has been cleared from them, and boil them with those of three or four undressed mutton-cutlets, a slice or two of carrot, or a few savoury herbs, and about a pint and a half of water or broth, until the liquid is reduced quite one third. Strain it off, let it cool, skim off all the fat, heat the gravy, thicken it when it boils with a dessertspoonful or rather more of arrowroot, or with a brown *roux*, mix the same sauce with it, and finish it exactly as the richer hash above. It may be served on sippets of fried bread or not, at choice.

* Minced collops of venison may be prepared exactly like those of beef; and venison-cutlets like those of mutton: the neck may be taken for both of these.

Hare trussed

TO ROAST A HARE

(In season from September to the 1st of March)

After the hare has been skinned, or cased,† as it is called, wash it very thoroughly in cold water, and afterwards in warm. If in any degree overkept, or musty in the inside, which it will sometimes be when emptied before it is hung up and neglected afterwards, use vinegar, or the pyroligneous acid, well diluted, to render it sweet; then again throw it into abundance of water, that it may retain no taste of the acid. Pierce with the point of a knife any parts in which the blood appears to have settled, and soak them in tepid water, that it may be well drawn out. Wipe the hare dry, fill it with the Common Forcemeat of Chapter 8, sew it up, truss and spit it firmly, baste it for ten minutes with lukewarm water mixed with a very little salt; throw this away, and put into the pan a quart or more of new milk; keep it constantly laded over the hare until it is nearly dried up, then add a large lump of butter, flour the hare, and continue the basting steadily until it is well browned; for unless this be done, and the roast be kept at a proper distance from the fire, the outside will become so dry and hard as to be quite uneatable. Serve the hare when done, with good brown gravy (of which a little should be poured round it in the dish), and with fine red currant jelly. This is an approved English method of dressing it, but we would recommend in preference, that it should be basted plentifully with butter from the beginning (the strict economist may substitute clarified beef-dripping, or marrow, and finish with a small quantity of butter only); and that the salt and water should be altogether omitted. First-rate cooks merely wipe the hare inside and out, and rub it with its own blood before it is laid to the fire, but there is generally a rankness about it, especially after it has been many days killed, which, we should say, renders the washing indispensable, unless a coarse game-flavour is liked.

1¼ to 1¾ hour.

† ['*Casing*' *or skinning a hare seems to have been the origin of the phrase 'First catch your hare', attributed to Mrs Glasse.*]

STEWED HARE

Wash and soak the hare thoroughly, wipe it very dry, cut it down into joints dividing the largest, flour and brown it slightly in butter with some bits of lean ham, pour to them by degrees a pint and a half of gravy, and stew the hare *very gently* for an hour and a half to two hours: when it is about one third done add the very thin rind of half a large lemon, and ten minutes before it is served stir to it a large dessertspoonful of rice-flour, smoothly mixed with two tablespoonsful of good mushroom catsup, a quarter of a teaspoonful or more of mace, and something less of cayenne. This is an excellent plain receipt for stewing a hare; but the dish may be enriched with forcemeat rolled into small balls, and simmered for ten minutes in the stew, or fried and added to it after it is dished; a higher seasoning of spice, a couple of glasses of port wine, with a little additional thickening and a tablespoonful of lemon-juice, will all serve to give it a heightened relish.

Hare, 1; lean of ham or bacon, 4 to 6 oz; butter, 2 oz; gravy, 1½ pint; lemon-rind: 1 hour and 20 to 50 minutes, Rice-flour, 1 large dessertspoonful; mushroom catsup, 2 tablespoonsful; mace, ⅓ of teaspoonful; little cayenne (salt, if needed): 10 minutes.

FRIED RABBIT

After the rabbit has been emptied, thoroughly washed and soaked, should it require it to remove any mustiness of smell, blanch it, that is to say, put it into boiling water and let it boil from five to seven minutes, drain it, and when cold or nearly so, cut it into joints, dip them into beaten egg, and then into fine bread-crumbs, seasoned with salt and pepper, and when all are ready, fry them in butter over a moderate fire, from twelve to fifteen minutes. Simmer two or three strips of lemon-rind in a little gravy, until it is well flavoured with it; boil the liver of the rabbit for five minutes, let it cool, and then mince it; thicken the gravy with an ounce of butter, and a small teaspoonful of flour, add the liver, give the sauce a minute's boil, stir in two tablespoonsful of cream if at hand, and last of all, a small quantity of lemon-juice. Dish the rabbit, pour the sauce *under* it, and serve it quickly. If preferred, a gravy can be made in the pan as for veal cutlets, and the rabbit may be simply fried.

(In season from the beginning of October to the end of January. The licensed term of pheasant shooting commences on the 1st of October, and terminates on the 2nd of February, but as the birds will remain perfectly good in cold weather for two or three weeks, if from that time hung in a well-ventilated larder, they continue, correctly speaking, in season so long as they can be preserved fit for table after the regular market for them is closed: the same rule applies equally to other varieties of game.)

Unless kept to the proper point, a pheasant is one of the most tough, dry, and flavourless birds that is sent to table; but when it has hung as many days as it can without becoming really tainted, and is well roasted and served, it is most excellent eating. Pluck off the feathers carefully, cut a slit in the back of the neck to remove the crop, then draw the bird in the usual way, and either wipe the inside very clean with a damp cloth, or pour water through it; wipe the outside also, but with a dry cloth; cut off the toes, turn the head of the bird *under* the wing, with the bill laid straight along the breast, skewer the legs, which must not be crossed, flour the pheasant well, lay it to a brisk fire, and baste it constantly and plentifully with well flavoured butter. Send bread-sauce and good brown gravy to table with it. When a brace is served, one is sometimes larded, and the other not; but a much handsomer appearance is given to the dish by larding both. About three-quarters of an hour will roast them.

3/4 hour; a few minutes less, if liked very much underdone; five or ten more for *thorough* roasting, with a *good* fire in both cases.

BOUDIN OF PHEASANT À LA RICHELIEU
(*Entrée*)

Take, quite clear from the bones, and from all skin and sinew, the flesh of a half-roasted pheasant; mince, and then pound it to the smoothest paste; add an equal bulk of the floury part of some fine roasted potatoes, or of such as have been boiled by Captain Kater's receipt (see Chapter 17), and beat them together until they are well blended; next throw into the mortar something less (in volume) of fresh butter than there was of the pheasant-flesh, with a high seasoning of mace, nutmeg, and cayenne, and a half-teaspoonful or more of salt; pound the mixture afresh for ten minutes or a quarter of an hour, keeping it turned from the sides of the mortar into the middle; then add one by one, after merely taking out the germs with the point of a fork, two whole eggs and a yolk or two without the whites, if these last will not render the mixture too moist. Mould it into the form of a roll, lay it into a stewpan rubbed with butter, pour boiling water on it and poach it gently from ten to fifteen minutes. Lift it out with care, drain it on a sieve, and when it is quite cold cover it equally with beaten egg, and then with the finest bread-crumbs, and broil it over a clear fire, or fry it in butter of a clear golden brown. A good gravy should be made of the remains of the bird and sent to table with it; the flavour may be heightened with ham and eschalots, and small mushrooms, sliced sideways, and stewed quite tender in butter, may be mixed with the *boudin* after it is taken from the mortar; or their flavour may be given more delicately by adding to it only the butter in which they have been simmered, well pressed from them through a strainer. The mixture, which should be set into a very cool place before it is moulded, may be made into several small rolls, which will require four or five minutes' poaching only. The flesh of partridges will answer quite as well as that of pheasants for this dish.

TO ROAST PARTRIDGES

(In season from the first of September to the second of February, and as long as they can be preserved fit for table from that time.)

Let the birds hang as long as they can possibly be kept without becoming offensive; pick them carefully, draw, and singe them; wipe the insides thoroughly with a clean cloth; truss them with the head turned under the wing and the legs drawn close together, not crossed. Flour them when first laid to the fire, and baste them plentifully with butter. Serve them with bread sauce, and good brown gravy: a little of this last should be poured over them. In some counties they are dished upon fried bread-crumbs, but these are better handed round the table by themselves. Where game is plentiful we recommend that the remains of a cold roasted partridge should be well bruised and boiled down with just so much water, or unflavoured broth, as will make gravy for a brace of other birds: this, seasoned with salt, and cayenne only, or flavoured with a few mushrooms, will be found a very superior accompaniment for roast partridges, to the best meat-gravy that can be made. A little eschalot, and a few herbs, can be added to it at pleasure. It should be served also with boiled or with broiled partridges in preference to any other.

30 to 40 minutes.

Obs. Rather less time must be allowed when the birds are liked underdressed. In preparing them for the spit, the crop must be removed through a slit cut in the back of the neck, the claws clipped close, and the legs held in boiling water for a minute, that they may be skinned the more easily.

BOILED PARTRIDGES

This is a delicate mode of dressing young and tender birds. Strip off the feathers, clean, and wash them well; cut off the heads, truss the legs like those of boiled fowls, and when ready, drop them into a large pan of boiling water; throw a little salt on them, and in fifteen, or at the utmost in eighteen minutes they will be ready to serve. Lift them out, dish them quickly, and send them to table with the white mushroom sauce, with bread sauce and game gravy (see preceding receipt), or with celery sauce. Our own mode of having them served is usually with a slice of fresh butter, about a tablespoonful of lemon-juice, and a good sprinkling of cayenne placed in a very hot dish, under them.

15 to 18 minutes.

For a brace of young well-kept birds, prepare from half to three-quarters of a pint of mushroom-buttons, or very small flaps [*flat mushrooms*], as for pickling. Dissolve over a gentle fire an ounce and a half of butter, throw in the mushrooms with a slight sprinkling of salt and cayenne, simmer them from eight to ten minutes, and turn them with the butter on to a plate; when they are quite cold, put the whole into the bodies of the partridges, sew them up, truss them securely, and roast them on a vertical jack with the heads downwards; or should an ordinary spit be used, tie them firmly to it, instead of passing it through them. Roast them the usual time, and serve them with brown mushroom sauce, or with gravy and bread sauce only. The birds may be trussed like boiled fowls, floured, and stewed slowly for thirty minutes; then turned, and simmered for another half hour with the addition of some mushrooms to the gravy; or they may be covered with small mushrooms stewed apart, when they are sent to table. They can also be served with their sauce only, simply thickened with a small quantity of fresh butter, smoothly mixed with less than a teaspoonful of arrowroot and flavoured with cayenne and a little catsup, wine, or store sauce.

Partridges, 2; mushrooms, ½ to ¾ pint; butter, 1½ oz; little mace and cayenne: roasted 30 to 40 minutes, or stewed 1 hour.

Obs. Nothing can be finer than the game flavour imbibed by the mushrooms with which the birds are filled, in this receipt.

BROILED PARTRIDGE
(*Breakfast Dish*)

'Split a young and well-kept partridge, and wipe it with a soft clean cloth inside and out, but do not wash it; broil it delicately over a very clear fire, sprinkling it with a little salt and cayenne; rub a bit of fresh butter over it the moment it is taken from the fire, and send it quickly to table with a sauce made of a good slice of butter browned with flour, a little water, cayenne, salt, and mushroom-catsup, poured over it.' We give this receipt exactly as we received it from a house where we know it to have been greatly approved by various guests who have partaken of it there.

TO ROAST THE LANDRAIL OR CORN-CRAKE†

This delicate and excellent bird is in its full season at the end of August and early in September, when it abounds often in the poulterers' shops. Its plumage resembles that of the partridge, but it is of smaller size and of much more slender shape. Strip off the feathers, draw and prepare the bird as usual for the spit, truss it like a snipe, and roast it quickly at a brisk but not a fierce fire from fifteen to eighteen minutes. Dish it on fried bread-crumbs, or omit these and serve it with gravy round it, and more in a tureen, and with well made bread sauce. Three or even four of the birds will be required for a dish. One makes a nice dinner for an invalid.

† [*This no longer abounds in the poulterers, but still occasionally appears on menus in Ireland.*]

TO ROAST GROUSE

Handle the birds very lightly in plucking off the feathers; draw them, and wipe the insides with clean damp cloths; or first wash, and then dry them well; though this latter mode would not be approved generally by epicures. Truss the grouse, and roast them about half an hour at a clear and brisk fire, keeping them basted almost without intermission. Serve them on a buttered toast which has been laid under them in the pan for ten minutes, or with gravy and bread sauce only.

½ hour to 35 minutes.

Obs. There are few occasions, we think, in which the contents of the dripping-pan can be introduced at table with advantage; but in dressing moor game, we would strongly recommend the toast to be laid in it under the birds, as it will afford a superior relish even to the birds themselves.

A SALMI OF MOOR FOWL, PHEASANTS, OR PARTRIDGES
(*Entrée*)

This is an excellent mode of serving the remains of roasted game, but when a superlative *salmi* is desired, the birds must be scarcely more than half roasted for it. In either case carve them very neatly, and strip every particle of skin and fat from the legs, wings, and breasts; bruise the bodies well, and put them with the skin and other trimmings into a very clean stewpan. If for a simple and inexpensive dinner, merely add to them two or three sliced eschalots, a bay leaf, a small blade of mace, and a few peppercorns; then pour in a pint or rather more of good veal gravy or strong broth, and boil it briskly until reduced nearly half; strain the gravy, pressing the bones well to obtain all the flavour, skim off the fat, add a little cayenne and lemon-juice, heat the game very gradually in it but do not on any account allow it to boil; place sippets of fried bread round a dish, arrange the birds in good form in the centre, give the sauce a boil, and pour it on them. This is but a homely sort of salmi, though of excellent flavour if well made; it may require perhaps the addition of a little thickening, and two or three glasses of dry white wine poured to the bodies of the birds with the broth, would bring it nearer to the French salmi in flavour. As the spongy substance in the inside of moor fowl and black game is apt to be extremely bitter when they have been long kept, care should be taken to remove such parts as would endanger the preparation.

TO ROAST WOODCOCKS OR SNIPES
(In season during the winter months, but not abundant until frost sets in.)

Handle them as little and as lightly as possible, and pluck off the feathers gently; for if this be violently done the skin of the birds will be broken. *Do not draw them,* but after having wiped them with clean soft cloths, truss them with the head under the wing, and the bill laid close along the breast; pass a slight skewer through the thighs, catch the ends with a bit of twine, and tie it across to keep the legs straight. Suspend the birds with the feet downwards to a bird-spit, flour them well, and baste them with butter, which should be ready dissolved in the pan or ladle. Before the trail [*insides, or entrail*] begins to drop, which it will do as soon as they are well heated, lay a thick round of bread, freed from the crust, toasted a delicate brown, and buttered on both sides, into the pan under them to catch it, as this is considered finer eating even than the flesh of the birds; continue the basting, letting the butter fall from them into the basting-spoon or ladle, as it cannot be collected again from the dripping-pan should it drop there, in consequences of the toast or *toasts* being in it. There should be one of these for each woodcock, and the trail should be spread equally over it. When the birds are done, which they will be, at a brisk fire, from twenty to twenty-five minutes, lay the toasts into a very hot dish, dress the birds upon them, pour a little gravy round the bread, and send more to table in a tureen.

Woodcock, 20 to 25 minutes; snipe, 5 minutes less.

TO ROAST THE PINTAIL, OR SEA PHEASANT

(All wild-fowl is in full season in mid-winter: the more severe the weather, the more abundant are the supplies of it in the markets. It may be had usually from November to March.)

This beautiful bird is by no means rare upon our eastern coast, but we know not whether it be much seen in the markets generally. It is most excellent eating, and should be roasted at a clear quick fire, well floured when first laid down, turned briskly, and basted with butter almost without cessation. If drawn from the spit in from twenty-five to thirty minutes, then dished and laid before the fire for two or three more, it will give forth a singularly rich gravy. Score the breast when it is carved, sprinkle on it a little cayenne, and fine salt, and let a cut lemon be handed round the table when the bird is served; or omit the scoring, and shed round with it brown gravy, and Christopher North's sauce made hot.

20 to 30 minutes.

TO ROAST WILD DUCKS

A bit of soft bread soaked in port wine, or in claret, is sometimes put into them, but nothing more. Flour them well, lay them rather near to a very clear and brisk fire, that they may be quickly browned, and yet retain their juices. Baste them plentifully and constantly with butter, and, if it can be so regulated, let the spit turn with them rapidly. From fifteen to twenty minutes will roast them sufficiently for the generality of eaters; but for those who object to them much underdressed, a few additional minutes must be allowed. Something less of time will suffice when they are prepared for persons who like them scarcely more than heated through.

Teal, which is a more delicate kind of wild-fowl, is roasted in the same way: in from ten to fifteen minutes it will be enough done for the fashionable mode of serving it, and twenty minutes will dress it *well* at a good fire.

16

CURRIES, POTTED MEATS, ETC.

REMARKS ON CURRIES

The great superiority of the oriental curries over those generally prepared in England is not, we believe, altogether the result of a want of skill or of experience on the part of our cooks, but is attributable in some measure to many of the ingredients, which in a *fresh and green state* add so much to their excellence, being here beyond our reach.

With us, turmeric and cayenne pepper prevail in them often far too powerfully: the prodigal use of the former should be especially avoided, as it injures both the quality and the *colour* of the currie, which ought to be of a dark green, rather than of a red or yellow hue. A couple of ounces of a sweet, sound cocoa-nut, lightly grated and stewed for nearly or quite an hour in the gravy of a currie, is a great improvement to its flavour: it will be found particularly agreeable with that of sweetbreads, and may be served in the currie, or strained from it at pleasure. Great care, however, should be taken not to use, for the purpose, a nut that is rancid. Spinach, cucumber, vegetable marrow, tomatas, acid apples, green gooseberries (seeded), and tamarinds imported *in the shell* – not preserved – may all, in their season, be added, with very good effect, to curries of different kinds. Potatoes and celery are also occasionally boiled down in them.

The rice for a currie should always be sent to table in a separate dish from it, and in serving them, it should be first helped, and the currie laid upon it.

MR ARNOTT'S CURRIE-POWDER

> Turmeric, eight ounces.*
> Coriander seed, four ounces.
> Cummin seed, two ounces.
> Foenugreek seed, two ounces.
> Cayenne, half an ounce.
> (More or less of this last to taste.)

Let the seeds be of the finest quality. Dry them well, pound, and sift them separately through a lawn sieve, then weigh, and mix them in the above proportions. This is an exceedingly agreeable and aromatic powder, when all the ingredients are perfectly fresh and good, but the preparing is rather a troublesome process. Mr Arnott recommends that when it is considered so, a 'high-caste' chemist should be applied to for it.

* We think it would be an improvement to diminish by two ounces the proportion of turmeric, and to increase that of the coriander seed; but we have not tried it.

MR ARNOTT'S CURRIE

'Take the heart of a cabbage, and nothing but the heart, that is to say, pull away all the outside leaves until it is about the size of an egg; chop it fine, add to it a couple of apples sliced thin, the juice of one lemon, half a teaspoonful of black pepper, with one large tablespoonful of *my* currie-powder, and mix the whole well together. Now take six onions that have been chopped fine and fried brown, a garlic head, the size of a nutmeg, also minced fine, two ounces of fresh butter, two tablespoonsful of flour, and one pint of strong mutton or beef gravy; and when these articles are boiling, add the former ingredients, and let the whole be well stewed up together: if not hot enough, add cayenne pepper. Next put in a fowl that has been roasted and nicely cut up; or a rabbit; or some lean chops of pork or mutton; or a lobster, or the remains of yesterday's calf's head; or anything else you may fancy; and you will have an excellent currie, fit for kings to partake of.

'Well! now for the rice! It should be put into water which should be frequently changed, and should remain in for half an hour at least; this both clears and soaks it. Have your saucepan full of water (the larger the better), and when it boils rapidly, throw the rice into it: it will be done in fifteen minutes. Strain it into a dish, wipe the saucepan dry, return the drained rice into it, and put it over a gentle fire for a few minutes, with a cloth over it: every grain will be separate. When served, do not cover the dish.'

Obs. We have already given testimony to the excellence of Mr Arnott's currie-powder, but we think the currie itself will be found somewhat too acid for English taste in general, and the proportion of onion and garlic by one half too much for any but well seasoned Anglo-Indian palates. After having tried his method of boiling the rice, we still give the preference to that of Chapter 1, page 16.

A BENGAL CURRIE

Slice and fry three large onions in two ounces of butter, and lift them out of the pan when done. Put into a stewpan three other large onions and a small clove of garlic which have been pounded together, and smoothly mixed with a dessertspoonful of the best pale turmeric, a teaspoonful of powdered ginger, one of salt, and one of cayenne pepper; add to these the butter in which the onions were fried, and half a cupful of good gravy; let them stew for about ten minutes, taking care that they shall not burn. Next, stir to them the fried onions and half a pint more gravy; add a pound and a half of mutton, or of any other meat, free from bone and fat, and simmer it gently for an hour, or more should it not then be perfectly tender.

Fried onions, 3 large; butter, 2 oz; onions pounded, 3 large; garlic, 1 clove, turmeric, 1 dessertspoonful; powdered ginger, salt, cayenne, each 1 teaspoonful; gravy, ½ cupful: 10 minutes. Gravy, ½ pint; meat, 1½ lb: 1 hour or more.

SELIM'S CURRIES
(*Captain White's*)

These curries are made with a sort of paste, which is labelled with the above names, and as it has attracted some attention of late, and the curries made with it are very good, and quickly and easily prepared, we give the directions for them. 'Cut a pound and a half of chicken, fowl, veal, rabbit, or mutton into pieces an inch and a half square. Put from two to three ounces of fresh butter in a stewpan, and when it is melted put in the meat, and give it a good stir with a wooden spoon; add from two to three dessertspoonsful of the currie-paste; mix the whole up well together, and continue the stirring over a brisk fire from five to ten minutes, and the currie will be done. This is a dry currie. For a gravy currie, add two or three tablespoonsful of boiling water after the paste is well mixed in, and continue the stewing and stirring from ten to twelve minutes longer, keeping the sauce of the consistency of cream. Prepare salmon and lobster in the same way, but very quickly, that they may come up firm. The paste may be rubbed over steaks, or cutlets, when they are nearly broiled; three or four minutes will finish them.'

Boil six ounces of ribband maccaroni for fifteen minutes, in water slightly salted, with a very small bit of butter dissolved in it; drain it perfectly, and then put it into a full pint and a quarter of good beef or veal stock or gravy, previously mixed and boiled for twenty minutes, with a small tablespoonful of fine currie-powder, a teaspoonful of arrowroot, and a little lemon-juice. Heat and toss the maccaroni gently in this until it is well and equally covered with it. A small quantity of rich cream, or a little *béchamel*, will very much improve the sauce, into which it should be stirred just before the maccaroni is added, and the lemon-juice should be thrown in afterwards. This dish is, to our taste, far better without the strong flavouring of onion or garlic, usually given to curries; which can, however, be imparted to the gravy in the usual way, when it is liked.

Ribband maccaroni, 6 oz: 15 to 18 minutes. Gravy, or good beef or veal stock, full pint and ¼; fine currie-powder, 1 small tablespoonful; arrowroot, 1 teaspoonful; little lemon-juice: 20 minutes. Maccaroni in sauce, 3 to 6 minutes.

Obs. An ounce or two of grated cocoa-nut, simmered in the gravy for half an hour or more, then strained and well pressed from it, is always an excellent addition. The pipe maccaroni, well curried, is extremely good: the sauce for both kinds should be made with *rich* gravy, especially when the onion is omitted. A few drops of eschalot vinegar can be added to it when the flavour is liked.

CURRIED EGGS

Boil six or eight fresh eggs quite hard, as for salad, and put them aside until they are cold. Mix well together from two to three ounces of good butter, and from three to four dessertspoonsful of currie-powder; shake them in a stewpan or thick saucepan, over a clear but moderate fire for some minutes, then throw in a couple of mild onions finely minced, and fry them gently until they are tolerably soft; pour to them, by degrees, from half to three-quarters of a pint of broth or gravy, and stew them slowly until they are reduced to pulp; mix smoothly a small cup of thick cream with two teaspoonsful of wheaten or of rice-flour, stir them to the currie, and simmer the whole until the raw taste of the thickening is gone. Cut the eggs into half-inch slices, heat them quite through in the sauce without boiling them, and serve them as hot as possible.

CURRIED SWEETBREADS

Wash and soak them as usual, then throw them into boiling water with a little salt in it, and a whole onion, and let them simmer for ten minutes; or, if at hand, substitute weak veal broth for the water. Lift them out, place them on a drainer, and leave them until they are perfectly cold; then cut them into half-inch slices, and either flour and fry them lightly in butter, or put them, without this, into as much curried gravy as will just cover them; stew them in it very gently, from twenty to thirty minutes; add as much lemon-juice or chili vinegar as will acidulate the sauce agreeably,* and serve the currie very hot. As we have already stated in two or three previous receipts, an ounce or more of sweet freshly-grated cocoa-nut, stewed tender in the gravy, and strained from it, before the sweetbreads are added, will give a peculiarly pleasant flavour to all curries.

Blanched 10 minutes; sliced (fried or not); stewed 20 to 30 minutes.

* We find that a small portion of Indian pickled mango, or of its liquor, is an agreeable addition to a currie as well as to mullagatawny soup.

Wedgwood Pestle and Mortar

POTTED MEATS

Any tender and well-roasted meat, taken free of fat, skin, and gristle, as well as from the dry outsides, will answer for potting admirably, better indeed than that which is generally baked for the purpose, and which is usually quite deprived of its juices by the process. Spiced or *corned* beef also is excellent when thus prepared; and any of these will remain good a long time if mixed with cold fresh butter, instead of that which is clarified; but no addition that can be made to it will render the meat eatable, unless it be *thoroughly pounded*; reduced, in fact, to the smoothest possible paste, free from a single lump or a morsel of unbroken fibre. If *rent* into fragments, instead of being quite cut through the grain in being minced, before it is put into the mortar, no beating will bring it to the proper state. Unless it be *very* dry, it is better to pound it for some time before any butter is added, and it must be long and patiently beaten after all the ingredients are mixed, that the whole may be equally blended and well mellowed in flavour.

The quantity of butter required will depend upon the nature of the meat; ham and salted beef will need a larger proportion than roast meat, or than the breasts of poultry and game; white fish, from being less dry, will require comparatively little. Salmon, lobsters, prawns, and shrimps are all extremely good, prepared in this way. They should, however, be perfectly fresh when they are pounded, and be set immediately afterwards into a very cool place. For these, and for white meats in general, mace, nutmeg, and cayenne or white pepper, are the appropriate spices. A small quantity of cloves may be added to hare and other brown meat, but allspice we would not recommend unless the taste is known to be in favour of it.

POTTED CHICKEN, PARTRIDGE, OR PHEASANT

Roast the birds as for table, but let them be thoroughly done, for if the gravy be left in, the meat will not keep half so well. Raise the flesh of the breast, wings, and merrythought, quite clear from the bones, take off the skin, mince, and then pound it very smoothly with about one third of its weight of fresh butter, or something less, if the meat should appear of a proper consistence without the full quantity; season it with salt, mace, and cayenne, only, and add these in small portions until the meat is rather highly flavoured with both the last; proceed with it as with other potted meats.

POTTED OX-TONGUE

Boil tender an unsmoked tongue of good flavour, and the following day cut from it the quantity desired for potting, or take for this purpose the remains of one which has already been served at table. Trim off the skin and rind, weigh the meat, mince it very small, then pound it as fine as possible with four ounces of butter to each pound of tongue, a small teaspoonful of mace, half as much of nutmeg and cloves, and a tolerably high seasoning of cayenne. After the spices are well beaten with the meat, taste it, and add more if required. A few ounces of any *well-roasted* meat, mixed with the tongue will give it firmness, in which it is apt to be deficient. The breasts of turkeys, fowls, partridges, or pheasants, may be used for the purpose with good effect.

Tongue, 1 lb; butter, 4 oz; mace, 1 teaspoonful; nutmeg and cloves each, 1/2 teaspoonful; cayenne, 5 to 10 grains.

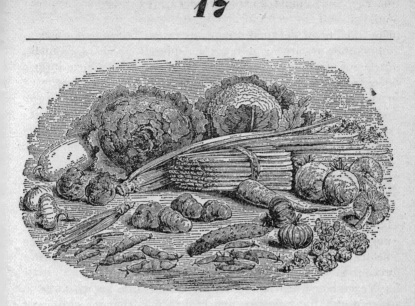

17

VEGETABLES

In this chapter it is interesting to note first of all, the different emphasis put on the vegetables compared with today. Lettuce, cucumber and 'tomatas' are all given as cooked dishes, not used as salad as they are today: asparagus was regarded as ordinary in those days, and not a luxury food (in a contemporary book, Cottage Cookery, it is given among the thrifty dishes for the poor): while vegetables, on the other hand, that we think of now as very ordinary and commonplace, such as cabbage, sprouts and onions, each have only one separate receipt, although cauliflower does better, and there is much more use made of the root vegetables.

The variety of vegetables used, though, before the day of the deep freeze must be astonishing to those whose horizons have shrunk so much that, 'there are no vegetables in the shops, so I bought a packet of peas', is the cry.

The quality of vegetables depends much both on the soil in which they are grown, and on the degree of care bestowed upon their culture; but if produced in ever so great perfection, their excellence will be entirely destroyed if they be badly cooked.

With the exception of artichokes, which are said to be improved by two or three days' keeping, all the summer varieties should be dressed before their first freshness has in any degree passed off (for their flavour is never so fine as within a few hours of their being cut or gathered); but when this cannot be done, precaution should be taken to prevent their withering. The stalk-ends of asparagus, cucumbers, and vegetable-marrow, should be placed in from one to two inches of cold water; and all other kinds should be spread on a cool brick floor. When this has been neglected, they must be thrown into cold water, for some time before they are boiled, to recover them, though they will prove even then but very inferior eating.

Vegetables when not sufficiently cooked are known to be so exceedingly unwholesome and indigestible, that the custom of serving them *crisp*, which means, in reality, only half-boiled, should be altogether disregarded when health is considered of more importance than fashion; but they should not be allowed to remain in the water after they are quite done, or both their nutritive properties and their flavour will be lost, and their good appearance destroyed. Care should be taken to *drain them thoroughly* in a warm strainer, and to serve them very hot, with well-made sauces, if with any.

Only dried peas or beans, Jerusalem artichokes, and potatoes, are put at first into cold water. All others require plenty of fast-boiling water, which should be ready salted and skimmed before they are thrown into it.

TO CLEAR VEGETABLES FROM INSECTS

Lay them for half an hour or more into a pan of strong brine, with the stalk ends uppermost; this will destroy the small snails

and other insects which cluster in the leaves, and they will fall
out and sink to the bottom. A pound and a half of salt to the
gallon of water will answer for this purpose, and if strained daily
it will last for some time.

POTATOES
(*Remarks on their properties and importance*)†

There is no vegetable commonly cultivated in this country, we
venture to assert, which is comparable in value to the potato
when it is of a good sort, has been grown in a suitable soil, and is
properly cooked and served. It *must* be very nutritious, or it
would not sustain the strength of thousands of people whose
almost sole food it constitutes, and who, when they can procure a
sufficient supply of it to satisfy fully the demands of hunger, are
capable of accomplishing the heaviest daily labour. It may not be
wise to depend for subsistence on a root of which the crop un-
happily is so frequently in these days destroyed or greatly injured
by disease, and for which it is so difficult to find a substitute that
is equally cheap, wholesome and satisfying; but we can easily
comprehend the predilection of an entire people for a tuber
which combines, like the potato, the solidity almost of bread,
with the healthful properties of various other fresh vegetables,
without their acidity; and which can also be cooked and served in
so many different forms. The wretched manner in which it is
dressed in many English houses renders it comparatively value-
less, and accounts in a measure for the prodigality with which it
is thrown away when cold, even in seasons when its price is highest.

† [*It is interesting to read these remarks and recall that they were written at the time of the Irish famine to which they obviously refer.*]

TO BOIL POTATOES
(*As in Ireland*)

Potatoes, to boil well together, should be all of the same sort, and
as nearly equal in size as may be. Wash off the mould, and scrub

them very clean with a hard brush, but neither scoop nor apply a knife to them in any way, even to clear the eyes.* Rinse them well, and arrange them compactly in a saucepan, so that they may not lie loose in the water, and that a small quantity may suffice to cover them. Pour this in cold, and when it boils, throw in about a large teaspoonful of salt, to the quart, and simmer the potatoes until they are nearly done, but for the last two or three minutes let them boil rapidly. When they are tender quite through, which may be known by probing them with a fork, pour all the water from them immediately, lift the lid of the saucepan to allow the steam to escape, and place them on a trivet, high over the fire, or by the side of it, until the moisture has entirely evaporated; then peel, and send them to table as quickly as possible, either in a hot napkin, or in a dish, of which the cover is so placed that the steam can pass off. There should be no delay in serving them after they are once taken from the fire. Irish families always prefer them served in their skins. Some kinds will be sufficiently boiled in twenty minutes, others in not less than three quarters of an hour.

20 minutes to 1 hour, or more.

Obs. The water in which they are boiled should barely cover the potatoes. After it is poured off, they should be steamed for twenty minutes or *half an hour*, if large.

Obs. 2. Habitual potato-eaters know well that this vegetable is never so good as when served in *the skin* the instant it is taken from the fire, dished in a hot napkin, or sent to table without a cover over it. It should also be clean and dry that it may at pleasure be taken in the fingers and broken like bread, or held in the dinner napkin while the inside is scooped out with the fork, thus forming it into a sort of cup.

* 'Because', in the words of our clever Irish correspondent, 'the water through these parts is then admitted into the very heart of the vegetable; and as the latent heat, after cooking, is not sufficient to throw it off, this renders the potatoes very unwholesome.'

TO BOIL POTATOES
(*The Lancashire Way*)

Pare the potatoes, cover them with cold water, and boil them slowly until they are quite tender, but watch them carefully, that they may not be overdone; drain off the water entirely, strew some salt over them, leave the saucepan uncovered by the side of the fire, and shake it forcibly every minute or two, until the whole of the potatoes appear dry and floury. Lancashire cooks dress the vegetable in this way to perfection, but it is far from an economical mode, as a large portion of the potato adheres to the saucepan; it has, however, many admirers.

NEW POTATOES IN BUTTER

Rub off the skins, wash the potatoes well and wipe them dry; put them with three ounces of good butter, for a small dish, and with four ounces or more for a large one, into a well-tinned stewpan or saucepan, and simmer them over a gentle fire for about half an hour. Keep them well shaken or tossed, that they may be equally done, and throw in some salt when they begin to stew. This is a good mode of dressing them when they are very young and watery.

TO BOIL POTATOES
(*Captain Kater's Receipt*)

Wash, wipe, and pare the potatoes, cover them with cold water, and boil them gently until they are done, pour off the water, and sprinkle a little fine salt over them; then take each potato separately with a spoon, and lay it into a clean *warm* cloth, twist this so as to press all the moisture from the vegetable, and render it quite round; turn it carefully into a dish placed before the fire, throw a cloth over, and when all are done, send them to table quickly. Potatoes dressed in this way are mashed without the slightest trouble; it is also by far the best method of preparing them for puddings or for cakes.

CRISPED POTATOES, OR POTATO-RIBBONS
(*Entremets – Or to serve with Cheese*)

Wash well, and wipe, some potatoes of good flavour; cut them up into slices of from half to a whole inch thick, free them from the skins, and then pare them round and round in very thin, and very long ribbons. Lay them into a pan of cold water, and half an hour before they are wanted for table lift them on to a sieve that they may be well drained. Fry them in good butter, which should be very hot when they are thrown in, until they are quite crisp, and lightly browned; drain and dry them on a soft cloth, pile them in a hot dish, strew over them a mixed seasoning of salt and cayenne in fine powder, and serve them without delay. For the second course, dress them in the same manner, but omit the cayenne. Five or six minutes will fry them.

FRIED POTATOES
(*Entremets – A Plainer Receipt*)

After having washed them, wipe and pare some raw potatoes, cut them into slices of equal thickness, or into thin shavings, and throw them into plenty of boiling butter, or very pure clarified dripping. Fry them of a fine light brown, and very crisp; lift them out with a skimmer, drain them on a soft warm cloth, dish them very hot, and sprinkle fine salt over them. This is an admirable way of dressing potatoes, very common on the Continent, but less so in England than the receipt above, and served dry and well fried, lightly piled in a dish, they make a handsome appearance, and are excellent eating. If sliced they should be something less than a quarter of an inch thick.

Boil some floury potatoes very dry, mash them as smoothly as possible, season them well with salt and white pepper, warm them with about an ounce of butter to the pound, or rather more if it will not render them too moist, and a few spoonsful of good cream. Boil them very dry; let them cool a little, roll them into balls, sprinkle over them vermicelli crushed slightly with the hand, and fry them a fine light brown. They may be dished round a shape of plain mashed potatoes, or piled on a napkin by themselves. They may likewise be rolled in egg and fine bread-crumbs instead of in the vermicelli, or in ground-rice, which answers very well for them.

POTATO BOULETTES
(*Entremets – Good*)

Boil some good potatoes as dry as possible; mash a pound of them very smoothly, and mix with them while they are still warm, two ounces of fresh butter, a teaspoonful of salt, a little nutmeg, the beaten and strained yolks of four eggs, and last of all the white thoroughly whisked. Mould the mixture with a teaspoon and drop it into a small pan of boiling butter, or of very pure lard, and fry the *boulettes* for five minutes over a moderate fire: they should be of a fine pale brown, and very light. Drain them well and dish them on a hot napkin.

Potatoes, 1 lb; butter, 2 oz; salt, 1 teaspoonful; eggs, 4: 5 minutes.

Obs. These *boulettes* are exceedingly light and delicate, and make an excellent dish for the second course; but we think that a few spoonsful of sweet fresh cream boiled with them until the mixture becomes dry, would both enrich them and improve their flavour. They should be dropped into the pan with the teaspoon, as they ought to be small, and they will swell in the cooking.

POTATO RISSOLES
(*French*)

Mash and season the potatoes with salt, and white pepper or cayenne, and mix them with plenty of minced parsley, and a small quantity of green onions, or eschalots; add sufficient yolks of eggs to bind the mixture together, roll it into small balls, and fry them in plenty of lard or butter over a moderate fire, or they will be too much browned before they are done through. Ham, or any other kind of meat finely minced, may be substituted for the herbs, or added to them.

TO BOIL SEA-KALE

Wash, trim, and tie the kale in bunches, and throw it into plenty of boiling water with some salt in it. When it is perfectly tender, lift it out, drain it well from the water, and send it to table with good melted butter. When fashion is not particularly regarded we would recommend its being served upon a toast like asparagus. About twenty minutes will boil it, rather less for persons who like it crisp.

18 to 20 minutes.

SPINACH
(*Common English mode*)

Boil the spinach very green in plenty of water, drain, and then press the moisture from it between two trenches; chop it small, put it into a clean saucepan, with a slice of fresh butter, and stir the whole until well mixed and very hot. Smooth it in a dish, mark it in dice, and send it quickly to table.

TO DRESS DANDELIONS LIKE SPINACH, OR AS A SALAD

(*Very wholesome*)

This common weed of the fields and highways is an excellent vegetable, the young leaves forming an admirable adjunct to a salad, and much resembling endive when boiled and prepared in the same way, or in any of the modes directed for spinach. The slight bitterness of its flavour is to many persons very agreeable; and it is often served at well-appointed tables. It has also, we believe, the advantage of possessing valuable medicinal qualities. Take the roots before the blossom is at all advanced, if they can readily be found in that state; if not, pluck off and use the young leaves only. Wash them as clean as possible, and boil them tender in a large quantity of water salted as for sprouts or spinach. Drain them well, press them dry with a wooden spoon, and serve them quite plain with melted butter in a tureen; or, squeeze, chop, and heat them afresh, with a seasoning of salt and pepper, a *morsel* of butter rolled in flour, and a spoonful or two of gravy or cream. A very large portion of the leaves will be required for a dish, as they shrink exceedingly in the cooking. For a salad, take them very young and serve them entire, or break them quite small with the fingers; then wash and drain them. Dress them with oil and vinegar, or with any other sauce which may be preferred with them.

STEWED LETTUCES

Strip off the outer leaves, and cut away the stalks; wash the lettuces with exceeding nicety, and throw them into water salted as for all green vegetables. When they are quite tender, which will be in from twenty to thirty minutes, according to their age, lift them out and press the water thoroughly from them; chop them a little, and heat them in a clean saucepan with a seasoning of pepper and salt, and a small slice of butter; then dredge in a little flour and stir them well; add next a small cup of broth or gravy, boil them quickly until they are tolerably dry, then stir in a little pale vinegar or lemon-juice, and serve them as hot as possible, with fried sippets round them.

ASPARAGUS POINTS DRESSED LIKE PEAS
(*Entremets*)

This is a convenient mode of dressing asparagus, when it is too small and green to make a good appearance plainly boiled. Cut the points so far only as they are perfectly tender, in bits of equal size, not more than the third of an inch in length; wash them very clean, and throw them into plenty of boiling water, with the usual quantity of salt, and a *few* grains of carbonate of soda. When they are tolerably tender, which will be in from ten to twelve minutes, drain them well, and spread them on a clean cloth; fold it over them, wipe them gently, and when they are quite dry put them into a clean stewpan with a good slice of butter, which should be just dissolved before the asparagus is added; stew them in this over a brisk fire, shaking them often, for eight or ten minutes; dredge in about a small teaspoonful of flour, and add half that quantity of white sugar; then pour in boiling water to nearly cover the asparagus, and boil it rapidly until but little liquid remains: stir in the beaten yolks of two eggs, heap the asparagus high in a dish, and serve it very hot. The sauce should adhere entirely to the vegetable as in green peas *à la Française*.

GREEN PEAS À LA FRANÇAISE, OR FRENCH FASHION
(*Entremets*)

Throw a quart of young and freshly-shelled peas into plenty of spring water with a couple of ounces of butter, and with the hand work them together until the butter adheres well to the peas; lift them out, and drain them in a cullender; put them into a stew-pan or thick saucepan without any water, and let them remain over a gentle fire, and be stirred occasionally for twenty minutes from the time of their first beginning to simmer; then pour to them as much boiling water as will just cover them; throw in a small quantity of salt, and keep them boiling quickly for forty minutes: stir well amongst them a small lump of sugar which has been dipped quickly into water, and a thickening of about half an ounce of butter very smoothly mixed with a teaspoonful of flour; shake them over the fire for two minutes, and serve them directly heaped high in a very hot dish. There will be no sauce except that which adheres to the peas if they be properly managed. We have found marrowfats excellent, dressed by this receipt. Fresh and good butter should be used with them always.

Peas, 1 quart; butter, 2 oz: 20 minutes. Water to cover the peas; little salt: 40 minutes. Sugar, small lump; butter, ½ oz; flour, 1 teaspoonful: 2 minutes.

GREEN PEAS WITH CREAM
(*Entremets*)

Boil a quart of young peas perfectly tender in salt and water, and drain them as dry as possible. Dissolve an ounce and a half of butter in a clean stewpan, stir smoothly to it when it boils a dessertspoonful of flour, and shake these over the fire for three or four minutes, but without allowing them to take the slightest colour; pour gradually to them a cup of rich cream, add a small lump of sugar pounded, let the sauce boil, then put in the peas and toss them gently in it until they are very hot: dish, and serve them quickly.

Peas, 1 quart: 18 to 25 minutes. Butter, 1½ oz; flour, 1 dessertspoonful: 3 to 5 minutes. Sugar, 1 saltspoonful; cream, 1 cupful.

AN EXCELLENT RECEIPT FOR
FRENCH BEANS À LA FRANÇAISE

Prepare as many young and freshly-gathered beans as will serve for a large dish, boil them tender, and drain the water well from them. Melt a couple of ounces of fresh butter, in a clean sauce-pan, and stir smoothly to it a small dessertspoonful of flour; keep these well shaken, and gently simmered until they are lightly browned, add salt and pepper, and pour to them by degrees a small cupful of good veal gravy (or, in lieu of this, of sweet rich cream), toss the beans in the sauce until they are as hot as possible; stir quickly in, as they are taken from the fire, the beaten yolks of two fresh eggs and a little lemon-juice, and serve them without delay. The eggs and lemon are sometimes omitted, and a tablespoonful of minced parsley is added to the butter and flour; but this, we think, is scarcely an improvement.

Beans, 1 to 2 quarts: boiled 15 to 20 minutes. Butter, 2 oz; flour, 1 dessertspoonful; salt and pepper; veal gravy, *small* cupful; yolks of eggs, 2; lemon-juice, a dessertspoonful.

DRESSED CUCUMBERS

Pare and slice them very thin, strew a little fine salt over them, and when they have stood a few minutes, drain off the water, by raising one side of the dish, and letting it flow to the other; pour it away, strew more salt, and a moderate seasoning of pepper on them, add two or three tablespoonsful of the purest salad-oil, and turn the cucumbers well, that the whole may receive a portion of it; then pour over them from one to three dessertspoonsful of chili vinegar, and a little common, should it be needed; turn them into a clean dish and serve them.

Obs. If very young, cucumbers are usually dressed without being pared, but the tough rind of full-grown ones being extremely indigestible, should be avoided. The vegetable, though apt to disagree with persons of delicate habit, when sauced in the common English mode, with salt, pepper, and vinegar only, may often be eaten by them with impunity when dressed with plenty of oil. It is difficult to obtain this perfectly fresh and pure here; and hence, perhaps arises in part the prejudice which, amongst us, is so often found to exist against the use of this most wholesome condiment.

MANDRANG, OR MANDRAM

(*West Indian Receipt*)

Chop together very small, two moderate-sized cucumbers, with half the quantity of mild onion; add the juice of a lemon, a salt-spoonful or more of salt, a third as much of cayenne, and one or two glasses of Madeira, or of any other dry white wine. The preparation is to be served with any kind of roast meat.

We are so used to eating cucumber raw, as a salad, that it is interesting to realize how much it was used as a cooked vegetable, as shown by the following receipts.

CUCUMBERS À LA POULETTE

The cucumbers for this dish may be pared and sliced very thin; or quartered, freed from the seeds, and cut into half-inch lengths; in either case they should be steeped in a little vinegar and sprinkled with salt for half an hour before they are dressed. Drain, and then press them dry in a soft cloth; flour them well, put a slice of butter into a stewpan or saucepan bright in the inside, and when it begins to boil throw in the cucumbers, and shake them over a gentle fire for ten minutes, but be careful to prevent their taking the slightest colour; pour to them gradually as much strong, but very pale veal stock or gravy as will nearly cover them; when it boils skim off the fat entirely, add salt and white pepper, if needed, and when the cucumbers are quite tender, strew in a large teaspoonful of finely minced parsley, and thicken the sauce with the yolks of two or three eggs. French cooks add the flour when the vegetable has stewed in the butter, instead of dredging it upon them at first, and this is perhaps the better method.

If very young they need not be pared, but otherwise, take off the rind, slice, and dredge them lightly with pepper and flour, but put no salt at first; throw them into very hot butter or clarified dripping, or they will not brown; when they are nearly done sprinkle some salt amongst them, and as soon as they are quite tender, lift them out with a slice, drain them well, and place them lightly over the hash or mince. A small portion of onion may be fried with them when it is liked.

CAULIFLOWERS
(French Receipt)

Cut the cauliflowers into small handsome tufts, and boil them until three parts done, drain them well, toss them for a moment in some *thick* melted butter or white sauce, and set them by to cool. When they are quite cold, dip them separately into the batter of Chapter 5, fry them a light brown, arrange them neatly in a dish, and serve them very hot.

CAULIFLOWERS À LA FRANÇAISE

Strip away all the green leaves, and divide each cauliflower into three or four parts, trimming the stalks quite close; put them, with the heads downwards, into a stewpan which will just hold them, half filled with boiling water, into which an ounce of good butter and some salt have previously been thrown; so soon as they are quite tender, drain the water from them, place a dish over the stewpan and turn it gently upside down; arrange the vegetables neatly in the form of one large cauliflower and cover it with good melted butter, into which a little lemon-juice has been stirred.

12 to 18 minutes.

ROAST TOMATAS

(To serve with roast leg, loin, or shoulder of mutton)

Select them nearly of the same size, take off the stalks, and roast them gently in a Dutch oven, or if more convenient, place them at the edge of the dripping-pan, taking care that no fat from the joint shall fall upon them, and keeping them turned that they may be equally done. From ten to fourteen minutes will roast them.

STEWED TOMATAS†

Arrange them in a single layer, and pour to them as much gravy as will reach half their height; stew them very softly until the under sides are done, then turn, and finish stewing them. Thicken the gravy with a little arrowroot and cream, or with flour and butter, and serve it round them.

† [*It was only about the time this book was first written that 'tomatas' were accepted as wholesome food. Previously they had been treated with suspicion and it had not been decided if they were vegetable or fruit. It is interesting to see so much use made of them by Eliza Acton. But they were always cooked and never eaten raw as salad.*]

FORCED† TOMATAS
(English Receipt)

Cut the stems quite close, slice off the tops of eight fine tomatas, and scoop out the insides; press the pulp through a sieve, and mix with it one ounce of fine crumbs of bread, one of butter broken very small, some pepper or cayenne, and salt. Fill the tomatas with the mixture and bake them for ten minutes in a moderate oven; serve them with brown gravy in the dish. A few small mushrooms stewed tender in a little butter, then minced and added to the tomata pulp, will very much improve this receipt.

Bake 10 minutes.

† [*'Forced' does not mean grown under glass, but stuffed – 'Farcé' – cf. forcemeat.*]

Divide a dozen fine ripe tomatas, squeeze out the seeds, and take off the stalks; put them with one small mild onion (or more, if liked), and about half a pint of very good gravy, into a well-tinned stewpan or saucepan, and simmer them for nearly or quite an hour; a couple of bay leaves, some cayenne, and as much salt as the dish may require, should be added when they begin to boil. Press them through a sieve, heat them again, and stir to them a quarter-pint of good cream, previously mixed and boiled for five minutes with a teaspoonful of flour. This purée is to be served with calf's head, veal cutlets, boiled knuckle of veal, calf's brains, or beef palates. For pork, beef, geese, and other brown meats, the tomatas should be reduced to a proper consistence in rich and highly-flavoured brown gravy, or Spanish sauce.

TO BOIL GREEN INDIAN CORN

When still quite green and tender, the ears of maize or Indian corn are very good boiled and served as a vegetable; and as they will not ripen well in this country unless the summer be un-usually warm and favourable, it is an advantageous mode of turn-ing them to account. Strip away the sheath which encloses them, and take off the long silken fibres from the tops; put the corn into boiling water salted as for asparagus, and boil it for about half an hour. Drain it well, dish it on a toast, and send it to table with melted butter. The Americans who have it served commonly at their tables, use it when more fully grown than we have recommended, and boil it without removing the inner leaves of the sheath; but it is sweeter and more delicate before it has reached so advanced a state. The grains may be freed from the corn-stalks with a knife, and tossed up with a slice of fresh butter and some pepper and salt, or served simply like green peas. Other modes of dressing the young maize will readily suggest themselves to an intelligent cook, and our space will not permit us to enumerate them.

25 to 30 minutes.

(*Delicious*)

Cut the stems from some fine meadow mushroom-buttons, and clean them with a bit of new flannel, and some fine salt; then either wipe them dry with a soft cloth, or rinse them in fresh water, drain them quickly, spread them in a clean cloth, fold it over them, and leave them for ten minutes, or more, to dry. For every pint of them thus prepared, put an ounce and a half of fresh butter into a thick iron saucepan, shake it over the fire until it *just* begins to brown, throw in the mushrooms, continue to shake the saucepan over a clear fire that they may not stick to it nor burn, and when they have simmered three or four minutes, strew over them a little salt, some cayenne, and pounded mace; stew them until they are perfectly tender, heap them in a dish, and serve them with their own sauce only, for breakfast, supper, or luncheon. Nothing can be finer than the flavour of the mushrooms thus prepared; and the addition of any liquid is far from an improvement to it. They are very good when drained from the butter, and served cold, and in a cool larder may be kept for several days. The butter in which they are stewed is admirable for flavouring gravies, sauces, or potted meats. Small flaps, freed from the fur and skin, may be stewed in the same way; and either these, or the buttons, served under roast poultry or partridges, will give a dish of very superior relish.

Meadow mushrooms, 3 pints; fresh butter, 4½ oz: 3 to 5 minutes. Salt, 1 small teaspoonful; mace, half as much; cayenne, third of saltspoonful: 10 to 15 minutes. More spices to be added if required – much depending on their quality; but they should not overpower the flavour of the mushrooms.

Obs. Persons inhabiting parts of the country where mushrooms are abundant, may send them easily, when thus prepared (or when potted by the following receipt), to their friends in cities, or in less productive counties. If poured into jars, with sufficient butter to cover them, they will travel any distance, and can be re-warmed for use.

Prepare either small flaps or buttons with great nicety, without wetting them, and wipe the former very dry, after the application of the salt and flannel. Stew them quite tender, with the same proportion of butter as the mushrooms *au beurre*, but increase a little the quantity of spice; when they are done turn them into a large dish, spread them over one end of it, and raise it two or three inches that they may be well drained from the butter. As soon as they are quite cold, press them very closely into small potting-pans; pour lukewarm clarified butter thickly over them, and store them in a cool dry place. If intended for present use, merely turn them down upon a clean shelf; but for longer keeping cover the tops first with very dry paper, and then with melted mutton-suet. We have ourselves had the mushrooms, after being simply spread upon a dish while hot, remain perfectly good in that state for seven or eight weeks: they were prepared late in the season, and the weather was consequently cool during the interval.

TRUFFLES AND THEIR USES

The truffle, or underground mushroom, as it has sometimes been called, is held in almost extravagant estimation by epicures,* and enters largely into what may be termed first-class cookery, both in England and abroad; though it is much less generally known and used here than in France, Germany, and other parts of the Continent, where it is far more abundant, and of very superior quality.

As it is in constant demand for luxuriously-served tables, and has hitherto, we believe, baffled all attempts to increase it by cultivation, it bears usually a high price in the English market, and is seldom to be had cheap in any; but although too costly for common consumption, where the expenditure is regulated by rational economy, it may at times be made to supply, at a reasonable expense, some excellent store-preparations for the breakfast and luncheon-table; as a small portion will impart its peculiar flavour to them.

The blackest truffles are considered the best. All are in their perfection during the latter part of November, December, and January; though they may be procured usually from October to March; yet as they are peculiarly subject to decay – or, properly speaking, become really putrid – from exposure to the air, it is an advantage to have them as early in their season as may be.

In sumptuous households the very finest foreign truffles are often served *as a vegetable* in the second course.

* It has been named by a celebrated gastronomer of past days, *Le diamant de la cuisine.*

TRUFFLES À L'ITALIENNE

Wash perfectly clean, wipe, and pare some truffles extremely thin; slice them about the size of a penny; put them into a sauté-pan (or small frying-pan), with a slice of fresh butter, some minced parsley and eschalot, salt and pepper; put them on the fire and stir them, that they may fry equally; when they are done, which will be in about ten minutes, drain off part of the butter, and throw in a bit of fresh butter, a small ladleful of Spanish sauce (see page 54) the juice of one lemon, and a little cayenne pepper. This is a dish of high relish.

TO BOIL SPROUTS, CABBAGES, SAVOYS, LETTUCES, OR ENDIVE†

All green vegetables should be thrown into abundance of fast boiling water ready salted and skimmed, with the addition of the small quantity of carbonate of soda which we have recommended, in a previous page of this chapter[p. 192]; the pan should be left uncovered, and every precaution taken to prevent the smoke from reaching its contents. Endive, sprouts, and spring greens, will only require copious washing before they are boiled; but savoys, large lettuces, and close-leaved cabbages should be thrown into salt and water for half an hour or more before they are dressed, with the tops downwards to draw out the insects. The stems of these last should be cut off, the decayed leaves stripped away, and the vegetable halved or quartered, or split deeply across the stalk-end, and divided entirely before it is dished.

Very young greens, 15 to 20 minutes; lettuces, 20 to 30 minutes, large savoys, or cabbages, 1 to 1½ hour, or more.

Obs. When the stalk of any kind of cabbage is tender it is ready to serve. Turnip-greens should be well washed in several waters, and boiled in a very large quantity to deprive them of their bitterness.

† [*Savoys are alternatively known as winter cabbages. Definitions of endive and chicory vary from country to country. In England 'endive' is a green, rather coarse-textured feathery lettuce, 'chicory' a blanched pale looking torpedo-shaped vegetable, often defined as Belgian chicory. In other countries the definition is often reversed. Here the English endive is meant.*]

STEWED CABBAGE†

Cut out the stalk entirely, and slice a fine firm cabbage or two in very thin strips; throw them after they have been well washed and drained, into a large pan of boiling water ready salted and skimmed, and when they are tender, which will be in from ten to fifteen minutes, pour them into a sieve or strainer, press the water thoroughly from them, and chop them slightly. Put into a very clean saucepan about a couple of ounces of butter, and when it is dissolved add the cabbage with sufficient pepper and salt to season it, and stir it over a clear fire until it appears tolerably dry; then shake lightly in a tablespoonful of flour, turn the whole well, and add by slow degrees a cup of thick cream: veal gravy or good white sauce may be substituted for this, when preferred to it.

† [*In contrast to the number of receipts for other vegetables, Eliza Acton only gives this one receipt for cabbage — apart from the general directions for boiling green vegetables. This always seems to be the poor relation of English vegetables although with children at any rate, it is coming into greater popularity now.*]

(*Good*)

This is an excellent way of dressing the vegetable when it is mild and finely grained; but its flavour otherwise is too strong to be agreeable. After they have been washed, wiped quite dry, and pared, slice the turnips nearly half an inch thick, and divide them into dice. Just dissolve an ounce of butter for each half-pound of the turnips, put them in as flat as they can be, and stew them very gently indeed, from three-quarters of an hour to a full hour. Add seasoning of salt and white pepper when they are half done. When thus prepared, they may be dished in the centre of fried or nicely broiled mutton cutlets, or served by themselves.

For a small dish: turnips, 1½ lb; butter, 3 oz; seasoning of white pepper; salt, ½ teaspoonful, or more: ¾ to 1 hour. Large dish: turnips, 2 lb; butter 4 oz.

CARROTS
(*Entrée – The Windsor Receipt*)

Select some good carrots of equal size, and cut the upper parts into even lengths of about two inches and a half, then trim one end of each into a point, so as to give the carrot the form of a sugar-loaf. When all are ready, throw them into plenty of ready-salted boiling water, and boil them three-quarters of an hour. Lift them out, and drain them well, then arrange them upright, and all on a level in a broad stewpan or saucepan, and pour in good hot beef-broth or veal gravy to half their height; add as much salt as may be needed, and a small teaspoonful of sugar, and boil them briskly for half an hour, or longer, should they require it. Place them again upright in dishing them, and keep them hot while a little good brown gravy is thickened to pour over them, and mixed with a large teaspoonful of parsley and a little lemon-juice; or sauce them with common *béchamel*, or white sauce, with or without the addition of parsley.

Thick part of carrots cut in cones: boiled ¾ hour. With gravy or broth, little salt and sugar: ½ hour, or more. Sauce: thickened gravy, *béchamel* made without meat, or common white sauce.

Obs. The carrots dressed thus are exceedingly good without any sauce beyond the small quantity of liquid which will remain in the stewpan with them, or with a few spoonsful more of gravy added to this, and thickened with butter and a little flour.

CARROTS AU BEURRE, OR BUTTERED CARROTS
(*French*)

Either boil sufficient carrots for a dish quite tender, and then cut them into slices a quarter of an inch thick, or first slice and then boil them: the latter method is the most expeditious, but the other best preserves the flavour of the vegetable. Drain them well, and while this is being done just dissolve from two to three ounces of butter in a saucepan, and strew in some minced parsley, some salt, and white pepper or cayenne; then add the carrots, and toss them very gently until they are equally covered with the sauce, which should not be allowed to boil: the parsley may be omitted at pleasure. Cold carrots may be re-warmed in this way.

CARROTS IN THEIR OWN JUICE
(*A simple but excellent Receipt*)

By the following mode of dressing carrots, whether young or old, their full flavour and all the nutriment they contain are entirely preserved; and they are at the same time rendered so palatable by it that they furnish at once an admirable dish to eat without meat, as well as with it. Wash the roots very clean, and scrape or lightly pare them, cutting out any discoloured parts. Have ready boiling and salted, as much water as will cover them; slice them rather thick, throw them into it, and should there be more than sufficient to just *float* them (and barely that), pour it away. Boil them gently until they are tolerably tender, and then very quickly, to evaporate the water, of which only a spoonful or so should be left in the saucepan. Dust a seasoning of pepper on them, throw in a morsel of butter rolled in flour, and turn and toss them gently until their juice is thickened by them and adheres to the roots. Send them immediately to table. They are excellent without *any* addition but the pepper; though they may be in many ways improved. A dessertspoonful of minced parsley may be strewed over them when the butter is added, and a little thick cream mixed with a *small* proportion of flour to prevent its curling, may be strewed amongst them, or a spoonful or two of good gravy.

FRIED PARSNEPS

Boil them until they are about half done, lift them out, and let them cool; slice them rather thickly, sprinkle them with fine salt and white pepper, and fry them a pale brown in good butter. Serve them with roast meat, or dish them under it.

JERUSALEM ARTICHOKES

Wash the artichokes, pare them quickly, and throw them as they are done into a saucepan of cold water, or of equal parts of milk and water; and when they are about half boiled add a little salt to them. Take them up the instant they are perfectly tender: this will be in from fifteen to twenty-five minutes, so much do they vary in size and as to the time necessary to dress them. If allowed to remain in the water after they are done, they become black and flavourless. Melted butter should always be sent to table with them.

15 to 25 minutes.

TO BOIL BEET ROOT

Wash the roots delicately clean, but neither scrape nor cut them, for should even the small fibres be taken off before they are cooked, their beautiful colour would be much injured. Throw them into boiling water, and according to their size, which varies greatly, as they are sometimes of enormous growth, boil them from one hour and a half to two and a half, or longer if requisite. Pare and serve them whole, or cut into thick slices and neatly dished in a close circle: send melted butter to table with them. Cold red beet root is often intermingled with other vegetables for winter salads; and it makes a pickle of remarkably brilliant hue. A common mode of serving it at the present day is in the last course of a dinner with the cheese: it is merely pared and sliced after having been baked or boiled tender.

1½ to 2½ hours, or longer.

TO BAKE BEET ROOT

Beet root if slowly and carefully baked until it is tender quite through, is very rich and sweet in flavour, although less bright in colour than when it is boiled: it is also, we believe, remarkably nutritious and wholesome. Wash and wipe it very dry, but neither cut nor break any part of it, then lay it into a coarse earthen dish, and bake it in a gentle oven for four or five hours: it will sometimes require even a longer time than this. Pare it quickly if it be served hot; but leave it to cool first, when it is to be sent to table cold.

In a slow oven from 4 to 6 hours.

TO STEW RED CABBAGE
(Flemish Receipt)

Strip the outer leaves from a fine and fresh red cabbage; wash it well, and cut it into the thinnest possible slices, beginning at the top; put it into a thick saucepan in which two or three ounces of good butter have been dissolved; add some pepper and salt, and stew it very slowly indeed for three or four hours in its own juice, keeping it often stirred, and well pressed down. When it is perfectly tender add a tablespoonful of vinegar; mix the whole up thoroughly, heap the cabbage in a hot dish, and serve broiled sausages round it; or omit these last, and substitute lemon-juice, cayenne pepper, and half a cupful of good gravy.

The stalk of the cabbage should be split in quarters and taken entirely out in the first instance.

3 to 4 hours.

BRUSSELS SPROUTS

These delicate little sprouts, or miniature cabbages, which at their fullest growth scarcely exceed a large walnut in size, should be quite freshly gathered. Free them from all discoloured leaves, cut the stems even, and wash the sprouts thoroughly. Throw them into a pan of water properly salted, and boil them quickly from eight to ten minutes; drain them *well*, and serve them upon a rather thick round of toasted bread buttered on both sides. Send good melted butter to table with them. This is the Belgian mode of dressing this excellent vegetable, which is served in France with the sauce poured over it, or it is tossed in a stewpan with a slice of butter and some pepper and salt: a spoonful or two of veal gravy (and sometimes a little lemon-juice) is added when these are perfectly mixed.

8 to 10 minutes.

SALSIFY

We are surprised that a vegetable so excellent as this should be so little cared for in England. Delicately fried in batter – which is a common mode of serving it abroad – it forms a delicious second course dish: it is also good when plain-boiled, drained, and served in gravy, or even with melted butter. Wash the roots, scrape gently off the dark outside skin, and throw them into cold water as they are done, to prevent their turning black; cut them into lengths of three or four inches, and when all are ready put them into plenty of boiling water with a little salt, a small bit of butter, and a couple of spoonsful of white vinegar or the juice of a lemon: they will be done in from three-quarters of an hour to an hour. Try them with a fork, and when perfectly tender, drain, and serve them with a white sauce, rich brown gravy, or melted butter.

¾ to 1 hour.

BOILED CELERY

This vegetable is extremely good dressed like sea-kale, and served on a toast with rich melted butter. Let it be freshly dug, wash it with great nicety, trim the ends, take off the coarse outer-leaves, cut the roots of equal length, tie them in bunches, and boil them in plenty of water, with the usual proportion of salt, from twenty to thirty minutes.

20 to 30 minutes.

STEWED ONIONS

Strip the outer skin from four to five fine Portugal onions, and trim the ends, but without cutting into the vegetable; arrange them in a saucepan of sufficient size to contain them all in one layer; just cover them with good beef or veal gravy, and stew them very gently indeed for a couple of hours: they should be tender quite through, but should not be allowed to fall to pieces. When large, but not *mild* onions are used, they should be first boiled for half an hour in plenty of water, then drained from it, and put into boiling gravy: strong, well-flavoured broth of veal or beef, is sometimes substituted for this, and with the addition of a little catsup, spice, and thickening, answers very well. The savour of this dish is heightened by flouring lightly and frying the onions of a pale brown before they are stewed.

Portugal onions, 4 or 5 (if fried, 15 to 20 minutes); broth or gravy, 1 to 1½ pint: nearly or quite 2 hours.

Obs. When the quantity of gravy is considered too much, the onions may be only half covered, and turned when the under side is tender, but longer time must then be allowed for stewing them.

STEWED CHESTNUTS

Strip the outer rind from forty or fifty fine sound Spanish chestnuts, throw them into a large saucepan of hot water, and bring it to the point of boiling; when the second skin parts from them easily, lift them out, and throw them into plenty of cold water; peel, and wipe them dry; then put them into a stewpan or bright saucepan, with as much highly-flavoured cold beef or veal gravy as will nearly cover them, and stew them very gently from three-quarters of an hour to a full hour: they should be quite tender, but unbroken. Add salt, cayenne, and thickening if required, and serve the chestnuts in their gravy. We have found it an improvement to have them floured and lightly browned in a little good butter before they are stewed, and also to add some thin strips of fresh lemon-rind to the gravy.

Chestnuts, 40 or 50; gravy, 3/4 pint, or more: 3/4 to 1 hour.

Obs. A couple of bay leaves and a slice of lean ham will give an improved flavour to the sauce should it not be sufficiently rich: the ham should be laid under the chestnuts, but not served with them. When these are to be browned, or even otherwise, they may be freed readily from the second skin by shaking them with a small bit of butter in a frying-pan over a gentle fire.

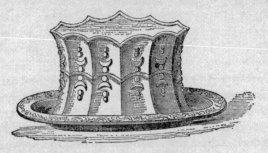

18

Timbale or Paté Chaud

PASTRY

INTRODUCTORY REMARKS

The greatest possible cleanliness and nicety should be observed in making pastry. The slab or board, paste-rollers, tins, cutters, moulds, everything, in fact, used for it, and especially the hands, should be equally free from the slightest soil or particle of dust. The more expeditiously the finer kinds of paste are made and dispatched to the oven, and the less they are touched the better.

In mixing paste, the water should be added gradually, and the whole gently drawn together with the finger, until sufficient has been added, when it should be lightly kneaded until it is as smooth as possible. When carelessly made, the surface is often left covered with small dry crumbs or lumps; or the water is poured in heedlessly in so large a proportion that it becomes necessary to add more flour to render it *workable* in any way; and this ought particularly to be avoided when a certain weight of all the ingredients has been taken.

The fine yellow glaze appropriate to meat pies is given with beaten yolk of egg, which should be laid on with a paste brush, or a small bunch of feathers: if a lighter colour be wished for, whisk the whole of the egg together, or mix a little milk with the yolk.

The best mode of icing fruit tarts before they are sent to the oven is, to moisten the paste with cold water, to sift sugar thickly upon it, and to press it lightly on with the hand; but when a *whiter* icing is preferred, the pastry must be drawn from the oven when nearly baked, and brushed with white of egg, whisked to a froth; then well covered with the sifted sugar, and sprinkled with a few drops of water before it is put in again: this glazing answers also very well, though it takes a slight colour, if used before the pastry is baked.

* For other pastry icing see chapter of 'cakes'.

FEUILLETAGE, OR FINE FRENCH PUFF PASTE

This, when made by a good French cook, is the perfection of rich light paste, and will rise in the oven from one to six inches in height: but some practice is, without doubt, necessary to accomplish this. In summer it is a great advantage to have ice at hand, and to harden the butter over it before it is used; the paste also between the intervals of rolling is improved by being laid on an oven-leaf [*flat metal sheet*] over a vessel containing it [*the ice*]. Take an equal weight of good butter free from the coarse salt which is found in some, and which is disadvantageous for this paste, and of fine dry, sifted flour; to each pound of these allow the yolks of a couple of eggs, and a small teaspoonful of salt. Break a few small bits of the butter very lightly into the flour, put the salt into the centre, and pour on it sufficient water to dissolve it (we do not understand why the doing this should be better than mixing it with the flour, as in other pastes, but such is the method always pursued for it); add a little more water to the eggs, moisten the flour gradually, and make it into a very smooth paste, rather lithe in summer, and never *exceedingly* stiff, though the opposite fault, in the extreme, would render the crust unmanageable. Press, in a soft thin cloth, all the moisture from the remainder of the butter, and form it into a ball, but in doing this be careful not to soften it too much. Should it be in an unfit state for pastry from the heat of the weather, put it into a basin, and set the basin into a pan of water mixed with plenty of salt and saltpetre, and let it remain in a cool place for an hour if possible before it is used. When it is ready (and the paste should never be commenced until it is so), roll the crust out square, and of sufficient size to enclose the butter, flatten this a little upon it in the centre, and then fold the crust well over it, and roll it out thin as lightly as possible, after having dredged the board and pasteroller with a little flour: this is called giving it *one turn*. Then fold it in three, give it another turn, and set it aside where it will be very cool, for a few minutes; give it two more turns in the same way, rolling it each time very lightly but of equal thickness, and to the full length that it will reach, taking always especial care that the butter shall not break through the paste. Let it again be set aside to become cold; and after it has been twice more rolled and folded in three, give it a half turn, by folding it once only, and it will be ready for use.

Equal weight of finest flour and good butter; to each pound of these, the yolks of two eggs, and a small teaspoonful of salt: 6½ turns to be given to the paste.

VERY GOOD LIGHT PASTE

Mix with a pound of sifted flour six ounces of fresh, pure lard, and make them into a smooth paste with cold water; press the buttermilk from ten ounces of butter, and form it into a ball, by twisting it in a clean cloth. Roll out the paste, put the ball of butter in the middle, close it like an apple-dumpling, and roll it very lightly until it is less than an inch thick; fold the ends into the middle, dust a little flour over the board and paste-roller, and roll the paste thin a second time, then set it aside for three or four minutes in a very cool place; give it two more *turns*, after it has again been left for a few minutes, roll it out twice more, folding it each time in three. This ought to render it fit for use. The sooner this paste is sent to the oven after it is made, the lighter it will be: if allowed to remain long before it is baked, it will be tough and heavy.

Flour, 1 lb; lard, 6 oz; butter, 10 oz; little salt.

ENGLISH PUFF PASTE

Break lightly into a couple of pounds of dried and sifted flour eight ounces of butter; add a pinch of salt, and sufficient cold water to make the paste; work it as quickly and as lightly as possible, until it is smooth and pliable, then level it with the paste-roller until it is three-quarters of an inch thick, and place regularly upon it six ounces of butter in small bits; fold the paste, roll it out again, lay on it six ounces more of butter, repeat the rolling, dusting each time a little flour over the board and paste, add again six ounces of butter, and roll the paste out thin three or four times, folding the ends into the middle.

Flour, 2 lb; little salt; butter, 1 lb 10 oz.

If very rich paste be required, equal portions of flour and butter must be used; and the latter may be divided into two, instead of three parts, when it is to be rolled in.

CREAM CRUST
(Author's Receipt – Very good)

Stir a little fine salt into a pound of dry flour, and mix gradually with it sufficient very thick, sweet cream to form a smooth paste; it will be found sufficiently good for common family dinners, without the addition of butter; but to make an excellent crust, roll in four ounces in the usual way, after having given the paste a couple of *turns*. Handle it as lightly as possible in making it, and send it to the oven as soon as it is ready: it may be used for fruit tarts, cannelons, puffs, and other varieties of small pastry, or for good meat pies. Six ounces of butter to the pound of flour will give a *very rich* crust.

Flour, 1 lb; salt, 1 small saltspoonful (more for meat pies); rich cream, ½ to ¾ pint; butter, 4 oz; for richest crust, 6 oz.

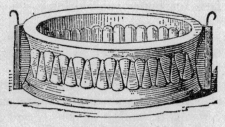

Raised Pie Mould

PÂTÉ BRISÉE, OR FRENCH CRUST FOR HOT OR COLD MEAT PIES

Sift two pounds and a quarter of fine dry flour, and break into it one pound of butter, work them together with the fingers until they resemble fine crumbs of bread, then add a small teaspoonful of salt, and make them into a firm paste, with the yolks of four eggs, well beaten, mixed with half a pint of cold water, and strained; or for a somewhat richer crust of the same kind, take two pounds of flour, one of butter, yolks of four eggs, half an ounce of salt, and less than the half-pint of water, and work the whole well until the paste is perfectly smooth.

Flour, 2¼ lb; butter, 1 lb; salt, 1 small teaspoonful; yolks of eggs, 4; water, ½ pint. Or: flour, 2 lb; butter, 1 lb; yolks of eggs, 4; salt, ½ oz; water, less than ½ pint.

VERY SUPERIOR SUET-CRUST

Strip the skin entirely from some fresh veal or beef kidney suet; chop, and then put it into the mortar, with a small quantity of pure-flavoured lard, oil, or butter, and pound it perfectly smooth: it may then be used for crust in the same way that butter is, in making puff paste, and in this form will be found a most excellent substitute for it, for *hot* pies or tarts. It is not quite so good for those which are to be served cold. Eight ounces of suet pounded with two of butter, and worked with the fingers into a pound of flour, will make an exceedingly good short crust; but for a very rich one the proportion must be increased.

Good short crust: flour, 1 lb; suet, 8 oz; salt, ½ teaspoonful. Richer crust: suet, 16 oz; butter, 4 oz; flour, 1½ lb; salt, 1 small teaspoonful.

VERY RICH SHORT CRUST FOR TARTS

Break lightly, with the least possible handling, six ounces of butter into eight of flour; add a dessertspoonful of pounded sugar, and two or three of water; roll the paste, for several minutes, to blend the ingredients well, folding it together like puff crust, and touch it as little as possible.

Flour, 8 oz; butter, 6 oz; pounded sugar, 1 dessertspoonful; water, 2 to 3 spoonsful.

EXCELLENT SHORT CRUST FOR SWEET PASTRY

Crumble down very lightly half a pound of butter into a pound of flour, breaking it quite small. Mix well with these a slight pinch of salt and two ounces of sifted sugar, and add sufficient milk to make them up into a very smooth and somewhat firm paste. Bake this slowly, and keep it pale. It will be found an admirable crust if well made and lightly handled, and will answer for many dishes much better than puff paste. It will rise in the oven too, and be extremely light. Ten ounces of butter will render it very rich, but we find eight quite sufficient.

CASSEROLE OF RICE

Proceed exactly as for Gabrielle's pudding (see Chapter 21), but substitute good veal broth or stock for the milk, and add a couple of ounces more of butter. Fill the casserole when it is emptied, with a rich mince or fricassee, or with stewed oysters in a *béchamel* sauce. French cooks make a very troublesome and elaborate affair of this dish, putting to the rice to make it *mellow*, a great deal of pot-top fat, slices of fat ham, etc., which must afterwards be well drained off, or picked out from it; but the dish, made as we have directed, will be found excellent eating, and of very elegant appearance, if it be moulded in a tasteful shape. It must have a *quick* oven to colour, without too much drying it. The rice for it must be boiled sufficiently tender to be crushed easily to a smooth paste, and it must be mashed with a strong wooden spoon against the sides of the stewpan until all the grains are broken. It may then, when cool, be made like a raised pie with the hands, and decorated with a design formed on it with a carrot cut into a point like a graver. For a large casserole, a pound of rice and a quart of gravy will be required: a bit of bread is sometimes used in filling the mould, cut to the shape, and occupying nearly half the inside, but always so as to leave a thick and compact crust in every part. Part of the rice which is scooped from the inside is sometimes mixed with the mince, or other preparation, with which the casserole is filled.

MODERN CHICKEN PIE

Skin, and cut down into joints a couple of fowls, take out all the bones, and season the flesh highly with salt, cayenne, pounded mace, and nutmeg; line a dish with a thin paste, and spread over it a layer of the finest sausage-meat, which has previously been moistened with a spoonful or two of cold water; over this place closely together some of the boned chicken joints, then more sausage-meat, and continue thus with alternate layers of each, until the dish is full; roll out, and fasten securely at the edge, a cover half an inch thick, trim off the superfluous paste, make an incision in the top, lay some paste leaves round it, glaze the whole with yolk of egg, and bake the pie from an hour and a half to two hours in a well heated oven. Lay a sheet or two of writing-paper over the crust, should it brown too quickly. Minced herbs can be mixed with the sausage-meat at pleasure, and a small quantity of eschalot also, when its flavour is much liked: it should be well moistened with water, or the whole will be unpalatably dry. The pie may be served hot or cold, but we would rather recommend the latter.

A couple of very young tender rabbits will answer exceedingly well for it instead of fowls, and a border, or half paste in the dish will generally be preferred to an entire lining of the crust, which is now but rarely served, unless for pastry which is to be taken out of the dish or mould in which it is baked before it is sent to table.

A COMMON CHICKEN PIE

Prepare the fowls as for boiling, cut them down into joints, and season them with salt, white pepper, and nutmeg or pounded mace; arrange them neatly in a dish bordered with paste, lay amongst them three or four fresh eggs boiled hard, and cut in halves, pour in some cold water, put on a thick cover, pare the edge, and ornament it, make a hole in the centre, lay a roll of paste, or a few leaves round it, and bake the pie in a moderate oven from an hour to an hour and a half. The back and neck bones may be boiled down with a bit or two of lean ham, to make a little additional gravy, which can be poured into the pie after it is baked.

Lay a border of fine puff paste round a large dish, and cover the bottom with a veal cutlet or tender rump steak, free from fat and bone, and seasoned with salt, cayenne, and nutmeg or pounded mace; prepare with great nicety as many freshly-killed young pigeons as the dish will contain in one layer; put into each a slice or ball of butter, seasoned with a little cayenne and mace, lay them into the dish with the breasts downwards, and between and over them put the yolks of half a dozen or more of hard-boiled eggs; stick plenty of butter on them, season the whole well with salt and spice, pour in some cold water or veal broth for the gravy, roll out the cover three-quarters of an inch thick, secure it well round the edge, ornament it highly, and bake the pie for an hour or more in a well-heated oven. It is a great improvement to fill the birds with small mushroom-buttons, prepared as for partridges (see Chapter 15): their livers also may be put into them.

A GOOD MUTTON PIE

Lay a half-paste of short or of puff crust round a buttered dish; take the whole or part of a loin of mutton, strip off the fat entirely, and raise the flesh clear from the bones without dividing it, then slice it into cutlets of equal thickness, season them well with salt and pepper, or cayenne, and strew between the layers some finely-minced herbs mixed with two or three eschalots, when the flavour of these last is liked; or omit them, and roll quite thin some good forcemeat (which can be flavoured with a little minced eschalot at pleasure), and lay it between the cutlets: two or three mutton kidneys intermingled with the meat will greatly enrich the gravy; pour in a little cold water, roll the cover half an inch thick, or more should the crust be short, as it will not rise like puff paste, close the pie very securely, trim the edges even with the dish, ornament the pie according to the taste, make a hole in the centre, and bake it from an hour and a half to a couple of hours. Gravy made with part of the bones, quite cleared from fat, and left to become cold, may be used to fill the pie instead of water.

PATTIES À LA PONTIFE
(*Entrée – A fast day, or Maigre dish*)

Mince, but not very small, the yolks of six fresh hard-boiled eggs; mince also and mix with them a couple of fine truffles, a large saltspoonful of salt, half the quantity of mace and nutmeg, and a fourth as much of cayenne. Moisten these ingredients with a spoonful of thick cream, or *béchamel maigre*, or with a dessert-spoonful of clarified butter; line the patty-moulds, fill them with the mixture, cover, and bake them from twelve to fifteen minutes in a moderate oven. They are excellent made with the cream-crust of page 213.

Yolks hard-boiled eggs, 6; truffles, 2 large; seasoning of salt, mace, nutmeg, and cayenne; cream, or *béchamel maigre*, 1 tablespoonful, or clarified butter, 1 dessertspoonful: baked moderate oven, 12 to 15 minutes.

Obs. A spoonful or two of jellied stock or gravy, or of good white sauce, converts these into admirable patties: the same ingredients make also very superior rolls or cannelons. For Patties *à la Cardinale*, small mushroom-buttons stewed as for partridges, Chapter 15, before they are minced, must be substituted for truffles; and the butter in which they are simmered should be added with them to the eggs.

EXCELLENT MEAT ROLLS

Pound, as for potting (see page 181), and with the same proportion of butter and of seasonings, some half-roasted veal, chicken, or turkey. Make some common forcemeat by the receipt in Chapter 8, and form it into small rolls, not larger than a finger; wrap twice or thrice as much of the pounded meat equally round each of these, first moistening it with a teaspoonful of water; fold them in good puffpaste, and bake them from fifteen to twenty minutes, or until the crust is perfectly done. A small quantity of the lean of a boiled ham may be finely minced and pounded with the veal, and very small mushrooms, prepared as for a partridge (see page 170) may be substituted for the force-meat.

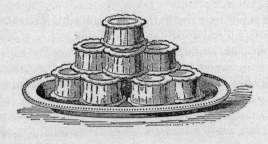

SMALL VOL-AU-VENTS, OR PATTY CASES

These are quickly and easily made with two round paste-cutters, of which one should be little more than half the size of the other: to give the pastry a better appearance, they should be fluted. Roll out some of the lightest puff paste to half-inch thickness, and with the larger of the tins cut the number of patties required; then dip the edge of the small shape into hot water, and press it about half through them. Bake them in a moderately quick oven from ten to twelve minutes, and when they are done, with the point of a sharp knife, take out the small rounds of crust from the tops, and scoop all the crumbs from the inside of the patties, which may then be filled with shrimps, oysters, lobster, chicken, pheasant, or any other of the ordinary varieties of patty meat, prepared with white sauce. Fried crumbs may be laid over them instead of the covers, or these last can be replaced.

For sweet dishes, glaze the pastry, and fill it with rich whipped cream, preserve, or boiled custard; if with the last of these, put it back into a very gentle oven until the custards are set.

Lay a band of fine paste round the rim of a tart-dish, fill it with any kind of fruit mixed with a moderate proportion of sugar, roll out the cover very evenly, moisten the edges of the paste, press them together carefully, and trim them off close to the dish; spread equally over the top, to within rather more than an inch of the edge all round, the whites of three fresh eggs beaten to a quite solid froth and mixed quickly at the moment of using them with three tablespoonsful of dry sifted sugar. Put the tart into a moderately brisk oven, and when the crust has risen well and the icing is set, either lay a sheet of writing-paper lightly over it, or draw it to a part of the oven where it will not take too much colour. This is now a fashionable mode of icing tarts, and greatly improves their appearance.

Bake half an hour.

A GOOD APPLE TART

A pound and a quarter of apples weighed after they are pared and cored, will be sufficient for a small tart, and four ounces more for one of moderate size. Lay a border of English puff paste, or of cream crust round the dish, just dip the apples into water, arrange them very compactly in it, higher in the centre than at the sides, and strew amongst them from three to four ounces of pounded sugar, or more should they be very acid: the grated rind and strained juice of half a lemon will much improve their flavour. Lay on the cover rolled thin, and ice it or not at pleasure. Send the tart to a moderate oven for about half an hour. This may be converted into the old-fashioned *creamed* apple tart, by cutting out the cover while it is still quite hot, leaving only about an inch-wide border of paste round the edge, and pouring over the apples when they have become cold, from half to three-quarters of a pint of rich boiled custard. The cover divided into triangular sippets, was formerly stuck round the inside of the tart, but ornamental leaves of pale puff paste have a better effect.

Well-drained whipped cream may be substituted for the custard, and be piled high, and lightly over the fruit.

SUPERLATIVE MINCEMEAT

Take four large lemons, with their weight of golden pippins pared and cored, of jar-raisins, currants, candied citron and orange-rind, and the finest suet, and a fourth part more of pounded sugar. Boil the lemons tender, chop them small, but be careful first to extract all the pips; add them to the other ingredients, after all have been prepared with great nicety, and mix the whole *well* with from three to four glasses of good brandy. We think that the weight of one lemon, in meat, improves this mixture; or, in lieu of it, a small quantity of crushed macaroons added just before it is baked.

MINCE PIES
(*Entremets*)

Butter some tin pattypans well, and line them evenly with fine puff paste rolled thin; fill them with mincemeat, moisten the edges of the covers, which should be nearly a quarter of an inch thick, close the pies carefully, trim off the superfluous paste, make a small aperture in the centre of the crust with a fork or the point of a knife, ice the pies or not, at pleasure, and bake them half an hour in a well-heated but not fierce oven: lay a paper over them when they are partially done, should they appear likely to take too much colour.

½ hour.

MINCE PIES ROYAL
(*Entremets*)

Add to half a pound of good mincemeat an ounce and a half of pounded sugar, the grated rind and the strained juice of a large lemon, one ounce of clarified butter, and the yolks of four eggs; beat these well together, and half fill, or rather more, with the mixture, some pattypans lined with fine paste; put them into a moderate oven and when the insides are just set, ice them thickly with the whites of the eggs beaten to snow, and mixed quickly at the moment with four heaped tablespoonsful of pounded sugar; set them immediately into the oven again, and bake them slowly of a fine light brown.

Mincemeat, ½ lb; sugar, 1½ oz; rind and juice, 1 large lemon; butter, 1 oz; yolks, 4 eggs. Icing: whites, 4 eggs; sugar, 4 table-spoonsful.

THE MONITOR'S TART, OR TOURTE À LA JUDD

Put into an enamelled stewpan, or into a delicately clean saucepan, three-quarters of a pound of well-flavoured apples, weighed after they are pared and cored; add to them from three to four ounces of pounded sugar, an ounce and a half of fresh butter cut small, and half a teaspoonful of pounded cinnamon, or the lightly grated rind of a small lemon. Let them stand over, or by the side of a gentle fire until they begin to soften, and toss them now and then to mingle the whole well, but do not stir them with a spoon; they should all remain unbroken and rather firm. Turn them into a dish, and let them become cold. Divide three-quarters of a pound of good light paste into two equal portions; roll out one quite thin and round, flour an oven-leaf and lay it on, as the tart cannot so well be moved after it is made; place the apples upon it in the form of a dome, but leave a clear space of an inch or more round the edge; moisten this with white of egg, and press the remaining half of the paste (which should be rolled out to the same size, and laid carefully over the apples) closely upon it: they should be well secured, that the syrup from the fruit may not burst through. Whisk the white of an egg to a froth, brush it over the tart with a paste brush or a small bunch of feathers, sift sugar thickly over, and then strew upon it some almonds blanched and roughly chopped; bake the tart in a moderate oven from thirty-five to forty-five minutes. It may be filled with peaches, or apricots, half stewed like the apples, or with cherries merely rolled in fine sugar.

Light paste, ½ to ¾ lb; apples, 12 oz; butter, 1½ oz; sugar, 4 oz; glazing of egg and sugar; some almonds: 35 to 45 minutes.

PUDDING PIES
(*Entremets*)

This form of pastry (or its name at least) is, we believe, peculiar to the county of Kent, where it is made in abundance, and eaten by all classes of people during Lent. Boil for fifteen minutes three ounces of ground rice in a pint and a half of new milk, and when taken from the fire stir into it three ounces of butter and four of sugar; add to these six well-beaten eggs, a grain or two of salt, and a flavouring of nutmeg or lemon-rind at pleasure. When the mixture is nearly cold, line some large pattypans or some saucers with thin puff paste, fill them with it three parts full, strew the tops thickly with currants which have been cleaned and dried, and bake the pudding pies from fifteen to twenty minutes in a gentle oven.

Milk, 1½ pint; ground rice, 3 oz: 15 minutes. Butter, 3 oz; sugar, ¼ lb; nutmeg or lemon-rind; eggs, 6; currants, 4 to 6 oz: 15 to 20 minutes.

COMMON LEMON TARTLETS

Beat four eggs until they are exceedingly light, add to them gradually four ounces of pounded sugar, and whisk these together for five minutes; strew lightly in, if it be at hand, a dessertspoonful of potato-flour, if not, of common flour well dried and sifted, then throw into the mixture by slow degrees, three ounces of good butter, which should be dissolved, but only just luke-warm: beat the whole well, then stir briskly in, the strained juice and the grated rind of one lemon and a half. Line some pattypans with fine puff paste rolled very thin, fill them two-thirds full, and bake the tartlets about twenty minutes, in a moderate oven.

Eggs, 4; sugar, 4 oz; potato-flour, or common flour, 1 dessert-spoonful; butter, 3 oz; juice and rind of 1½ full-sized lemon: baked 15 to 20 minutes.

MADAME WERNER'S ROSENVIK CHEESE-CAKES

Blanch and pound to the finest possible paste, four ounces of fine fresh Jordan almonds, with a few drops of lemon-juice or water, then mix with them, very gradually indeed, six fresh, and thoroughly well-whisked eggs; throw in by degrees twelve ounces of pounded sugar, and beat the mixture without intermission all the time: add then the finely grated rinds of four small, or of three large lemons, and afterwards, by very slow degrees, the strained juice of all. When these ingredients are perfectly blended, pour to them in small portions, four ounces of just liquefied butter (six of clarified if exceedingly rich cheese-cakes are wished for), and again whisk the mixture lightly for several minutes; thicken it over the fire like boiled custard, and either put it into small pans or jars for storing,* or fill with it, one-third full, some pattypans lined with the finest paste; place lightly on it a layer of apricot, orange, or lemon-marmalade, and on this pour as much more of the mixture. Bake the cheese-cakes from fifteen to twenty minutes in a moderate oven. They are very good *without* the layer of preserves.

Jordan almonds, 4 oz; eggs, 6; sugar, 12 oz; rinds and strained juice of 4 small, or of 3 quite large lemons; butter, 4 oz (6 for *rich* cheese-cakes); layers of preserve. Baked 15 to 20 minutes, moderate oven.

* This preparation will make excellent *fanchonnettes*, or pastry-sandwiches. It will not curdle if gently boiled for two or three minutes (and stirred without ceasing), and it may be long kept afterwards.

APPEL KRAPFEN
(*German Receipt*)

Boil down three-quarters of a pound of good apples with four ounces of pounded sugar, and a small glass of white wine, or the strained juice of a lemon; when they are stewed quite to a pulp, keep them stirred until they are thick and dry; then mix them gradually with four ounces of almonds, beaten to a paste, or very finely chopped, two ounces of candied orange or lemon-rind shred extremely small, and six ounces of jar raisins stoned and quartered: to these the Germans add a rather high flavouring of cinnamon, which is a very favourite spice with them, but a grating of nutmeg, and some fresh lemon-peel, are, we think, preferable for this composition. Mix all the ingredients well together; roll out some butter-crust a full back-of-knife thickness, cut it into four-inch squares, brush the edges to the depth of an inch round with beaten egg, fill them with the mixture, lay another square of paste on each, press them very securely together, make, with the point of a knife a small incision in the top of each, glaze them or not at pleasure, and bake them rather slowly, that the raisins may have time to become tender. They are very good. The proportion of sugar must be regulated by the nature of the fruit; and that of the almonds can be diminished when it is thought too much. A delicious tart of the kind is made by substituting for the raisins and candied orange-rind, two heaped tablespoonsful of very fine apricot jam.

STRAWBERRY TARTLETS
(*Good*)

Take a full half-pint of freshly-gathered strawberries, without the stalks; first crush, and then mix them with two ounces and a half of powdered sugar; stir to them by degrees four well-whisked eggs, beat the mixture a little, and put it into pattypans lined with fine paste: they should be only three parts filled. Bake the tartlets from ten to twelve minutes.

Line some pattypans with very fine paste, and put into each a layer of apricot jam; on this pour some thick boiled custard. Whisk the whites of a couple of eggs to a solid froth, mix a couple of tablespoonsful of sifted sugar with them, lay this icing lightly over the tartlets, and bake them in a gentle oven from twenty to thirty minutes, unless they should be very small, when less time must be allowed for them.

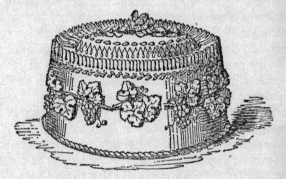

Raised Pie

19

SOUFFLÉS, OMLETS, ETC.

A FONDU, OR CHEESE SOUFFLÉ

Mix to a smooth batter, with a quarter-pint of new milk, two
ounces of potato-flour, arrowroot, or *tous les mois*; pour boiling to
them three-quarters of a pint more of milk, or of cream in preference: stir them well together, and then throw in two ounces of
butter cut small. When this is melted, and well-beaten into the
mixture, add the well-whisked yolks of four large or of five small
eggs, half a teaspoonful of salt, something less of cayenne, and
three ounces of lightly-grated cheese, Parmesan or English, or
equal parts of both. Whisk the whites of the eggs to a quite firm
and solid froth; then proceed, as for a *soufflé*, to mix and bake
the *fondu*. Fill the *soufflé*-pan less than half full; set it instantly
into the oven, which should be gentle, but not exceedingly slow
close the door immediately and do not open it for fifteen or
twenty minutes: in from thirty to forty the *soufflé* will be ready
for table unless the oven should be very cool: a fierce degree of
heat will have a most unfavourable effect upon it.

A COMMON OMLET

Six eggs are sufficient for an omlet of moderate size. Let them be
very fresh; break them singly and carefully; clear them from
specks with the point of a fork while they are in the cup; or, when
they are sufficiently whisked pour them through a sieve, and
resume the beating until they are very light. Add to them from
half to a whole teaspoonful of salt, and a seasoning of pepper.
Dissolve in a small frying-pan a couple of ounces of butter, pour
in the eggs, and as soon as the omlet is well risen and firm

throughout, slide it on to a hot dish, fold it together like a turn-over, and serve it *immediately*; from five to seven minutes will fry it.

Eggs, 6; butter, 2 oz; seasoning of salt and pepper: 5 to 7 minutes.

PLAIN COMMON FRITTERS

Mix with three well-whisked eggs a quarter-pint of milk, and strain them through a fine sieve; add them gradually to three large tablespoonsful of flour, and thin the batter with as much more milk as will bring it to the consistence of cream; beat it up thoroughly at the moment of using it, that the fritters may be light. Drop it in small portions from a spouted jug or basin into boiling lard; when lightly coloured on one side, turn the fritters, drain them well from the lard as they are lifted out, and serve them very quickly. They are eaten generally with fine sugar, and orange or lemon juice: the first of these may be sifted quickly over them after they are dished, and the oranges or lemons halved or quartered, and sent to table with them. The lard used for frying them should be fresh and pure-flavoured: it renders them more crisp and light than butter, and is, therefore, better suited to the purpose. These fritters may be agreeably varied by mingling with the batter just before it is used two or three ounces of well cleaned and well dried currants, or three or four apples of a good boiling kind *not* very finely minced. Double the quantity of batter will be required for a large dish.

Eggs, 3; flour, 3 tablespoonsful; milk, ¼ to ½ pint.

FRITTERS OF CAKE AND PUDDING†

Cut plain pound, or rice cake, or rich seed cake, into small square slices half-inch thick; trim away the crust, fry them slowly a light brown in a small quantity of fresh butter, and spread over them when done a layer of apricot-jam, or of any other preserve, and serve them immediately. These fritters are improved by being moistened with a little good cream before they are fried: they must then be slightly floured. Cold plum-pudding sliced down as thick as the cake, and divided into portions of equal size and good form, then dipped into French or English batter and gently fried, will also make an agreeable variety of fritter. Orange marmalade and Devonshire cream may be served in separate layers on the *seed cake* fritters. The whole of the above may be cut of uniform size and shaped with a round cake-cutter.

† [*'Cake fritters' seem a rather solid diet for present-day taste, but I can imagine they are a great treat for those who favour the solid suety pudding.*]

MINCEMEAT FRITTERS

With half a pound of mincemeat mix two ounces of fine bread-crumbs (or a tablespoonful of flour), two eggs well beaten, and the strained juice of half a small lemon. Mix these well, and drop the fritters with a dessertspoon into plenty of very pure lard or fresh butter; fry them from seven to eight minutes, drain them on a napkin or on white blotting paper, and send them very hot to table; they should be quite small.

Mincemeat, ½ lb; bread-crumbs, 2 oz (or flour, 1 table-spoonful); eggs, 2; juice of ½ lemon: 7 to 8 minutes.

POTATO FRITTERS†
(*Entremets*)

The same mixture as for potato puddings, Chapter 21, if dropped in small portions into boiling butter, and fried until brown on both sides, will make potato fritters. Half the proportion of ingredients will be quite sufficient for a dish of these.

† [*These sound delicious but I cannot think at what point of the meal they should be eaten.*]

Croquettes

CROQUETTES OF RICE†
(*Entremets*)

Wipe very clean, in a dry cloth, seven ounces of rice, put it into a clean stewpan, and pour on it a quart of new milk; let it swell gently by the side of the fire, and stir it often that it may not stick to the pan, nor burn; when it is about half done, stir to it five ounces of pounded sugar, and six bitter almonds beaten extremely fine: the thin rind of half a fresh lemon may be added in the first instance. The rice must be simmered until it is soft, and very thick and dry; it should then be spread on a dish, and left until cold, when it is to be rolled into small balls, which must be dipped into beaten egg, and then covered in every part with the finest bread-crumbs. When all are ready, fry them a light brown in fresh butter, and dry them well before the fire, upon a sieve reversed and covered with a very soft cloth, or with a sheet of white blotting paper. Pile them in a hot dish, and send them to table quickly.

Rice, 7 oz; milk, 1 quart; rind of lemon: ¾ hour. Sugar, 5 oz; bitter almonds, 6: 40 to 60 minutes, or more. Fried, 5 to 7 minutes.

Obs. As, from the difference of quality, the same proportions of rice and milk will not always produce the same effect, the cook must use her discretion in adding, should it be needed, sufficient liquid to soften the rice perfectly: but she must bear in mind that if not boiled extremely thick and dry, it will be difficult to make it into croquettes.

We must repeat here what we have elsewhere stated as the result of *many* trials of it, that good rice will absorb and become tender with three times its own bulk or measure of liquid. Thus, an exact half-pint (or half pound) will require a pint and a half, with an extremely gentle degree of heat, to convert it into a thoroughly soft but firm mass; which would, perhaps, be rather too dry for *croquettes*. A pint of milk to four ounces of rice, if well managed, would answer better.

† [*The directions for cooking rice should be well observed.*]

VERY SAVOURY ENGLISH RISSOLES
(*Entrée*)

Make the common forcemeat of Chapter 8, sufficiently firm with unbeaten yolk of egg, to roll rather thin on a well-floured board; cut it into very small rounds, put a little pounded chicken in the centre of one half, moistening the edges with water, or white of egg, lay the remaining rounds over these, close them securely, and fry them in butter a fine light brown; drain and dry them well, and heap them in the middle of a hot dish, upon a napkin folded flat: these *rissoles* may be egged and crumbed before they are fried.

SAVOURY TOASTS

Cut some slices of bread free from crust, about half-inch thick, and two inches and a half square; butter the tops thickly, spread a little mustard on them, and then cover them with a deep layer of grated cheese and of ham seasoned rather highly with cayenne; fry them in good butter, but do not turn them in the pan; lift them out, and place them in a Dutch oven for three or four minutes to dissolve the cheese: serve them very hot.

To 4 tablespoonsful of grated English cheese, an equal portion of very finely minced, or grated ham; but if Parmesan, or Gruyere, 6 tablespoonsful. Seasoning of mustard and cayenne.

Obs. These toasts, for which we give the original receipt unaltered, may be served in the cheese-course of a dinner. Such mere '*relishes*' as they are called, do not seem to us to demand much of our space, or many of them which are very easy of preparation might be inserted here: a good cook, however, will easily supply them at slight expense. Truffles minced, seasoned, and stewed tender in butter with an eschalot or two, may be served on fried toasts or *croûtons* and will generally be liked.

MACCARONI À LA REINE†

This is a very excellent and delicate mode of dressing maccaroni. Boil eight ounces in the usual way, and by the time it is sufficiently tender, dissolve gently ten ounces of any rich, well flavoured white cheese in full three-quarters of a pint of good cream; add a little salt, a rather full seasoning of cayenne, from half to a whole saltspoonful of pounded mace, and a couple of ounces of sweet fresh butter. The cheese should, in the first instance, be sliced very thin, and taken quite free of the hard part adjoining the rind; it should be stirred in the cream without intermission until it is entirely dissolved, and the whole is perfectly smooth: the maccaroni, previously well drained, may then be tossed gently in it, or after it is dished, the cheese may be poured equally over the maccaroni. The whole, in either case, may be thickly covered before it is sent to table, with fine crumbs of bread fried of a pale gold colour, and dried perfectly, either before the fire or in an oven, when such an addition is considered an improvement. As a matter of precaution, it is better to boil the cream before the cheese is melted in it; rich white sauce, or *béchamel*, made not very thick, with an additional ounce or two of butter, may be used to vary and enrich this preparation. If Parmesan cheese be used for it, it must of course be grated; but, as we have said before, it will not easily blend with the other ingredients so as to be smooth. A portion of Stilton, free from the blue mould, would have a good effect in the present receipt. Half the quantity may be served.

Maccaroni, ½ lb; cheese, 10 oz; good cream, ¾ pint (or rich white sauce); butter, 2 oz (or more); little salt, *fine* cayenne, and mace.

† [*This is really maccaroni cheese, but made with a good deal more cream and care than many a present-day version.*]

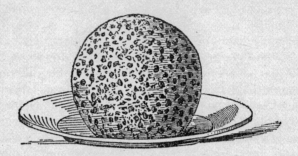

20

BOILED PUDDINGS

GENERAL DIRECTIONS

Custard pudding to have a good appearance, must be *simmered* only but without ceasing; for if boiled in a quick and careless manner, the surface instead of being smooth and velvety, will be full of holes, or honey-combed, as it is called, and the whey will flow from it and mingle with the sauce. A thickly buttered sheet of writing-paper should be laid between the custard mixture and the cloth before it is tied over, or the cover of the mould is closed upon it; and the mould itself or the basin in which it is boiled, and which should always be quite full, must likewise be well buttered; and after it is lifted from the water the pudding should be left in it for quite five minutes before it is dished, to prevent its breaking or spreading about.

Batter is much lighter when boiled in a cloth, and allowed full room to swell, than when confined in a mould: it should be well beaten the instant before it is poured into it, and put into the water immediately after it is securely tied. The cloth should be moist and thickly floured, and the pudding should be sent to table as expeditiously as possible after it is done, as it will quickly become heavy. This applies equally to all puddings made with paste, which are rendered uneatable by any delay in serving them after they are ready: they should be opened a little at the top as soon as they are taken from the boiler or stewpan to permit the escape of the steam from within.

A *very* little salt improves all sweet puddings, by taking off the insipidity, and bringing out the full flavour of the other ingredients, but its presence should not be in the slightest degree *perceptible*. When brandy, wine, or lemon-juice is added to them it should be stirred in briskly, and by degrees, quite at last, as it would be likely otherwise to curdle the milk or eggs.

TO MIX BATTER FOR PUDDINGS

Put the flour and salt into a bowl, and stir them together; whisk the eggs thoroughly, strain them through a fine hair-sieve, and add them *very gradually* to the flour; for if too much liquid be poured to it at once it will be full of lumps, and it is easy with care to keep the batter perfectly smooth. Beat it well and lightly with the back of a strong wooden spoon, and after the eggs are added thin it with milk to a proper consistence. The whites of the eggs beaten separately to a solid froth, and stirred gently into the mixture the instant before it is tied up for boiling, or before it is put into the oven to be baked, will render it remarkably light. When fruit is added to the batter, it must be made thicker than when it is served plain, or it will sink to the bottom of the pudding. Batter should never *stick to the knife* when it is sent to table: it will do this both when a sufficient number of eggs are not mixed with it, and when it is not enough cooked. About four eggs to the half pound of flour will make it firm enough to cut smoothly.

SUET CRUST, FOR MEAT OR FRUIT PUDDINGS

Clear off the skin from some fresh beef kidney-suet, hold it firmly with a fork, and with a sharp knife slice it thin, free it entirely from fibre, and mince it very fine: six ounces thus prepared will be found quite sufficient for a pound of flour. Mix them well together, add half a teaspoonful of salt for meat puddings, and a third as much for fruit ones, and sufficient cold water to make the whole into a very firm paste; work it smooth, and roll it out of equal thickness when it is used. The weight of suet should be taken after it is minced. This crust is so much lighter, and more wholesome than that which is made with butter, that we cannot refrain from recommending it in preference to our readers. Some cooks merely slice the suet in thin shavings, mix it with the flour, and beat the crust with a paste-roller, until the flour and suet are perfectly incorporated; but it is better minced.

Flour, 2 lb; suet, 12 oz; salt, 1 teaspoonful; water, 1 pint.

BUTTER CRUST FOR PUDDINGS

When suet is disliked for crust, butter must supply its place, but there must be no intermixture of lard in paste which is to be boiled. Eight ounces to the pound of flour will render it sufficiently rich for most eaters, and less will generally be preferred; rich crust of this kind being more indigestible by far than that which is baked. The butter may be lightly broken into the flour before the water is added or it may be laid on, and rolled into the paste as for puff crust. A small portion of salt must be added to it always, and for a meat pudding the same proportion as directed in the preceding receipt. For kitchen, or for quite common family puddings, butter and clarified dripping are used sometimes in equal proportions. From three to four ounces of each will be sufficient for the pound and a quarter of flour.

Flour, 1 lb; butter, 8 oz; salt, for fruit puddings, ½ saltspoonful; for meat puddings, ½ teaspoonful.

SMALL BEEF-STEAK PUDDING

Make into a very firm smooth paste, one pound of flour, six ounces of beef-suet finely minced, half a teaspoonful of salt, and half-pint of cold water. Line with this a basin which holds a pint and a half. Season a pound of tender steak, free from bone and skin, with half an ounce of salt and half a teaspoonful of pepper well mixed together; lay it in the crust, pour in a quarter-pint of water, roll out the cover, close the pudding carefully, tie a floured cloth over, and boil it for three hours and a half. We give this receipt as an exact guide for the proportions of meat puddings in general.

Flour, 1 lb; suet, 6 oz; salt, ½ teaspoonful; water, ½ pint; rump steak, 1 lb; salt, ½ oz; pepper, ½ teaspoonful; water, ¼ pint: 3½ hours.

RUTH PINCH'S BEEF-STEAK PUDDING

To make *Ruth Pinch's* celebrated pudding (known also as beef-steak pudding *à la Dickens*), substitute six ounces of butter for the suet in this receipt, and moisten the paste with the well-beaten yolks of four eggs, or with three whole ones, mixed with a little water; butter the basin very thickly before the paste is laid in, as the pudding is to be turned out of it for table. In all else proceed exactly as above.

PARTRIDGE PUDDING
(*Very good*)

Skin a brace of well-kept partridges and cut them down into joints; line a deep basin with suet crust, observing the directions given in the preceding receipts; lay in the birds, which should be rather highly seasoned with pepper or cayenne, and moderately with salt; pour in water for the gravy, close the pudding with care, and boil it from three hours to three and a half. The true flavour of the game is admirably preserved by this mode of cooking. When mushrooms are plentiful, put a layer of buttons, or small flaps, cleaned as for pickling, alternately with a layer of partridge, in filling the pudding, which will then be most excellent eating: the crust may be left untouched, and merely emptied of its contents, where it is objected to, or its place may be supplied with a richer one made of butter. A seasoning of pounded mace or nutmeg can be used at discretion. Puddings of veal, chickens, and young rabbits, may all be made by this receipt, or with the addition of oysters, which we have already noticed.

WINE SAUCE FOR SWEET PUDDINGS

Boil gently together for ten or fifteen minutes the very thin rind of half a small lemon, about an ounce and a half of sugar, and a wineglassful of water. Take out the lemon-peel and stir into the sauce until it has boiled for one minute, an ounce of butter smoothly mixed with a large half-teaspoonful of flour; add a wineglassful and a half of sherry or Madeira or other good white wine, and when quite hot serve the sauce without delay. Port wine sauce is made in the same way with the addition of a dessertspoonful of lemon-juice, some grated nutmeg and a little more sugar. Orange-rind and juice may be used for it instead of lemon.

A GERMAN CUSTARD PUDDING-SAUCE

Boil very gently together half-pint of new milk or of milk and cream mixed, a very thin strip or two of fresh lemon-rind, a bit of cinnamon, half-inch of a vanilla bean, and an ounce and a half or two ounces of sugar, until the milk is strongly flavoured; then strain, and pour it, by slow degrees, to the well-beaten yolks of three eggs, smoothly mixed with a *knife-end-full* (about half a teaspoonful) of flour, a grain or two of salt, and a tablespoonful of cold milk; and stir these very quickly round as the milk is added. Put the sauce again into the stewpan, and whisk or stir it rapidly until it thickens, and looks creamy. It must not be placed *upon* the fire, but should be held over it, when this is done. The Germans *mill* their sauces to a froth; but they may be whisked with almost equally good effect, though a small mill for the purpose – formed like a chocolate mill – may be had at a very trifling cost.

A DELICIOUS GERMAN PUDDING-SAUCE

Dissolve in half-pint of sherry or of Madeira, from three to four ounces of fine sugar, but do not allow the wine to boil; stir it hot to the well-beaten yolks of six fresh eggs, and mill the sauce over a gentle fire until it is well thickened and highly frothed; pour it over a plum, or any other kind of sweet boiled pudding, of which it much improves the appearance. Half the quantity will be sufficient for one of moderate size. We recommend the addition of a dessertspoonful of strained lemon-juice to the wine.

For large pudding, sherry or Madeira, ½ pint; fine sugar, 3 to 4 oz; yolks of eggs, 6; lemon-juice (if added), 1 dessertspoonful.

Obs. Great care must be taken not to allow these sauces to curdle. The safer plan is to put any preparation of the kind into a white jar, and to place it over the fire in a pan of boiling water, and then to stir or mill it until it is sufficiently thickened: the jar should not be half filled, and it should be large enough to allow the sauce to be worked easily. The water should not reach to within two or three inches of the brim. We give these minute details for inexperienced cooks.

COMMON RASPBERRY-SAUCE

Put three ounces of sugar broken into small lumps, and a wine-glassful and a half of water into a small stewpan, and boil them for four or five minutes. Add half-pint of fresh ripe raspberries, well mashed with the back of a spoon. Mix them with the syrup, and boil them for six or seven minutes; the sauce should then be quite smooth and clear. The quantity of it with these proportions will not be large, but can be increased at pleasure.

Obs. We have generally found that the most simple, and consequently the most refreshing fruit-sauces have been much liked by the persons who have partaken of them; and they are, we think, preferable to the foreign ones – German principally – to which wine and cinnamon are commonly added, and which are often composed of dried fruit. Their number can easily be augmented by an intelligent cook; and they can be varied through all the summer and autumnal months with the fruit in season at the time.

A VERY FINE PINE-APPLE SAUCE OR SYRUP, FOR PUDDINGS OR OTHER SWEET DISHES

After having pared away every morsel of the rind from a ripe and highly flavoured pine-apple, cut three-quarters of a pound of it into very thin slices, and then into quite small dice. Pour to it nearly half-pint of spring water; heat, and boil it very gently until it is extremely tender, then strain and press the juice closely from it through a cloth or through a muslin strainer folded in four; strain it clear, mix it with ten ounces of the finest sugar in small lumps, and when this is dissolved, boil the syrup gently for a quarter of an hour. It will be delicious in flavour and very bright in colour if well made. If put into a jar, and stored with a paper tied over it, it will remain excellent for weeks; and it will become almost a jelly with an additional ounce of sugar and rather quicker boiling. It may be poured round moulded creams, rice, or sago; or mingled with various sweet preparations for which the juice of fruit is admissible.

BATTER PUDDING

Mix the yolks of three eggs smoothly with three heaped table-spoonsful of flour, thin the batter with new milk until it is of the consistence of cream, whisk the whites of eggs apart, stir them into the batter, and boil the pudding in a floured cloth or in a buttered mould or basin for an hour. Before it is served, cut the top quickly into large dice half through the pudding, pour over it a small jarful of fine currant, raspberry, or strawberry jelly, and send it to table without the *slightest* delay.

Flour, 3 tablespoonsful; eggs, 3; salt, ½ teaspoonful; milk, from ½ to whole pint: 1 hour.

KENTISH SUET PUDDING

To a pound and a quarter of flour add half a pound of finely minced beef-suet,* half a teaspoonful of salt, and a quarter one of pepper; mix these into a smooth paste with one well-beaten egg, and a little cold milk or water; make it into the shape of a paste-roller, fold a floured cloth round it, tie the ends tightly, and boil it for two hours. In Kentish farmhouses, and at very plain family dinners, this pudding is usually sent to table with boiled beef, and is sometimes cooked with it also. It is very good sliced and broiled, or browned in a Dutch oven, after having become quite cold.

Flour, 1¼ lb; suet, ½ lb; salt, ½ teaspoonful; half as much pepper; 1 egg; little milk or water: boiled 2 hours.

* A very common fault with bad and careless cooks is, that of using for paste and puddings suet *coarsely chopped,* which is, to many eaters, distasteful to the last degree.

HERODOTUS' PUDDING†
(*A Genuine Classical Receipt*)

'Prepare and mix in the usual manner one pound of fine raisins stoned, one pound of minced beef-suet, half a pound of bread-crumbs, four figs chopped small, two tablespoonsful of moist sugar (*honey*, in the original), two wineglassesful of sherry, and the rind of half a large lemon (grated). Boil the pudding for *fourteen hours.*'

Obs. This receipt is really to be found in Herodotus. The only variations made in it are the substitution of sugar for honey, and sherry for the wine of ancient Greece. We are indebted for it to an accomplished scholar, who has had it served at his own table on more than one occasion; and we have given it on his authority, without testing it: but we venture to suggest that *seven* hours would boil it quite sufficiently.

† [*I have tried this, using honey, and it makes a very fruity, moist pudding, with a good lemony tang.*]

THE PUBLISHER'S PUDDING

This pudding can scarcely be made *too* rich. First blanch, and then beat to the smoothest possible paste, six ounces of fresh Jordan almonds, and a dozen bitter ones; pour very gradually to them, in the mortar, three-quarters of a pint of boiling cream; then turn them into a cloth, and wring it from them again with strong expression. Heat a full half-pint of it afresh, and pour it, as soon as it boils, upon four ounces of fine bread-crumbs, set a plate over, and leave them to become nearly cold; then mix thoroughly with them four ounces of maccaroons, crushed tolerably small; five of finely minced beef-suet, five of marrow, cleared very carefully from fibre, and from the splinters of bone which are sometimes found in it, and shred not very small, two ounces of flour, six of pounded sugar, four of dried cherries, four of the best Muscatel raisins, weighed after they are stoned, half a pound of candied citron, or of citron and orange-rind mixed, a quarter saltspoonful of salt, half a nutmeg, the yolks only of seven full-sized eggs, the grated rind of a large lemon, and last of all, a glass of the best Cognac brandy, which must be stirred briskly in by slow degrees. Pour the mixture into a *thickly* buttered mould or basin, which contains a full quart, fill it to the brim, lay a sheet of buttered writing-paper over, then a well-floured cloth, tie them securely, and boil the pudding for four hours and a quarter; let it stand for two minutes before it is turned out; dish it carefully, and serve it with the German pudding-sauce of page 238.

Jordan almonds, 6 oz; bitter almonds, 12; cream, ¾ pint; bread-crumbs, 4 oz; cream wrung from almonds, ½ pint; crushed maccaroons, 4 oz; flour, 2 oz; beef-suet, 5 oz; marrow, 5 oz; dried cherries, 4 oz; stoned muscatel raisins, 4 oz; pounded sugar, 6 oz; candied citron (or citron and orange-rind mixed), ½ lb; pinch of salt; ½ nutmeg; grated rind, 1 lemon; yolks of eggs, 7; best cognac, 1 wineglassful: boiled in mould or basin, 4¼ hours.

Obs. This pudding, which, if well made, is very light as well as rich, will be sufficiently good for most tastes without the almonds: when they are omitted, the boiling cream must be poured at once to the bread-crumbs.

THE WELCOME GUEST'S OWN PUDDING
(Light and Wholesome – Author's Receipt)

Pour, quite boiling, on four ounces of fine bread-crumbs, an exact half-pint of new milk, or of thin cream; lay a plate over the basin and let them remain until cold; then stir to them four ounces of dry crumbs of bread, four of very finely minced beef kidney suet, a small pinch of salt, three ounces of coarsely crushed ratifias, three ounces of candied citron and orange-rind sliced thin, and the grated rind of one large or of two small lemons. Clear, and whisk four large eggs well, throw to them by degrees four ounces of pounded sugar, and continue to whisk them until it is dissolved, and they are very light; stir them to, and beat them well up with the other ingredients; pour the mixture into a thickly buttered mould, or basin which will contain nearly a quart, and which it should fill to within half-inch of the brim; lay first a buttered paper, then a well floured pudding-cloth over the top, tie them tightly and very securely round, gather up and fasten the corners of the cloth, and boil the pudding for two hours at the utmost. Let it stand for a minute or two before it is dished, and serve it with simple wine sauce, or with that which follows; or with pine-apple or any other *clear* fruit-sauce. (For these last, see page 240.)

Boil very gently, for about ten minutes, a full quarter-pint of water, with the very thin rind of half a fresh lemon, and an ounce and a half of lump sugar; then take out the lemon peel, and stir in a small teaspoonful of arrowroot, smoothly mixed with the strained juice of the lemon (with or without the addition of a little orange juice); take the sauce from the fire, throw in nearly half a glass of pale French brandy, or substitute for this a large wineglassful of sherry, or of any other white wine which may be preferred, but increase a little, in that case, the proportion of arrowroot.

SIR EDWIN LANDSEER'S PUDDING

To convert the preceding into *Sir Edwin Landseer's pudding*, ornament the mould tastefully with small leaves of thin citron-rind and split muscatel raisins in a pattern, and strew the inter-mediate spaces with well cleaned and well dried currants mingled with plenty of candied orange- or lemon-rind shred small. Pour gently in the above pudding mixture, when quite cold, after having added one egg-yolk to it, and steam or boil it the same length of time.

A VERY FINE CABINET PUDDING

Butter thickly a quart mould, and ornament it tastefully with dried cherries, or with the finest muscatel raisins opened and stoned; lay lightly into it a quarter-pound of sponge biscuit† cut in slices, and intermixed with an equal weight of ratifias; sweeten with three ounces of sugar in lumps, and flavour highly with vanilla, or with the thin rind of half a fine lemon, and six sound bitter almonds bruised (should these be preferred), three-quarters of a pint, or rather more, of thin cream, or of cream and new milk mixed; strain and pour this hot to the well-beaten yolks of six eggs and the white of two, and when the mixture is nearly cold, throw in gradually a wineglassful of good brandy; pour it gently, and by degrees, into the mould, and steam or boil the pud-ding very softly for an hour. Serve it with well made wine sauce. Never omit a buttered paper over any sort of custard-mixture; and remember that quick boiling will destroy the good appearance of this kind of pudding. The liquid should be quite cold before it is added to the cake, or the butter on the mould will melt off, and the decorations with it; preserved ginger, and candied citron in slices, may be used to vary these, and the syrup of the former may be added to give flavour to the other ingredients.

Dried cherries, 3 to 4 oz; sponge-biscuits, ¼ lb; ratifias, 4 oz; thin cream, or cream and milk, ¾ pint; sugar, 3 oz; vanilla, ½ pod (or thin rind of ½ lemon and 6 bitter almonds bruised); yolks of 6 eggs, white of 2; brandy, 1 wineglassful (preserved ginger and candied citron at choice): steamed, or gently boiled, 1 hour.

† [*Sometimes called Savoy fingers – a kind of crisp sponge cake shaped like narrow fingers; by ratifias Miss Acton here means small almond-flavoured biscuits: cf. p. 252.*]

THE ELEGANT ECONOMIST'S PUDDING

Butter thickly a plain mould or basin, and line it entirely with slices of cold plum or raisin pudding, cut so as to join closely and neatly together; fill it quite with a good custard; lay, first a buttered paper, and then a floured cloth over it, tie them securely, and boil the pudding gently for an hour; let it stand for ten minutes after it is taken up before it is turned out of the mould. This is a more tasteful mode of serving the remains of a plum-pudding than the usual one of broiling them in slices, or converting them into fritters. The German sauce, well milled or frothed, is generally much relished with sweet boiled puddings, and adds greatly to their good appearance; but common wine or punch sauce, may be sent to table with the above quite as appropriately.

Mould or basin holding 1½ pint, lined with thin slices of plum-pudding; ¾ pint new milk boiled gently 5 minutes with grain of salt, 5 bitter almonds, bruised; sugar in lumps, 2½ oz; thin rind of ½ lemon, strained and mixed directly with 4 large well-beaten eggs; poured into mould while just warm: boiled gently 1 hour.

SMALL AND VERY LIGHT PLUM PUDDING

With three ounces of the crumb of a stale loaf finely grated and soaked in a quarter-pint of boiling milk, mix six ounces of suet minced very small, one ounce of dry bread-crumbs, ten ounces of stoned raisins, a little salt, the grated rind of a China orange, and three eggs, leaving out one white. Boil the pudding for two hours, and serve it with very sweet sauce; put no sugar in it.

VEGETABLE PLUM PUDDING
(*Cheap and good*)

Mix well together one pound of smoothly-mashed potatoes, half a pound of carrots boiled quite tender, and beaten to a paste, one pound of flour, one of currants, and one of raisins (full weight after they are stoned), three-quarters of a pound of sugar, eight ounces of suet, one nutmeg, and quarter of a teaspoonful of salt. Put the pudding into a well-floured cloth, tie it up very closely, and boil it for four hours. The correspondent to whom we are indebted for this receipt says, that the cost of the ingredients does not exceed half a crown, and that the pudding is of sufficient size for a party of sixteen persons. We can vouch for its excellence, but as it is rather apt to break when turned out of the cloth, a couple of eggs would perhaps improve it. It is excellent cold. Sweetmeats, brandy, and spices can be added at pleasure.

Mashed potatoes, 1 lb; carrots, 8 oz; flour, 1 lb; suet, ½ lb; sugar, ¾ lb; currants and raisins, 1 lb each; nutmeg, 1; little salt: 4 hours.

THE AUTHOR'S CHRISTMAS PUDDING

To three ounces of flour, and the same weight of fine, lightly-grated bread-crumbs, add six of beef kidney-suet, chopped small, six of raisins, weighed after they are stoned, six of well-cleaned currants, four ounces of minced apples, five of sugar, two of candied orange-rind, half a teaspoonful of nutmeg, mixed with pounded mace, a very little salt, a small glass of brandy, and three whole eggs. Mix and beat these ingredients well together, tie them tightly in a thickly-floured cloth, and boil them for three hours and a half. We can recommend this as a remarkably light small rich pudding: it may be served with German wine, or punch sauce.

Flour, 3 oz; bread-crumbs, 3 oz; suet, stoned raisins, and currants, each, 6 oz; minced apples, 4 oz; sugar, 5 oz; candied peel, 2 oz; spice, ½ teaspoonful; salt, few grains; brandy, small wineglassful; eggs, 3: 3½ hours.

A BREAD PUDDING

Sweeten a pint of new milk with three ounces of fine sugar, throw in a few grains of salt, and pour it boiling on half a pound of fine and lightly-grated bread-crumbs; add an ounce of fresh butter, and cover them with a plate; let them remain for half an hour or more, and then stir to them four large well-whisked eggs, and a flavouring of nutmeg or of lemon-rind; pour the mixture into a thickly-buttered mould or basin, which holds a pint and a half, and which ought to be quite full; tie a paper and a cloth tightly over, and boil the pudding for exactly an hour and ten minutes. This is quite a plain receipt, but by omitting two ounces of the bread, and adding more butter, one egg, a small glass of brandy, the grated rind of a lemon, and as much sugar as will sweeten the whole richly, a very excellent pudding will be obtained; candied orange-peel also has a good effect when sliced thinly into it; and half a pound of currants, is generally considered a further improvement.

New milk, 1 pint; sugar, 3 oz; salt, few grains; bread-crumbs, ½ lb; eggs, 4 (5, if very small); nutmeg or lemon-rind at pleasure: 1 hour and 10 minutes.

Or: milk, 1 pint; bread-crumbs, 6 oz; butter, 2 to 3 oz; sugar,

4 oz; eggs, 5; brandy, small glassful; rind, 1 lemon. Further additions at choice: candied peel, 1½ oz; currants ½ lb.

CHEAP RICE PUDDING

Wash six ounces of rice, mix it with three-quarters of a pound of raisins, tie them in a well-floured cloth, giving them plenty of room to swell; boil them exactly an hour and three-quarters, and serve the pudding with very sweet sauce: this is a nice dish for the nursery. A pound of apples pared, cored, and quartered, will also make a very wholesome pudding, mixed with the rice, and boiled from an hour and a quarter to an hour and a half; and *sultana* raisins and rice will give another good variety of this simple pudding.

Rice, 6 oz; raisins, ¾ lb: 1¾ hour. Or, rice, 6 oz; apples, 1 lb: 1¼ to 1½ hour.

FASHIONABLE APPLE DUMPLINGS†

These are boiled in small *knitted* or closely-netted cloths (the former have, we think, the prettiest effect), which give quite an ornamental appearance to an otherwise homely dish. Take out the cores without dividing the apples, which should be large, and of a good boiling kind, and fill the cavities with orange or lemon marmalade; enclose them in a good crust rolled thin, draw the cloths round them, tie them closely, and boil them for three-quarters of an hour. Lemon dumplings may be boiled in the same way.

¾ to 1 hour, if the apples be *not* of the best boiling kind.

† [*These are probably delicious. I have not tried them, but it makes Miss Acton's day seem remote and leisured that one should* knit *cloths for dumplings!*]

SUFFOLK, OR HARD DUMPLINGS

Mix a little salt with some flour, and make it into smooth and rather lithe paste, with cold water or skimmed milk; form it into dumplings, and throw them into boiling water: in half an hour they will be ready to serve. A better kind of dumpling is made by adding sufficient milk to the flour to form a thick batter, and then tying the dumplings in small well-floured cloths. In Suffolk farm-houses, they are served with the dripping-pan gravy of roast meat; and they are sometimes made very small indeed, and boiled with stewed shin of beef.

BOILED RICE, TO BE SERVED WITH STEWED FRUITS, PRESERVES, OR RASPBERRY VINEGAR

Take out the discoloured grains from half a pound of good rice; and wash it in several waters; tie it very loosely in a pudding cloth, put it into cold water; heat it slowly, and boil it for quite an hour, it will then be quite solid and resemble a pudding in appearance. Sufficient room must be given to allow the grain to swell to its full size, or it will be hard; but too much space will render the whole watery. With a little experience, the cook will easily ascertain the exact degree to be allowed for it. Four ounces of rice will require quite three-quarters of an hour's boiling; a little more or less of time will sometimes be needed, from the difference of quality in the grain. It should be put into an abundant quantity of water, which should be cold, and then very slowly heated.

Carolina rice, ½ lb: boiled 1 hour. 4 oz: ¾ hour.

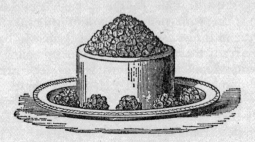

21

Pudding garnished with Preserves

BAKED PUDDINGS

THE PRINTER'S PUDDING

Grate very lightly six ounces of the crumb of a stale loaf, and put it into a deep dish. Dissolve in a quart of cold new milk four ounces of good Lisbon sugar; add it to five large, well-whisked eggs, strain, and mix them with the bread-crumbs; stir in two ounces of a fresh finely-grated cocoa-nut; add a flavouring of nutmeg or of lemon-rind, and the slightest pinch of salt; let the pudding stand for a couple of hours to soak the bread; and bake it in a gentle oven for three-quarters of an hour: it will be excellent if carefully made, and not too quickly baked. When the cocoa-nut is not at hand, an ounce of butter just dissolved, should be poured over the dish before the crumbs are put into it; and the rind of an entire lemon may be used to give it flavour; but the cocoa-nut imparts a peculiar richness when it is good and fresh.

Bread-crumbs, 6 oz; new milk, 1 quart; sugar, 4 oz; eggs, 5; cocoa-nut, 2 oz (or rind, 1 large lemon, and 1 oz butter); slightest pinch of salt: to stand 2 hours. Baked in gentle oven full ¾ hour.

Obs. When a very sweet pudding is liked, the proportion of sugar may be increased.

THE YOUNG WIFE'S PUDDING
(Author's Receipt)

Break separately into a cup four perfectly sweet eggs, and with the point of a small three-pronged fork clear them from the specks. Throw them, as they are done, into a large basin, or a bowl, and beat them up lightly for four or five minutes; then add by degrees two ounces and a half of pounded sugar, with a very small pinch of salt, and whisk the mixture well, holding the fork rather loosely between the thumb and fingers; next, grate in the rind of a quite fresh lemon, or substitute for it a tablespoonful of lemon-brandy, or of orange-flower water, which should be thrown in by degrees and stirred briskly to the eggs. Add a pint of cold new milk, and pour the pudding into a well buttered dish. Slice some stale bread, something more than a quarter of an inch thick, and with a very small cake-cutter cut sufficient rounds from it to cover the top of the pudding; butter them thickly with good butter; lay them, with the dry side undermost, upon the pudding, sift sugar thickly on them, and set the dish gently into a Dutch or American oven, which should be placed at the distance of a foot or more from a moderate fire. An hour of very *slow baking* will be just sufficient to render the pudding firm throughout; but should the fire be fierce, or the oven placed too near it, the receipt will fail.

Obs. We give minute directions for this dish, because though simple, it is very delicate and good, and the same instructions will serve for all the varieties of it which follow. The cook who desires to succeed with them, must take the trouble to regulate properly the heat of the oven in which they are baked. When it is necessary to place them in that of the kitchen-range the door should be left open for a time to cool it down (should it be very hot), before they are placed in it; and they may be set upon a plate or dish reversed, if the iron should still remain greatly heated.

(Author's Receipt)

Lay into a rather deep tart-dish some thin slices of French roll very slightly spread with butter and covered with a thick layer of mincemeat; place a second tier lightly on these, covered in the same way with the mincemeat; then pour gently in a custard made with three well-whisked eggs, three-quarters of a pint of new milk or thin cream, the slightest pinch of salt, and two ounces of sugar. Let the pudding stand to soak for an hour, then bake it gently until it is quite firm in the centre: this will be in from three-quarters of an hour to a full hour.

BAKEWELL PUDDING

This pudding is famous not only in Derbyshire, but in several of our northern counties, where it is usually served on all holiday-occasions. Line a shallow tart-dish with quite an inch-deep layer of several kinds of good preserve mixed together, and inter-mingle with them from two to three ounces of candied citron or orange-rind. Beat well the yolks of ten eggs, and add to them gradually half a pound of sifted sugar; when they are well mixed, pour in by degrees half a pound of good clarified butter, and a little ratifia† or any other flavour that may be preferred; fill the dish two-thirds full with this mixture, and bake the pudding for nearly an hour in a moderate oven. Half the quantity will be sufficient for a small dish.

Mixed preserves, 1½ to 2 lb; yolks of eggs, 10; sugar, ½ lb; butter, ½ lb; ratifia,† lemon-brandy, or other flavouring, to the taste: baked, moderate oven, ¾ to 1 hour.

Obs. This is a rich and expensive, but not very refined pudding. A variation of it, known in the south as an Alderman's Pudding, is we think, superior to it. It is made without the candied peel, and with a layer of apricot-jam only, six ounces of butter, six of sugar, the yolks of six, and the whites of two eggs.

† [*A liqueur flavoured with almonds or peach kernels.*]

We have already given a receipt for an exceedingly good boiled pudding bearing this title, but we think the baked one answers even better, and it is made with rather more facility. Butter a deep tart-dish well, cut the slices of plum-pudding to join exactly in lining it, and press them against it lightly to make them adhere, as without this precaution they are apt to float off; pour in as much custard (previously thickened and left to become cold), or any other sweet pudding mixture, as will fill the dish almost to the brim; cover the top with thin slices of the plum pudding, and bake it in a slow oven from thirty minutes to a full hour, according to the quantity and quality of the contents. One pint of new milk poured boiling on an ounce and a half of *tous-les-mois*, smoothly mixed with a quarter of a pint of cold milk, makes with the addition of four ounces of sugar, four small eggs, a little lemon-grate, and two or three bitter almonds, or a few drops of ratifia, an excellent pudding of this kind; it should be baked nearly three-quarters of an hour in quite a slow oven. Two ounces and a half of arrowroot may be used in lieu of the *tous-les-mois*.

RICH BREAD AND BUTTER PUDDING

Give a good flavour of lemon-rind and bitter almonds, or of cinnamon, if preferred, to a pint of new milk, and when it has simmered a sufficient time for this, strain and mix it with a quarter-pint of rich cream; sweeten it with four ounces of sugar in lumps, and stir it while still hot to five well-beaten eggs; throw in a few grains of salt, and move the mixture briskly with a spoon as a glass of brandy is added to it. Have ready in a thickly-buttered dish three layers of thin bread and butter cut from a half-quartern loaf, with four ounces of currants, and one and a half of finely shred candied peel, strewed between and over them; pour the eggs and milk on them by degrees, letting the bread absorb one portion before another is added: it should soak for a couple of hours before the pudding is taken to the oven, which should be a moderate one. Half an hour will bake it. It is very good when made with new milk only; and some persons use no more than a pint of liquid in all, but part of the whites of the eggs may then be omitted. Cream may be substituted for the entire quantity of milk at pleasure.

New milk, 1 pint; rind of small lemon, and 6 bitter almonds bruised (or ½ drachm of cinnamon): simmered 10 to 20 minutes. Cream, ¼ pint; sugar, 4 oz; eggs, 5; brandy, 1 wineglassful. Bread and butter, 3 layers; currants, 4 oz; candied orange- or lemon-rind, 1½ oz: to stand 2 hours, and to be baked 30 minutes in a moderate oven.

SUTHERLAND, OR CASTLE PUDDINGS

Take an equal weight of eggs in the shell, of good butter, of fine dry flour, and of sifted sugar. First, whisk the eggs for ten minutes or until they appear extremely light: then throw in the sugar by degrees, and continue the whisking for four or five minutes; next, strew in the flour, also gradually, and when it appears smoothly blended with the other ingredients, pour the butter to them in small portions, each of which should be beaten in until there is no appearance of it left. It should previously be just liquefied with the least possible degree of heat: this may be effected by putting it into a well-warmed saucepan, and shaking it round until it is dissolved. A grain or two of salt should be thrown in with the flour; and the rind of half a fine lemon rasped on sugar or grated, or some pounded mace, or any other flavour can be added at choice. Pour the mixture directly it is ready into well-buttered cups, and bake the puddings from twenty to twenty-five minutes. When cold they resemble good pound cakes, and may be served as such. Wine sauce should be sent to table with them.

Eggs, 4; their weight in flour, sugar, and butter; *little* salt; flavouring of pounded mace or lemon-rind.

Obs. Three eggs are sufficient for a small dish of these

puddings, They may be varied with an ounce or two of candied citron; or with a spoonful of brandy, or a little orange-flower water. The mode we have given of making them will be found perfectly successful if our directions be followed with exactness. In a slow oven they will not be too much baked in half an hour.

MADELEINE PUDDINGS
(To be served cold)

Take the same ingredients as for the Sutherland puddings, but clarify an additional ounce of butter; skim, and then fill some round tin pattypans with it almost to the brim; pour it from one to the other until all have received a sufficient coating to prevent the puddings from adhering to them, and leave half a teaspoonful in each; mix the remainder with the eggs, sugar, and flour, beat the whole up very lightly, fill the pans about two-thirds full, and put them directly into a rather brisk oven, but draw them towards the mouth of it when they are sufficiently coloured; from fifteen to eighteen minutes will bake them. Turn them out, and drain them on a sheet of paper. When they are quite cold, with the point of the knife take out a portion of the tops, hollow the puddings a little, and fill them with rich apricot jam, well mixed with half its weight of pounded almonds, of which two in every ounce should be bitter ones.

A GOOD FRENCH RICE PUDDING, OR GÂTEAU DE RIZ

Swell gently in a quart of new milk, or in equal parts of milk and cream, seven ounces of the best Carolina rice, which has been cleared of the discoloured grains, and washed and drained; when it is tolerably tender, add to it three ounces of fresh butter, and five of sugar roughly powdered, a *few* grains of salt, and the lightly grated rind of a fine lemon, and simmer the whole until the rice is swollen to the utmost; then take it from the fire, let it cool a little, and stir to it quickly, and by degrees, the well-beaten yolks of six full-sized eggs. Pour into a small copper stewpan a couple of ounces of clarified butter, and incline it in such a manner that it may receive an equal coating in every part; then turn it upside down for an instant, to drain off the superfluous butter; next, throw in some exceedingly fine light crumbs of stale bread, and shake them entirely over it, turn out those which do not adhere, and with a small brush or feather sprinkle more clarified butter slightly on those which line the pan. Whisk quickly the whites of the eggs to snow, stir them gently to the rice, and pour the mixture softly into the stewpan, that the bread-crumbs may not be displaced; put it immediately into a *moderate* oven, and let it remain in a full hour. It will then, if properly baked, turn out from the mould or pan well browned, quite firm, and having the appearance of a cake; but a fierce heat will cause it to break, and present an altogether unsightly appearance. In a very slow oven, a longer time must be allowed for it.

New milk, or milk and cream, 1 quart; Carolina rice, 7 oz: ¾ hour. Fresh butter, 3 oz; sugar, in lumps, 5 oz; rind, 1 large lemon: ¾ to 1¼ hours. Eggs, 6: baked in a moderate oven, 1 hour.

Obs. An excellent variety of this *gâteau* is made with cocoa-nut flavoured milk, or cream, or with either of these poured boiling on six ounces of Jordan almonds, finely pounded, and mixed with a dozen bitter ones, then wrung from them with strong pressure; it may likewise be flavoured with vanilla, or with candied orange-blossoms, and covered at the instant it is dished with strawberry, apple, or any other clear jelly.

RICE PUDDING MERINGUÉ

Swell gently four ounces of Carolina rice in a pint and a quarter of milk or of thin cream; let it cool a little, and stir to it an ounce and a half of butter, three of pounded sugar, a grain or two of salt, the grated rind of a small lemon, and the yolks of four large, or of five small eggs. Pour the mixture into a well-buttered dish, and lay lightly and equally over the top the whites of four eggs beaten as for sponge cakes, and mixed at the instant with from four to five heaped tablespoonsful of sifted sugar. Bake the pudding half an hour in a moderate oven, but do not allow the *meringue* to be too deeply coloured; it should be of a clear brown, and very crisp. Serve it directly it is taken from the oven.

Rice, 4 oz; milk, or cream, 1¼ pint; butter, 1½ oz; sugar, 3 oz; rind, 1 lemon; yolks of eggs, 4 or 5; the whites beaten to snow, and mixed with as many tablespoonsful of sifted sugar: baked ½ hour, moderate oven.

COMMON GROUND-RICE PUDDING

One pint and a half of milk, three ounces and a half of rice, three of Lisbon sugar, one and a half of butter, some nutmeg, or lemon-grate, and four eggs, baked slowly for half an hour, or more, if not quite firm.

POTATO PUDDING

With a pound and a quarter of fine mealy potatoes, boiled very dry, and mashed perfectly smooth while hot, mix three ounces of butter, five or six of sugar, five eggs, a few grains of salt, and the grated rind of a small lemon. Pour the mixture into a well-buttered dish, and bake it in a moderate oven for nearly three-quarters of an hour. It should be turned out and sent to table with fine sugar sifted over it, or for variety, red currant jelly, or any other preserve, may be spread on it as soon as it is dished.

Potatoes, 1¼ lb; butter, 3 oz; sugar, 5 or 6 oz; eggs, 5 or 6; lemon-rind, 1; salt, few grains: 40 to 45 minutes.

Obs. When cold, this pudding eats like cake, and may be served as such, omitting of course, the sugar or preserve when it is dished.

Beat well together fourteen ounces of mashed potatoes, four ounces of butter, four of fine sugar, five eggs, the grated rind of a small lemon, and a slight pinch of salt; add half a glass of brandy, and pour the pudding into a thickly-buttered dish or mould, ornamented with slices of candied orange- or lemon-rind; pour a little clarified butter on the top, and then sift plenty of white sugar over it.

Potatoes, 14 oz; butter, 4 oz; sugar, 4 oz; eggs, 5; lemon-rind, 1; little salt; brandy, ½ glassful; candied peel, 1 to 2 oz: 40 minutes.

Obs. The potatoes for these receipts should be lightly and carefully mashed, but never pounded in a mortar as that will convert them into a heavy paste, or they may be grated while hot through a wire sieve. From a quarter to a half-pint of cream is, by many cooks, added always to potato puddings.

CAKE AND CUSTARD, AND VARIOUS OTHER INEXPENSIVE PUDDINGS

Even when very dry, the remains of a sponge or a Savoy cake will serve excellently for a pudding, if lightly broken up, or crumbled and intermixed or not, with a few ratifias or macaroons, which should also be broken up. A custard composed of four eggs to the pint of milk if small, and three if very large and fresh, and not very highly sweetened, should be poured over the cake half an hour at least before it is placed in the oven (which should be *slow*); and any flavour given to it which may be liked. An economical and clever cook will seldom be at a loss for compounding an inexpensive and good pudding in this way. More or less of the cake can be used as may be convenient. Part of a mould of sweet rice and various other preparations may be turned to account in a similar manner; but the custard should be perfectly and equally mingled with whatever other ingredients are used. Macaroni boiled tender in milk, or in milk and water, will make an excellent pudding; and sago stewed very thick, will supply another; the custard may be mixed with this last while it is still just warm. Two ounces well washed, and slowly heated in a pint of liquid will be tender in from fifteen to twenty minutes. All these puddings will require a gentle oven, and will be ready to serve when they are firm in the centre, and do not stick to a knife when plunged into it.

BAKED APPLE PUDDING, OR CUSTARD

Weigh a pound of good boiling apples after they are pared and cored, and stew them to a perfectly smooth marmalade, with six ounces of sugar, and a spoonful or two of wine; stir them often that they may not stick to the pan. Mix with them while they are still quite hot, three ounces of butter, the grated rind and the strained juice of a lemon, and lastly stir in by degrees the well-beaten yolks of five eggs, and a dessertspoonful of flour, or in lieu of the last, three or four Naples' biscuits, or macaroons crushed small. Bake the pudding for a full half hour in a moderate oven, or longer should it be not quite firm in the middle. A little clarified butter poured on the top, with sugar sifted over, improves all baked puddings.

Apples, 1 lb; sugar, 6 oz; wine, 1 glassful; butter, 3 oz; juice and rind, 1 lemon; 5 eggs: ½ hour, or more.

Obs. Many cooks press the apples through a sieve after they are boiled, but this is not needful when they are of a good kind, and stewed, and beaten smooth.

GABRIELLE'S PUDDING, OR SWEET CASSEROLE OF RICE

Wash half a pound of the best Carolina rice, drain it on a hair-sieve, put it into a very clean stewpan or saucepan, and pour on it a quart of cold new milk. Stir them well together, and place them near the fire that the rice may swell very gradually; then let it simmer as gently as possible for about half an hour, or until it begins to be quite tender; mix with it then, two ounces of fresh butter and two and a half of pounded sugar, and let it continue to simmer softly until it is dry and sufficiently tender,* to be easily crushed to a smooth paste with a strong wooden spoon. Work it to this point, and then let it cool. Before it is taken from the fire, scrape into it the outside of some sugar which has been rubbed upon the rind of a fresh lemon. Have ready a tin mould of pretty form, well buttered in every part; press the rice into it while it is still warm, smooth the surface, and let it remain until cold. Should the mould be one which opens at the ends, the pudding will come out easily; but if it should be in a plain common one, just dip it into hot water to loosen it; turn out the rice, and then again reverse it on to a tin or dish, and with the point of a knife mark round the top a rim of about an inch wide; then brush some clarified butter over the whole pudding, and set it into a brisk oven. When it is of an equal light golden brown draw it out, raise the cover carefully where it is marked, scoop out the rice from the inside, leaving only a crust of about an inch thick in every part, and pour into it some preserved fruit warmed in its own syrup, or fill it with a *compôte* of plums or peaches (see Chapter 23); or with some good apples boiled with fine sugar to a smooth rich marmalade. This is a very good as well as an elegant dish: it may be enriched with more butter, and by substituting cream for the milk in part or entirely, but it is excellent without either.

Rice, ½ lb; new milk, 1 quart: ½ hour. Fresh butter, 2 oz; pounded sugar, 2½ oz; rasped rind, 1 lemon: ½ hour or more.

Obs. The precise time of baking the pudding cannot well be specified: it only requires colour.

* Unless the rice be boiled slowly, and *very dry*, it will not answer for the casserole.

THE POOR AUTHOR'S PUDDING†

Flavour a quart of new milk by boiling in it for a few minutes half a stick of well-bruised cinnamon, or the thin rind of a small lemon; add a few grains of salt, and three ounces of sugar, and turn the whole into a deep basin: when it is quite cold, stir to it three well-beaten eggs, and strain the mixture into a pie-dish. Cover the top entirely with slices of bread free from crust, and half an inch thick, cut so as to join neatly, and buttered on both sides: bake the pudding in a moderate oven for about half an hour, or in a Dutch oven before the fire.

New milk, 1 quart; cinnamon, or lemon-rind; sugar, 3 oz; little salt; eggs, 3; buttered bread: baked ½ hour.

† [*A marked contrast to 'Publisher's Pudding' which 'can scarcely be made too rich'. In fact, this is very good, and a rather richer and grander version of it appears nowadays (as 'Bread and Butter Pudding') as a speciality of the Connaught Hotel, London.*]

THE CURATE'S PUDDING

Wash, wipe, and pare some quickly grown rhubarb-stalks, cut them into short lengths, and put a layer of them into a deep dish with a spoonful or two of Lisbon sugar; cover these evenly with part of a penny roll [*or thin slices of bread*] sliced thin; and add another thick layer of fruit and sugar, then one of bread, then another of the rhubarb; cover this last with a deep layer of fine bread-crumbs well mingled with about a tablespoonful of sugar, pour a little clarified butter over them, and send the pudding to a brisk oven. From thirty to forty minutes will bake it. Good boiling apples sliced, sweetened, and flavoured with nutmeg or grated lemon-rind, and covered with well buttered slices of bread, make an excellent pudding of this kind, and so do black currants likewise, without the butter.

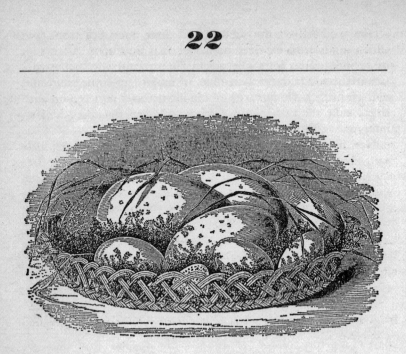

22

EGGS AND MILK

TO COOK EGGS IN THE SHELL WITHOUT BOILING THEM
(An admirable Receipt)

This mode of dressing eggs is not *new*; it seems, indeed, to have been known in years long past, but not to have received the attention which its excellence deserved. We saw it mentioned with much commendation in a most useful little periodical, called the *Cottage Gardener*, and had it tested immediately with various modifications and with entire success. After many trials, we give the following as the *best* and most uniform in its results of our numerous experiments. First, put some boiling water into a large basin – a slop-basin for example – and let it remain for a few seconds, then turn it out, lay in the egg (or eggs), and roll it over, to take the chill off the shell, that it may not crack from the sudden application of heat; and pour in – and upon the egg – *quite boiling* water from a kettle, until it is completely immersed; put a plate over it instantly, and let it remain, upon the table, for twelve minutes, when it will be found perfectly and beautifully cooked, entirely free from all flavour and appearance of *rawness*, and yet so lightly and delicately dressed as to suit even persons who cannot take eggs at all when boiled in the usual way. It should be turned when something more than half done, but the plate should be replaced as quickly as possible. Two eggs will require scarcely more time than one; but some additional minutes must be allowed for any number beyond that. The process may always be quickened by changing the water when it has cooled a little, for more that is fast boiling: the eggs may, in fact, be rendered quite hard by the same means, but then no advantage is obtained over the old method of cooking them.

12 minutes.

Obs. This is one of the receipts which we have re-produced here from our cookery for invalids, on account of its adaptation to the taste generally.

TO POACH EGGS

Take for this purpose a wide and delicately clean pan about half-filled with the clearest spring-water; throw in a small salt-spoonful of salt, and place it over a fire quite free from smoke. Break some new-laid eggs into separate cups, and do this with care, that the yolks may not be injured. When the water boils, draw back the pan, glide the eggs gently into it, and let them stand until the whites appear almost set, which will be in about a minute: then, without shaking them, move the pan over the fire, and just simmer them from two minutes and a half to three minutes. Lift them out separately with a slice, trim quickly off the ragged edges, and serve them upon dressed spinach, or upon minced veal, turkey, or chicken; or dish them for an invalid, upon delicately toasted bread, sliced thick, and freed from crust:

it is an improvement to have the bread buttered, but it is then less wholesome.

Comparative time of poaching eggs. Swans' eggs, 5 to 6 minutes. (In basin, 10 minutes.) Turkeys' eggs, 4 minutes. Hens' eggs, 3 to 3½ minutes. Guinea-fowls', 2 to 3 minutes. Bantams', 2 minutes.

Obs. All eggs may be poached *without boiling* if kept just at simmering point, but *one boil* quite at last will assist to detach them from the stewpan, from which they should always be very carefully lifted on what is called a fish or *egg-slice*. There are pans made on purpose for poaching and frying them in good form; but they do not, we believe, answer particularly well. If broken into cups slightly rubbed with butter, and simmered in them, their roundness of shape will be best preserved.

POACHED EGGS WITH GRAVY
(*Entremets – Oeufs Pochés au Jus*)

Dress the eggs as above, giving them as good an appearance as possible, lay them into a very hot dish, and sauce them with some rich, clear, boiling veal gravy, or with some *Espagnole*. Each egg, for variety, may be dished upon a *croûton* of bread cut with a fluted paste-cutter, and fried a pale brown: the sauce should then be poured round not over them.

Poaching is the best mode of dressing a swan's egg,* as it renders it more than any other delicate in flavour; it is usually served on a bed of spinach. Only the eggs of quite young swans are suited to the table; one is sufficient for a dish. It may be laid on a large *croûton* of fried bread, and sauced with highly flavoured gravy, or with tomata-sauce well seasoned with eschalots.

* We fear that want of space must compel us to omit some other receipts for swans' eggs, which we had prepared for this chapter.

A pewter or any other metal plate or dish which will bear the fire, must be used for these. Just melt a slice of butter in it, then put in some very fresh eggs broken as for poaching; strew a little pepper and salt on the top of each, and place them over a gentle fire until the whites are quite set, but keep them free from colour.

This is a very common mode of preparing eggs on the continent; but there is generally a slight rawness of the surface of the yolks which is in a measure removed by ladling the boiling butter over them with a spoon as they are cooking, though a salamander held above them for a minute would have a better effect. Four or five minutes will dress them.

DEVONSHIRE, OR CLOTTED CREAM

From the mode adopted in Devonshire, and in some other counties, of scalding the milk in the following manner, the cream becomes very rich and thick, and is easily converted into excellent butter. It is strained into large shallow metal pans as soon as it is brought into the dairy and left for twelve hours at least in summer, and thirty-six in cold weather. It is then gently carried to a hot plate – heated by a fire from below – and brought *slowly* to a quite scalding heat but without being allowed to boil or even to simmer. When it is ready to be removed, distinct rings appear on the surface, and small bubbles of air. It must then be carried carefully back to the dairy, and may be skimmed in twelve hours afterwards. The cream should be well drained from the milk – which will be very poor – as this is done. It may then be converted into excellent butter, merely by beating it with the hand in a shallow wooden tub, which is, we are informed, the usual manner of making it in small Devonshire dairies.

Boil a quart of new milk, and let it cool sufficiently to allow the cream to be taken off; then rinse an earthen jar well in every part with buttermilk, and while the boiled milk is still rather warm, pour it in and add the cream gently on the top. Let it remain twenty-four hours, turn it into a deep dish, mix it with pounded sugar, and it will be ready to serve. This preparation is much eaten abroad during the summer, and is considered very wholesome. The milk by the foregoing process, becomes a very soft curd, *slightly*, but not at all unpleasantly, acid in flavour. A cover, or thick folded cloth, should be placed on the jar after the milk is poured in, and it should be kept in a moderately warm place. In very sultry weather less time may be allowed for the milk to stand.

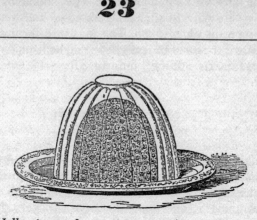

23

Jelly of two colours, with macedoine *of fruit*

SWEET DISHES, OR ENTREMETS

PREPARED, APPLE OR QUINCE JUICE

Pour into a clean earthen pan two quarts of spring water, and throw into it as quickly as they can be pared, quartered, and weighed, four pounds of nonsuches, pearmains, Ripstone pippins, or any other good boiling apples of fine flavour. When all are done, stew them gently until they are well broken, but not reduced quite to pulp; turn them into a jelly-bag, or strain the juice from them without pressure through a closely-woven cloth, which should be gathered over the fruit, and tied, and suspended above a deep pan until the juice ceases to drop from it: this, if not very clear, must be rendered so before it is used for syrup or jelly, but for all other purposes once straining it will be sufficient. Quinces are prepared in the same way, and with the same proportions of fruit and water, but they must not be too long boiled, or the juice will become red. We have found it answer well to have them simmered until they are perfectly tender, and then to leave them with their liquor in a bowl until the following day, when the juice will be rich and clear. They should be thrown into the water very quickly after they are pared and weighed, as the air will soon discolour them. The juice will form a jelly much more easily if the cores and pips be left in the fruit.

Water, 2 quarts; apples or quinces, 4 lb.

COMPÔTES OF FRUIT
(*Or Fruit stewed in Syrup*)

We would especially recommend these delicate and very agreeable preparations for trial to such of our readers as may be unacquainted with them, as well as to those who may have a distaste to the common '*stewed fruit*' of English cookery. If well made they are peculiarly delicious and refreshing, preserving the pure flavour of the fruit of which they are composed; while its acidity is much softened by the small quantity of water added to form the syrup in which it is boiled. They are also more economical than tarts or puddings, and infinitely more wholesome. In the second course pastry-crust can always be served with them, if desired, in the form of ready baked leaves, round cakes, or any more fanciful shapes; or a border of these may be fastened with a little white of egg and flour round the edge of the dish in which the *compôte* is served; but rice, or maccaroni simply boiled, or a very plain pudding is a more usual accompaniment.

Compôte of spring fruit. – (Rhubarb). Take a pound of the stalks after they are pared, and cut them into short lengths; have ready a quarter-pint of water boiled gently for ten minutes with five ounces of sugar, or with six should the fruit be very acid; put it in, and simmer it for about ten minutes. Some kinds will be tender in rather less time, some will require more.

Compôte of green gooseberries. – This is an excellent *compôte* if made with fine sugar, and very good with any kind. Break five ounces into small lumps and pour on them half-pint of water; boil these gently for ten minutes, and clear off all the scum; then add to them a pint of fresh gooseberries freed from the tops and stalks, washed, and well drained. Simmer them gently from eight

268

to ten minutes, and serve them hot or cold. Increase the quantity for a large dish.

Compôte of red currants. – A quarter-pint of water and five ounces of sugar: ten minutes. One pint of currants free from the stalks to be just simmered in the syrup from five to seven minutes. This receipt will serve equally for raspberries, or for a *compôte* of the two fruits mixed together. Either of them will be found an admirable accompaniment to a pudding of batter, custard, bread, or ground-rice, and also to various other kinds of puddings, as well as to whole rice plainly boiled.

Compôte of Kentish or Flemish cherries. – Simmer five ounces of sugar with half-pint of water for ten minutes; throw into the syrup a pound of cherries weighed after they are stalked, and let them stew gently for twenty minutes: it is a great improvement to stone the fruit, but a large quantity will then be required for a dish.

Compôte of the green Magnum-Bonum or Mogul plum. – The green Mogul plums are often brought abundantly into the market when the fruit is thinned from the trees, and they make admirable tarts or *compôtes*, possessing the fine slightly bitter flavour of the unripe apricot, to which they are quite equal. Measure a pint of the plums without their stalks, and wash them very clean; then throw them into a syrup made with seven ounces of sugar in lumps, and half-pint of water, boiled together for eight or ten minutes. Give the plums one quick boil, and then let them stew quite softly for about five minutes, or until they are tender, which occasionally will be in less time even. Take off the scum, and serve the *compôte* hot or cold.

Compôte of Siberian crabs. – To three-quarters of a pint of water add six ounces of fine sugar, boil them for ten or twelve minutes, and skim them well. Add a pound and a half of Siberian crabs [*small, very sharp-flavoured apples*] without their stalks, and keep them just at the point of boiling for twenty minutes; they will then become tender without bursting. A few strips of lemon-rind and a little of the juice are sometimes added to this *compôte*.

Obs. In a dry warm summer, when fruit ripens freely, and is rich in quality, the proportion of sugar directed for these *compôtes* would generally be found sufficient; but in a cold or wet season it would certainly, in many instances, require to be increased. The present slight difference in the cost of sugars, renders it a poor economy to use the raw for dishes of this class, instead of that which is well refined. To make a clear syrup it should be broken into lumps, not crushed to powder. Almost every kind of fruit may be converted into a good *compôte*.

COMPÔTE OF PEACHES

Pare half a dozen ripe peaches, and stew them very softly from eighteen to twenty minutes, keeping them often turned in a light syrup, made with five ounces of sugar, and half-pint of water boiled together for ten minutes. Dish the fruit; reduce the syrup by quick boiling, pour it over the peaches, and serve them hot for a second-course dish, or cold for dessert. They should be quite ripe, and will be found delicious dressed thus. A little lemon-juice may be added to the syrup, and the blanched kernels of two or three peach or apricot stones.

Sugar, 5 oz; water, ½ pint: 10 minutes. Peaches, 6: 18 to 20 minutes.

Obs. Nectarines, without being pared, may be dressed in the same way, but will require to be stewed somewhat longer, unless they be quite ripe.

BLACK CAPS PAR EXCELLENCE
(*For the Second-course, or for Dessert*)

Cut a dozen fine Norfolk biffins in two without paring them, scoop out the cores, and fill the cavities with thin strips of fresh lemon-rind and with candied orange-peel. Cover the bottom of a flat shallow tin with a thick layer of fine pale brown sugar, press the two halves of each apple together, and place them close in the tin; pour half a bottle of raisin or of any other sweet wine over them, and be careful to moisten the tops of all; sift white sugar thickly on them, and set the tin into a very hot oven at first, that the outsides of the apples may catch or become black; then draw them to the mouth of the oven, and bake them gently until they are soft quite through. The Norfolk biffin answers for this dish far better than any other kind of apple, but the winter queening, and some few firm sorts beside, can be used for it with fair success. These for variety may be cored without being divided, and filled with orange marmalade. The black caps served hot, as a second-course dish, are excellent.

Norfolk biffins, 12; rinds fresh lemons, 1 to 2; candied orange-rind, 2 to 3 oz; pale brown sugar, ¾ lb; raisin or other wine, ½ bottle; little sifted sugar: ¾ to 1 hour, or more.

Obs. The apples dressed as above, resemble a *rich confection*, and will remain good for ten days or a fortnight; sometimes much longer even. The receipt is an admirable one.

GÂTEAU DE POMMES

Boil together for fifteen minutes a pound of well-refined sugar and half-pint of water; then add a couple of pounds of non-suches, or of any other finely-flavoured apples which can be boiled easily to a smooth pulp, and the juice of a couple of small, or of one very large lemon. Stew these gently until the mixture is perfectly free from lumps, then boil it quickly, keeping it stirred, without quitting it, until it forms a very thick and dry mar-malade. A few minutes before it is done add the finely grated rinds of a couple of lemons; when it leaves the bottom of the preserving-pan visible and dry, press it into moulds of tasteful form; and either store it for winter use, or if wanted for table, serve it plain for dessert, or ornament it with spikes of blanched almonds, and pour a custard round it for a second-course dish (*entremets*).

Sugar, 1 lb; water, ½ pint: 15 minutes. Nonsuches or other apples, 2 lb; juice, 1 large or 2 small lemons: 2 hours or more.

Modern Jelly Mould

MODERN VARIETIES OF CALF'S FEET JELLY

In modern cookery a number of excellent jellies are made with the stock of calves' feet, variously flavoured. Many of them are compounded entirely without wine, a small quantity of some fine liqueur being used as a substitute; and sometimes cinnamon, or vanilla, or Seville orange-rind with a slight portion of acid, takes place of this. For aristocratic tables, indeed, it is the present fashion to serve them very lightly and delicately flavoured. Their cost is thus materially diminished. Fresh strawberries dropped into clear calf's feet jelly just before it sets, impart a delicious fragrance to it, when they are of a choice kind; and other fruit is mingled with it often; but none has so good an effect, though many sorts when tastefully employed give an excellent appearance to it.

ORANGE ISINGLASS JELLY

To render this perfectly transparent the juice of the fruit must be filtered, and the isinglass clarified; but it is not usual to take so much trouble for it. Strain as clear as possible; first through a sieve or muslin, then through a thick cloth or jelly bag, one quart of China orange-juice, mixed with as much lemon-juice as will give it an agreeable degree of acidity, or with a small proportion of Seville orange-juice. Dissolve two ounces and a half of isinglass in a pint of water, skim it well, throw in half a pound of sugar, and a few strips of the orange-rind, pour in the orange-juice, stir the whole well together, skim it clean without allowing it to boil, strain it through a cloth or through a muslin, many times folded, and when nearly cold put it into the moulds.* This jelly is sometimes made without any water, by dissolving the isinglass and sugar in the juice of the fruit.

Orange-juice, 1 quart; water, 1 pint; isinglass, 2½ oz;† sugar, ½ lb.

* In France, orange-jelly is very commonly served in the halved rinds of the fruit, or in little baskets made as we shall hereafter direct.

† [*Gelatine now takes the place of isinglass.*]

ORANGES FILLED WITH JELLY

This is one of the fanciful dishes which make a pretty appearance on a supper table, and are acceptable when much variety is desired. Take some very fine China oranges, and with the point of a small knife cut out from the top of each a round about the size of a shilling; then with the small end of a tea or an egg spoon, empty them entirely, taking great care not to break the rinds. Throw these into cold water, and make jelly of the juice, which must be well pressed from the pulp, and strained as clear as possible. Colour one half a fine rose colour with prepared cochineal, and leave the other very pale; when it is nearly cold, drain and wipe the orange-rinds, and fill them with alternate stripes of the two jellies; when they are perfectly cold cut them into quarters, and dispose them tastefully in a dish with a few light branches of myrtle between them. Calf's feet or any other variety of jelly, or different blanc-manges, may be used at choice to fill the rinds; the colours, however, should contrast as much as possible.

TO MAKE ORANGE BASKETS FOR JELLY

The oranges for these should be large. First, mark the handle of the basket evenly across the stalk end of the fruit with the back of a small knife, or with a silver one, and let it be quite half-inch wide; then trace a line across from one end of the handle to the other exactly in the middle of the orange, and when the other side is marked in the same way, cut just through the rind with the point of a penknife, being careful not to pierce the fruit itself; next, with a tea or dessertspoon, take off the quartered rind on either side of the handle; pass a penknife under the handle itself; work the point of a spoon gently between the orange and the basket, until they are separated in every part; then take the fruit between the thumb and fingers, and press it carefully out through one of the spaces on either side of the handle.

Baskets thus made may be filled with any of the jellies of which the receipts are given here: but they should be nearly cold before they are poured in; and they ought also to be very clear. Some of the baskets may be filled with ratifias, and dished alternately with those which contain the jelly.

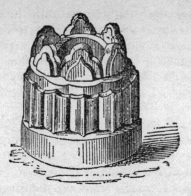

CONSTANTIA JELLY†

Infuse in a pint of water for five minutes the rind of half a Seville orange, pared extremely thin; add an ounce of isinglass; and when this is dissolved throw in four ounces of good sugar in lumps; stir well, and simmer the whole for a few minutes, then mix with it four large wineglassesful of Constantia, and strain the jelly through a fine cloth of close texture; let it settle and cool, then pour it gently from any sediment there may be, into a mould which has been laid for an hour or two into water. We had this jelly made in the first instance for an invalid who was forbidden to take acids, and it proved so agreeable in flavour that we can recommend it for the table. The isinglass, with an additional quarter of an ounce, might be clarified, and the sugar and orange-rind boiled with it afterwards.

Water, 1 pint; rind, ½ Seville orange: 5 minutes. Isinglass, 1 oz; sugar, 4 oz: 5 to 7 minutes. Constantia, 4 large wineglassesful.

† [*Constantia was a sweet wine from South Africa very popular at this time. It was made from the muscatel grape and very fragrant.*]

STRAWBERRY ISINGLASS JELLY

A great variety of equally elegant and excellent jellies for the table may be made with clarified isinglass, clear syrup, and the juice of almost any kind of fresh fruit; but as the process of making them is nearly the same for all, we shall limit our receipts to one or two, which will serve to direct the makers for the rest. Boil together quickly for fifteen minutes one pint of water and three-quarters of a pound of very good sugar; measure a quart of ripe richly-flavoured strawberries without their stalks; the scarlet answer best, from the colour which they give: on these pour the boiling syrup, and let them stand all night. The next day clarify two ounces and a half of isinglass in a pint of water; drain the syrup from the strawberries very closely, add to it two or three tablespoonsful of red currant juice, and the clear juice of one large or two small lemons; and when the isinglass is nearly cold mix the whole, and put it into moulds. The French, who excel in these fruit-jellies, always mix the separate ingredients when they are almost cold; and they also place them over ice for an hour or so after they are moulded, which is a great advantage, as they then require less isinglass, and are in consequence much more delicate. When the fruit abounds, instead of throwing it into the syrup, bruise lightly from three to four pints, throw two table-spoonsful of sugar over it, and let the juice flow from it for an hour or two; then pour a little water over, and use the juice without boiling, which will give a jelly of finer flavour than the other.

Water, 1 pint; sugar, ¾ lb: 15 minutes. Strawberries, 1 quart; isinglass, 2½ oz; water, 1 pint; juice, 1 large or 2 small lemons.

QUEEN MAB'S PUDDING
(*An Elegant Summer Dish*)

Throw into a pint of new milk the thin rind of a small lemon, and six or eight bitter almonds, blanched and bruised; or substitute for these half a pod of vanilla cut small, heat it slowly by the side of the fire, and keep it at the point of boiling until it is strongly flavoured, then add a small pinch of salt, and three-quarters of an ounce of the finest isinglass, or a full ounce should the weather be extremely warm; when this is dissolved, strain the milk through a muslin, and put it into a clean saucepan, with from four to five ounces and a half of sugar in lumps, and half-pint of rich cream; give the whole one boil, and then stir it, briskly and by degrees, to the well-beaten yolks of six fresh eggs; next, thicken the mixture as a custard, over a gentle fire, but do not hazard its curdling; when it is of tolerable consistence, pour it out, and continue the stirring until it is half cold, then mix with it an ounce and a half of candied citron, cut in small spikes, and a couple of ounces of dried cherries, and pour it into a mould rubbed with a drop of oil: when turned out it will have the appearance of a pudding. From two to three ounces of preserved ginger, well drained and sliced, may be substituted for the cherries, and an ounce of pistachio-nuts, blanched and split, for the citron; these will make an elegant variety of the dish, and the syrup of the ginger, poured round as sauce, will be a further improvement. Currants steamed until tender, and candied orange or lemon-rind, are often used instead of the cherries, and the well-sweetened juice of strawberries, raspberries (white or red), apricots, peaches, or syrup of pine-apple, will make an agreeable sauce; a small quantity of this last will also give a delicious flavour to the pudding itself, when mixed with the other ingredients. Cream may be substituted entirely for the milk, when its richness is considered desirable.

New milk, 1 pint; rind 1 small lemon; bitter almonds, 6 to 8 (or, vanilla, ½ pod); salt, few grains; isinglass, ¾ oz (1 oz in sultry weather); sugar, 4½ oz; cream, ½ pint; yolks, 6 eggs; dried cherries, 2 oz; candied citron, 1½ oz; (or, preserved ginger, 2 to 3 oz and the syrup as sauce, and 1 oz of blanched pistachio-nuts; or 4 oz currants steamed 20 minutes, and 2 oz candied orange-rind). For sauce, sweetened juice of strawberries, raspberries, or plums, or pine-apple syrup.

Obs. The currants should be steamed in an earthen cullender, placed over a saucepan of boiling water, and covered with the lid. It will be a *great* improvement to place the pudding over ice for an hour before it is served.

Shell and blanch (see page 209) twenty-four fine Spanish chestnuts, and put them with three-quarters of a pint of water into a small and delicately clean saucepan. When they have simmered from six to eight minutes, add to them two ounces of fine sugar, and let them stew very gently until they are perfectly tender; then drain them from the water, pound them, while still warm, to a smooth paste, and press them through the back of a fine sieve. While this is being done, dissolve half an ounce of isinglass in two or three spoonsful of water, and put to it as much cream as will, with the small quantity of water used, make half-pint, two ounces of sugar, about the third of a pod of vanilla, cut small, and well bruised, and a strip or two of fresh lemon-rind, pared extremely thin. Give these a minute's boil, and then keep them quite hot by the side of the fire, until a strong flavour of the vanilla is obtained. Now, mix gradually with the chestnuts half-pint of rich, unboiled cream, strain the other half-pint through a fine muslin, and work the whole well together until it becomes very thick; then stir to it a couple of ounces of dried cherries, cut into quarters, and two of candied citron, divided into very small dice. Press the mixture into a mould which has been rubbed with a particle of the purest salad oil, and in a few hours it will be ready for table. The cream should be sufficiently stiff, when the fruit is added, to prevent its sinking to the bottom, and both kinds should be dry when they are used.

Chestnuts, large, 24; water, 3/4 pint; sugar, 2 oz; isinglass, 1/2 oz; water, 2 to 3 tablespoonsful; cream, nearly 1/2 pint; vanilla, 1/3 of pod; lemon-rind, 1/4 of 1 large: infuse 20 minutes or more. Unboiled cream, 1/2 pint; dried cherries, 2 oz; candied citron, 2 oz.

Obs. When vanilla cannot easily be obtained, a little noyau [*a nut liqueur*] may be substituted for it, but a full weight of isinglass must then be used.

Take equal parts of wine and brandy, about a wineglassful of each, or two-thirds of good sherry or Madeira, and one of spirit, and soak in the mixture four sponge-biscuits, and half a pound of macaroons and ratafias; cover the bottom of the trifle-dish with part of these, and pour upon them a full pint of rich boiled custard made with three-quarters of a pint, or rather more, of milk and cream taken in equal portions, and six eggs; and sweetened, flavoured and thickened by the receipt of page 285; lay the remainder of the soaked cakes upon it, and pile over the whole, to the depth of two or three inches, the whipped syllabub of page 281, previously well drained; then sweeten and flavour slightly with wine only, less than half-pint of thin cream (or of cream and milk mixed); wash and wipe the whisk, and whip it to the lightest possible froth: take it off with a skimmer and heap it gently over the trifle.

Macaroons and ratafias, ½ lb; wine and brandy mixed, ¼ pint; rich boiled custard, 1 pint; whipped syllabub (see page 281); light froth to cover the whole, short ½ pint of cream and milk mixed;† sugar, dessertspoonful; wine, ½ glassful.

† [*The cream of those days would appear to be richer than ours, as it would be difficult to whip thin, or single, cream today.*]

CHANTILLY BASKET FILLED WITH
WHIPPED CREAM AND FRESH STRAWBERRIES

Take a mould of any sort that will serve to form the basket on, just dip the edge of some macaroons into melted barley sugar, and fasten them together with it; take it out of the mould, keep it in a dry place until wanted, then fill it high with whipped strawberry cream which has been drained on a sieve from the preceding day, and stick very fine ripe strawberries over it. It should not be filled until just before it is served.

Chantilly Basket

VERY GOOD LEMON CREAMS MADE WITHOUT CREAM

Pour over the very thin rinds of two moderate-sized but perfectly sound fresh lemons and six ounces of sugar, half-pint of spring water, and let them remain for six hours; then add the strained juice of the lemons, and five fresh eggs well beaten and also strained; take out the lemon-rind, and stir the mixture without ceasing over a gentle fire until it has boiled softly from six to eight minutes: it will not curdle as it would did milk supply the place of the water and lemon-juice. The creams are, we think, more delicate, though not quite so thick, when the yolks only of six eggs are used for them. They will keep well for nearly a week in really cold weather.

Rinds of lemons, 2; sugar, 6 oz (or 8 when a very sweet dish is preferred); cold water, ½ pint: 6 hours. Juice of lemons, 2; eggs, 5: to be boiled softly 6 to 8 minutes.

Obs. Lemon creams may, on occasion, be more expeditiously prepared, by rasping the rind of the fruit upon the sugar which is used for them; or, by paring it thin, and boiling it for a few minutes with the lemon-juice, sugar, and water, before they are stirred to the eggs.

Weigh seven ounces of fine sugar and rasp on it the rinds of two fresh sound lemons of good size, then pound or roll it to powder, and put it into a bowl with the strained juice of the lemons, two large glasses of sherry, and two of brandy; when the sugar is dissolved add a pint of very fresh cream, and whisk or mill the mixture well; take off the froth as it rises, and put it into glasses. These syllabubs will remain good for several days, and should always be made if possible, four-and-twenty hours before they are wanted for table. The full flavour of the lemon-rind is obtained with less trouble than in rasping, by paring it very thin indeed, and infusing it for some hours in the juice of the fruit.

Sugar, 7 oz; rind and juice of lemons, 2; sherry, 2 large wine-glassesful; brandy, 2 wineglassesful; cream, 1 pint.

Obs. These proportions are sufficient for two dozens or more of syllabubs: they are often made with almost equal quantities of wine and cream, but are considered less wholesome without a portion of brandy.

† [*This is a delicious sweet and easy to make, but the above is probably too sweet for present-day tastes, and the amount of sugar could be halved.*]

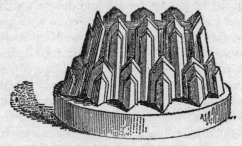

Blamange or Cake Mould

GOOD COMMON BLANC-MANGE OR BLANC MANGER
(*Author's Receipt*)

Infuse for an hour in a pint and a half of new milk the very thin rind of one small, or of half a large lemon and four or five bitter almonds, blanched and bruised,* then add two ounces of sugar, or rather more for persons who like the blanc-mange very sweet, and an ounce and a half of isinglass. Boil them gently over a clear fire, stirring them often until this last is dissolved; take off the scum, stir in half-pint, or rather more, of rich cream, and strain the blanc-mange into a bowl; it should be moved gently with a spoon until nearly cold to prevent the cream from settling on the surface. Before it is moulded, mix with it by degrees a wineglassful of brandy.

New milk, 1½ pints; rind of lemon, ½ large or whole small; bitter almonds, 4: infuse 1 hour. Sugar, 2 to 3 oz; isinglass, 1½ oz: 10 minutes. Cream, ½ pint; brandy, 1 wineglassful.

* These should always be very sparingly used.

JAUMANGE, OR JAUNE MANGER, SOMETIMES CALLED DUTCH FLUMMERY

Pour on the very thin rind of a large lemon and half a pound of sugar broken small, a pint of water, and keep them stirred over a gentle fire until they have simmered for three or four minutes, then leave the saucepan by the side of the stove that the syrup may taste well of the lemon. In ten or fifteen minutes afterwards, add two ounces of isinglass, and stir the mixture often until this is dissolved, then throw in the strained juice of four sound moderate-sized lemons, and a pint of sherry; mix the whole briskly with the beaten yolks of eight fresh eggs, and pass it through a delicately clean hair-sieve: next thicken it in a jar or jug placed in a pan of boiling water, turn it into a bowl, and when it has become cool and been allowed to settle for a minute or two, pour it into moulds, which have been laid in water. Some persons add a small glass of brandy to it, and deduct so much from the quantity of water.

Rind of 1 lemon; sugar, 8 oz; water, 1 pint: 3 or 4 minutes. Isinglass, 2 oz; juice, 4 lemons; yolks of eggs, 8; wine, 1 pint; brandy (at pleasure), 1 wineglassful.

(Delicious)

This, if carefully made, and with ripe quinces, is one of the most richly-flavoured preparations of fruit that we have ever tasted; and the receipt, we may venture to say, will be altogether new to the reader. Dissolve in a pint of prepared juice of quinces (see page 267) an ounce of the best isinglass; next, add ten ounces of sugar, roughly pounded, and stir these together gently over a clear fire, from twenty to thirty minutes, or until the juice jellies in falling from the spoon. Remove the scum carefully, and pour the boiling jelly gradually to half-pint of thick cream, stirring them briskly together as they are mixed: they must be stirred until very nearly cold, and then poured into a mould which has been rubbed in every part with the smallest possible quantity of very pure salad oil, or if more convenient, into one that has been dipped into cold water.

Obs. This blanc manger which we had made originally on the thought of the moment for a friend, proved so very rich in flavour, that we inserted the exact receipt for it, as we had had it made on our first trial; but it might be simplified by merely boiling the juice, sugar, and isinglass, together for a few minutes, and then mixing them with the cream. An ounce and a half of isinglass and three-quarters of a pint of cream might then be used for it. The juice of other fruit may be substituted for that of the quinces.

Juice of quinces, 1 pint; isinglass, 1 oz: 5 to 10 minutes. Sugar, 10 oz: 20 to 30 minutes. Cream, ½ pint.

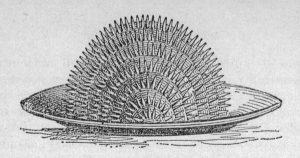

AN APPLE HEDGEHOG, OR SUÉDOISE

This dish is formed of apples, pared, cored without being divided, and stewed tolerably tender in a light syrup. These are placed in a dish, after being well drained, and filled with apricot, or any other rich marmalade,† and arranged in two or more layers, so as to give, when the whole is complete, the form shown in the engraving. The number required must depend on the size of the dish. From three to five pounds more must be stewed down into a smooth and dry marmalade, and with this all the spaces between them are to be filled up, and the whole are to be covered with it; an icing of two eggs, beaten to a very solid froth, and mixed with two heaped teaspoonsful of sugar, must then be spread evenly over the suédoise, fine sugar sifted on this, and spikes of blanched almonds, cut lengthwise, stuck over the entire surface; the dish is then to be placed in a moderate oven until the almonds are browned, but not too deeply, and the apples are hot through. It is not easy to give the required form with less than fifteen apples; eight of these may first be simmered in a syrup made with half-pint of water and six ounces of sugar, and the remainder may be thrown in after these are lifted out. Care must be taken to keep them firm. The marmalade should be sweet, and pleasantly flavoured with lemon.

† [*'Marmalade' in this context means a* purée *of fruit.*]

RICH BOILED CUSTARD

Take a small cupful from a quart of fresh cream, and simmer the remainder for a few minutes with four ounces of sugar and the rind of a lemon, or give it any other flavour that may be preferred. Beat and strain the yolks of eight eggs, mix them with the cupful of cream, and stir the rest boiling to them: thicken the custard in a deep jug set over the fire in a pan of boiling water.

Cream, 1 quart; sugar, 4 oz; yolks of eggs, 8.

THE QUEEN'S CUSTARD

On the beaten and strained yolks of twelve new-laid eggs pour a pint and a half of boiling cream which has been sweetened, with three ounces of sugar; add the smallest pinch of salt, and thicken the custard as usual. When nearly cold, flavour it with a glass and a half of noyau, maraschino, or cuirasseau [*curaçao*], and add the sliced almonds or not, at pleasure.

Yolks of eggs, 12; cream, 1½ pint; sugar, 3 oz; little salt; noyau, maraschino, or cuirasseau, 1½ wineglassful.

THE DUKE'S CUSTARD

Drain well from their juice, and then roll in dry sifted sugar, as many fine brandied Morella cherries as will cover thickly the bottom of the dish in which this is to be sent to table; arrange them in it, and pour over them from a pint to a pint and a half of rich cold boiled custard; garnish the edge with macaroons, or Naples biscuits, or pile upon the custard some solid rose-coloured whipped cream, highly flavoured with brandy.

Brandied Morella cherries, ½ to whole pint; boiled custard, from 1 to 1½ pint; thick cream, ½ pint or more; brandy, 1 to 2 glassesful; sugar, 2 to 3 oz; juice of ½ large lemon; prepared cochineal, or carmine, 20 to 40 drops.

Dissolve gently by the side of the fire an ounce and a half of the best chocolate in rather more than a wineglassful of water, and then boil it until it is perfectly smooth; mix with it a pint of milk well flavoured with lemon peel or vanilla, add two ounces of fine sugar, and when the whole boils, stir it to five well-beaten eggs which have been strained. Put the custard into a jar or jug, set it into a pan of boiling water, and stir it without ceasing until it is thick. Do not put it into glasses or a dish until it is nearly or quite cold. These, as well as all other custards, are infinitely finer when made with the yolks only of the eggs, of which the number must then be increased. Two ounces of chocolates, a pint of milk, half-pint of cream, two or three ounces of sugar, and eight yolks of eggs, will make very superior custards of this kind.

Rasped chocolate, 1½ oz; water, 1 *large* wineglassful: 5 to 8 minutes. New milk, 1 pint; eggs, 5; sugar, 2 oz. Or: chocolate, 2 oz; water, ¼ pint; new milk, 1 pint; sugar, 2½ to 3 oz; cream, ½ pint; yolks of eggs, 8.

Obs. Either of these may be moulded by dissolving from half to three-quarters of an ounce of isinglass in the milk. The proportion of chocolate can be increased to the taste.

COMMON BAKED CUSTARD

Mix a quart of new milk with eight well beaten eggs, strain the mixture through a fine sieve, and sweeten it with from five to eight ounces of sugar, according to the taste; add a small pinch of salt and pour the custard into a deep dish, grate nutmeg or lemon-rind over the top, and bake it in a very slow oven from twenty to thirty minutes, or longer, should it not be firm in the centre. A custard, if well made, and properly baked, will be quite smooth when cut, without the honey-combed appearance which a hot oven gives; and there will be no whey in the dish.

New milk, 1 quart; eggs, 8; sugar, 5 to 8 oz; salt, ¼ saltspoonful; nutmeg or lemon-grate: baked, slow oven, 20 to 30 minutes, or more.

QUINCE OR APPLE CUSTARDS†

Add to a pint of apple-juice prepared as for jelly, a tablespoonful of strained lemon-juice, and from four to six ounces of sugar according to the acidity of the fruit; stir these boiling, quickly, and in small portions, to eight well-beaten eggs, and thicken the custard in a jug placed in a pan of boiling water, in the usual manner. A large proportion of lemon-juice and a high flavouring of a rind can be given when approved. For quince custards, which if well made are excellent, observe the same directions as for the apple, but omit the lemon-juice. As we have before observed, all custards are much finer when made with the yolks only of the eggs, of which the number must be increased nearly half, when this is done.

Prepared apple-juice (see page 267, 1 pint; lemon-juice, 1 tablespoonful; sugar, 4 to 6 oz; eggs, 8. Quince custards, same proportions, but no lemon-juice.

Obs. In making lemon creams, the apple-juice may be substituted very advantageously for water, without varying the receipt in other respects.

† [*Quinces are delicious, but like many fruits seem to be going out of favour. This receipt is very good, and I have eaten in Greece, where quinces are still much used, a dish of large quinces poached in syrup, and the hollow made by the removal of the pips filled with quince custard — and excellent.*]

A MERINGUE OF RHUBARB, OR GREEN GOOSEBERRIES

Weigh a pound of delicate young rhubarb-stems after they have been carefully pared and cut into short lengths; mix eight ounces of pounded sugar with them, and stew them gently until they form a smooth pulp; then quicken the boiling, and stir them often until they are reduced to a tolerably dry marmalade. When the fruit has reached this point turn it from the pan and let it stand until it is quite cold. Separate the whites of four fresh eggs carefully from the yolks, and whisk them to a froth sufficiently solid to remain standing in points when it is dropped from the whisk or fork. Common cooks sometimes fail entirely in very light preparations from not properly understanding this extremely easy process, which requires nothing beyond plenty of space in the bowl or basin used, and regular but not violent whisking until the eggs whiten, and gradually assume the appearance of snow. No drop of liquid must remain at the bottom of the basin, and the mass must be firm enough to stand up, as has been said, in points. When in this state, mingle with it four heaped tablespoonsful of dry sifted sugar, stir these gently together, and when they are quite mixed, lay them lightly over the rhubarb in a rather deep tart-dish. Place the *meringue* in a moderate oven and bake it for about half an hour, but ascertain, before it is served, that the centre is quite firm. The crust formed by the white of egg and sugar, which is in fact the *meringue*, should be of a light equal brown, and crisp quite through. If placed in an exceedingly slow oven, the underpart of it will remain half liquid, and give an uninviting appearance to the fruit when it is served. Unless the rhubarb should be very acid, six ounces of sugar will be sufficient to sweeten it for many tastes. It is a great improvement to this dish to diminish the proportion of fruit, and to pour some thick boiled custard upon it before the *meringue* is laid on.

Obs. When gooseberries are substituted for spring-fruit, a pint and a half will be sufficient for this preparation, or even a smaller proportion when only one of quite moderate size is required. In the early part of the season they will be more acid even than the rhubarb, and rather more sugar must be allowed for them.

MERINGUE OF PEARS, OR OTHER FRUIT

Fill a deep tart-dish nearly to the brim with stewed pears, and let them be something more than half covered with their juice.

Whisk to a solid froth the whites of five eggs; stir to them five tablespoonsful of dry sifted sugar and lay them lightly and equally over the fruit; put the *meringue* immediately into a moderate oven, and bake it half an hour. Cherries, bullaces, and damsons, with various other kinds of plums, first either stewed as for *compôtes* (see page 268) or baked with sugar, as for winter use, answer as well as pears for this dish; which may, likewise, be made of apples, peaches, apricots, or common plums boiled down quite to a marmalade, with sufficient sugar to sweeten them moderately: the skins and stones of these last should be removed, but a few of the blanched kernels may be added to the fruit.

Dish filled with stewed pears or other fruit; whites of eggs, 5; pounded sugar, 5 tablespoonsful: baked, ½ hour.

AN APPLE CHARLOTTE, OR CHARLOTTE DE POMMES

Butter a plain mould (a round or square cake-tin will answer the purpose quite well), and line it entirely with thin slices of the crumb of a stale loaf [*i.e. slices of bread with the crusts removed*], cut so as to fit into it with great exactness, and dipped into clarified butter. When this is done, fill the mould to the brim with apple marmalade; cover the top with slices of bread dipped in butter, and on these place a dish, a large plate, or the cover of a French stewpan with a weight upon it. Send the Charlotte to a brisk oven for three-quarters of an hour should it be small, and for an hour if large. Turn it out with great care, and serve it hot. If baked in a slack oven it will not take a proper degree of colour, and it will be liable to break in the dishing. The strips of bread must of course join very perfectly for if any spaces were left between them the syrup of the fruit would escape and destroy the good appearance of the dish: should there not have been sufficient marmalade prepared to fill the mould entirely, a jar of quince or apricot jam, or of preserved cherries even, may be added to it with advantage. The butter should be well drained from the Charlotte before it is taken from the mould; and sugar may be sifted thickly over it before it is served, or it may be covered with any kind of clear red jelly.

A more elegant, and we think an easier mode of forming the crust, is to line the mould with small rounds of bread stamped out with a plain cake or paste cutter, then dipped in butter, and placed with the edges sufficiently one over the other to hold the fruit securely: the strips of bread are sometimes arranged in the same way.

¾ to 1 hour, quick oven.

MARMALADE FOR THE CHARLOTTE

Weigh three pounds of good boiling apples, after they have been pared, cored, and quartered; put them into a stewpan with six ounces of fresh butter, three-quarters of a pound of sugar beaten to powder, three-quarters of a teaspoonful of pounded cinnamon, and the strained juice of a lemon; let these stew over a gentle fire, until they form a perfectly smooth and dry marmalade; keep them often stirred that they may not burn, and let them cool before they are put into the crust. This quantity is for a moderate-sized Charlotte.

A CHARLOTTE À LA PARISIENNE

This dish is sometimes called in England a Vienna cake; and it is known here also, we believe, as a *Gâteau de Bordeaux*. Cut horizontally into half-inch slices a Savoy or sponge cake, and cover each slice with a different kind of preserve; replace them in their original form, and spread equally over the cake an icing made with the whites of three eggs, and four ounces of the finest pounded sugar; sift more sugar over it in every part, and put it into a very gentle oven to dry. The eggs should be whisked to snow before they are used. One kind of preserve, instead of several, can be used for this dish; and a rice or a pound cake may supply the place of the Savoy or sponge biscuit.

POMMES AU BEURRE
(*Buttered apples – Excellent*)

Pare six or eight fine apples of a firm but good boiling kind, and core without piercing them through, or dividing them; fill the cavities with fresh butter, put a quarter of a pound more, cut small, into a stewpan just large enough to contain the apples in a single layer, place them closely together on it, and stew them as softly as possible, turning them occasionally until they are almost sufficiently tender to serve; then strew upon them as much sifted sugar as will sweeten the dish highly, and a teaspoonful of pounded cinnamon; shake these well in and upon the fruit, and stew it for a few minutes longer. Lift it out, arrange it in a hot dish, put into each apple as much warm apricot jam as it will contain, and lay a small quantity on the top; pour the syrup from the pan round, but not on the fruit, and serve it immediately.

Apples, 6 to 8; fresh butter, 4 oz, just simmered till tender. Sugar, 6 to 8 oz; cinnamon, 1 teaspoonful: 5 minutes. Apricot jam as needed.

Obs. Particular care must be taken to keep the apples entire: they should rather steam in a gentle heat than boil. It is impossible to specify the precise time which will render them sufficiently tender, as this must depend greatly on the time of year and the sort of fruit. If the stewpan were placed in a very slow oven, the more regular heat of it would perhaps be better in its effect than the stewing.

SWEET MACCARONI

Drop gently into a pint and a half of new milk, when it is boiling fast, four ounces of fine pipe maccaroni, add a grain or two of salt, and some thin strips of lemon- or orange-rind: cinnamon can be substituted for these when preferred. Simmer the maccaroni by a gentle fire until it is tolerably tender, then add from two to three ounces of sugar broken small, and boil it till the pipes are soft, and swollen to their full size; drain, and arrange it in a hot dish; stir the milk quickly to the well-beaten yolks of three large, or of four small eggs, shake them round briskly over the fire until they thicken, pour them over the maccaroni and serve it immediately; or instead of the eggs, heat and sweeten some very rich cream, pour it on the drained maccaroni, and dust finely-powdered cinnamon over through a muslin, or strew it thickly with crushed macaroons. For variety, cover it with the German sauce of page 238 milled to a light froth.

New milk, 1½ pint; pipe maccaroni, 4 oz; strips of lemon-rind or cinnamon; sugar, 2 to 3 oz: ¾ to 1 hour, or more.

BERMUDA WITCHES

Slice equally some rice, pound, or Savoy cake, not more than the sixth of an inch thick; take off the brown edges, and spread one half of it with Guava jelly, or, if more convenient, with fine strawberry, raspberry, or currant jelly of the best quality (see Norman receipt, page 299), on this strew thickly some fresh cocoa-nut grated small and lightly; press over it the remainder of the cake, and trim the whole into good form; divide the slices if large, pile them slopingly in the centre of a dish upon a very white napkin folded flat, and garnish or intersperse them with small sprigs of myrtle. For very young people a French roll or two, and good currant jelly, red or white, will supply a wholesome and inexpensive dish.

24

PRESERVES

A FEW GENERAL RULES AND DIRECTIONS FOR PRESERVING

1. Let everything used for the purpose be delicately clean and *dry*; bottles especially so.

2. Never place a preserving pan *flat upon the fire*, as this will render the preserve liable to *burn to*, as it is called; that is to say, to adhere closely to the metal, and then to burn; it should rest always on a trivet, or on the lowered bar of a kitchen range when there is no regular preserving stove in a house.

3. After the sugar is added to them, stir the preserves gently at first, and more quickly towards the end, without quitting them until they are done: this precaution will always prevent the chance of their being spoiled.

4. All preserves should be perfectly cleared from the scum as it rises.

5. Fruit which is to be preserved in syrup must first be blanched or boiled gently, until it is sufficiently softened to absorb the sugar; and a thin syrup must be poured on it at first, or it will shrivel instead of remaining plump, and becoming clear. Thus, if its weight of sugar is to be allowed, and boiled to a syrup with a pint of water to the pound, only half the weight must be taken at first, and this must not be boiled with the water more than fifteen or twenty minutes at the commencement of the process; a part of the remaining sugar must be added every time the syrup is re-boiled, unless it should be otherwise directed in the receipt.

6. To preserve both the true flavour and the colour of fruit in jams and jellies, boil them rapidly until they are well reduced, *before* the sugar is added, and quickly afterwards, but do not allow them to become so much thickened that the sugar will not dissolve in them easily, and throw up its scum. In some seasons, the juice is so much richer than in others, that this effect takes place almost before one is aware of it; but the drop which adheres to the skimmer when it is held up, will show the state it has reached.

7. Never use tin, iron, or pewter spoons, or skimmers, for preserves, as they will convert the colour of red fruit into a dingy purple, and impart, besides, a very unpleasant flavour.†

8. When cheap jams or jellies are required, make them at once with Lisbon sugar, but use that which is *well refined* always, for preserves in general; it is a false economy, as we have elsewhere observed, to purchase an inferior kind, as there is great waste from it in the quantity of scum which it throws up. The *best* has been used for all the receipts given here.

9. Let fruit for preserving be gathered always in perfectly dry weather, and be free both from the morning and evening dew, and as much so as possible from dust. When bottled, it must be steamed or baked during the day on which it is gathered, or there will be a great loss from the bursting of the bottles; and for jams and jellies it cannot be too soon boiled down after it is taken from the trees.

† [*Use a wooden spoon only.*]

Wash some freshly gathered gooseberries very clean; after having taken off the tops and stalks, then to each pound pour three-quarters of a pint of spring water, and simmer them until they are well broken; turn the whole into a jelly-bag or cloth, and let all the juice drain through; weigh and boil it rapidly for fifteen minutes. Draw it from the fire, and stir in it until entirely dissolved, an equal weight of good sugar reduced to powder; boil the jelly from fifteen to twenty minutes longer, or until it jellies strongly on the spoon or skimmer; clear it perfectly from scum, and pour it into small jars, moulds, or glasses. It ought to be very pale and transparent. The sugar may be added to the juice at first, and the preserve boiled from twenty-five to thirty-five minutes, but the colour will not then be so good. When the fruit abounds, the juice may be drawn from it with very little water, when it will require much less boiling.

Gooseberries, 6 lb; water, 4½ pints: 20 to 30 minutes. Juice boiled quickly, 15 minutes; to each pound, 1 lb sugar: 15 to 20 minutes.

GREEN GOOSEBERRY JAM
(*Firm and of good colour*)

Cut the stalks and tops from the fruit, weigh and bruise it slightly, boil it for six or seven minutes, keeping it well turned during the time, then to every three pounds of gooseberries add two and a half of sugar beaten to a powder, and boil the preserve quickly for three-quarters of an hour. It must be constantly stirred, and carefully cleared from scum. This makes a fine, firm, and refreshing preserve if the fruit be rubbed through a sieve before the sugar is added. If well reduced afterwards, it may be converted into a gâteau, or gooseberry-solid, with three pounds of sugar, or even a smaller proportion. The preceding jam will often turn in perfect form from the moulds or jars which contain it; and if freed from the seeds, would be very excellent: it is extremely good even made as above. For all preserves, the reduction, or boiling down to a certain consistence, should take place principally before the sugar is mingled with them; and this has the best effect when added to the fruit and dissolved in it by degrees.

Green gooseberries, 6 lb: 6 to 7 minutes. Sugar, 5 lb: ¾ hour.

JAM OF KENTISH OR FLEMISH CHERRIES

This is a very agreeable preserve when it is made as we shall direct; but if long boiled with a large proportion of sugar, as it frequently is, both the bright colour and the pleasant flavour of the cherries will be destroyed.

Stone, and then weigh the fruit; heat it rather slowly so that the juice may be well drawn out before it begins to boil, and stew the cherries until they are tolerably tender, then boil them quickly, keeping them well turned and stirred from the bottom of the pan, for three-quarters of an hour or somewhat longer, should there still remain a large quantity of juice. Draw the pan from the fire, and stir in gradually half a pound of sugar for each pound of cherries. An ounce or two more may occasionally be required when the fruit is more than usually acid, and also when a quite sweet preserve is liked. When the sugar is dissolved continue the boiling rapidly for about twenty minutes longer; clear off all the scum as it appears, and keep the jam stirred *well* and constantly, but not quickly, to prevent its adhering to the bottom of the preserving-pan.

Stoned Kentish or Flemish cherries, 6 lb: without sugar, 1 hour or rather more. Sugar roughly powdered, 3 lb (or 3½ lb). About 20 minutes quick boiling.

Obs. Heat the fruit and boil it gently until it is quite tender, turning it often, and pressing it down into the juice; then quicken the boiling to evaporate the juice before the sugar is added. Cherries which are bruised will not make good preserves: they always remain tough.

Stone the fruit, or if this trouble be objected to, bruise and boil it without, until it is sufficiently tender to press through a sieve, which it will be in from twenty to thirty minutes. Weigh the pulp in this case, and boil it quickly to a dry paste, then stir to it six ounces of sugar for the pound of fruit, and when this is dissolved, place the pan again over, but not upon, a brisk fire, and stir the preserve without ceasing, until it is so dry as not to adhere to the finger when touched; then press it immediately into small moulds or pans, and turn it from them when wanted for table. When the cherries have been stoned, a good common preserve may be made of them without passing them through a sieve, with the addition of five ounces of sugar to the pound of fruit, which must be boiled very dry both before and after it is added.

Kentish or Flemish cherries without stoning: 20 to 30 minutes. Passed through a sieve. To each pound of pulp (first boiled dry), 6 oz sugar. To each pound of cherries stoned and boiled to a dry paste, 5 oz sugar.

STRAWBERRY JAM

Strip the stalks from some fine scarlet strawberries, weigh, and boil them for thirty-five minutes, keeping them very constantly stirred; throw in eight ounces of good sugar, beaten small, to the pound of fruit; mix them well off the fire, then boil the preserve again quickly for twenty-five minutes.

Strawberries, 6 lb: 35 minutes. Sugar, 3 lb: 25 minutes.

Obs. We do not think it needful to give directions with each separate receipt for skimming the preserve with care, and keeping it constantly stirred, but neither should in any case be neglected.

Let the fruit be gathered in the middle of a warm day, in very dry weather; strip it from the stalks directly, weigh it, bruise it *slightly*, turn it into a bowl or deep pan, and mix with it an equal weight of fine dry sifted sugar, and put it immediately into small, wide-necked bottles; cork these firmly without delay, and tie bladders over the tops. Keep them in a cool place, or the fruit will ferment. The mixture should be stirred softly, and only just sufficiently to blend the sugar and the fruit. The bottles must be perfectly dry, and the bladders, after having been cleaned in the usual way, and allowed to become nearly so, should be moistened with a little spirit on the side which is to be next to the cork. Unless these precautions be observed, there will be some danger of the whole being spoiled.

Equal weight of fruit and sugar.

RASPBERRY JAM

This is a very favourite English preserve, and one of the most easily made that can be. The fruit for it should be ripe and perfectly sound; and as it soon decays or become mouldy after it is gathered, it should be fresh from the bushes when it is used. That which grows in the shade has less flavour than the fruit which received the full warmth of the sun.

Excellent jam for common family use may be made as follows:

Bruise gently with the back of a wooden spoon, six pound of ripe and freshly-gathered raspberries, and boil them over a brisk fire for twenty-five minutes; stir to them half their weight of good sugar, roughly powdered, and when it is dissolved, boil the preserve quickly for ten minutes, keeping it well stirred and skimmed.

Raspberries, 6 lb: 25 minutes. Sugar, 3 lb: 10 minutes.

SUPERLATIVE RED CURRANT JELLY
(*Norman Receipt*)

Strip carefully from the stems some quite ripe currants of the finest quality, and mix with them an equal weight of good sugar reduced to powder; boil these together quickly for exactly eight minutes, keep them stirred all the time, and clear off the scum – which will be very abundant – as it rises; then turn the preserve into a very clean sieve, and put into small jars the jelly which runs through it, and which will be delicious in flavour, and of the brightest colour. It should be carried immediately, when this is practicable, to an extremely cool but not a damp place, and left there until perfectly cold. The currants which remain in the sieve make an excellent jam, particularly if only part of the jelly be taken from them. In Normandy, where the fruit is of richer quality than in England, this preserve is boiled only two minutes, and is both firm and beautifully transparent.

Currants, 3 lb; sugar, 3 lb: 8 minutes.

Obs. This receipt we are told by some of our correspondents is not generally quite successful in this country, as the jelly, though it keeps well and is of the finest possible flavour, is scarcely firm enough for table. We have ourselves found this to be the case in cold damp seasons; but the preserve even then was valuable for many purposes, and always agreeable eating.†

† [*This is quite true – I have made this often and it is never very firm, but of a delicious flavour.*]

WHITE CURRANT JAM, A BEAUTIFUL PRESERVE

Boil together quickly for seven minutes an equal weight of fine white currants, stalked with the greatest nicety, and of the best sugar pounded and passed through a sieve. Stir the preserve gently the whole time, and be careful to skim it thoroughly.

White currants, 4 lb; best sugar, 4 lb: 7 minutes.

Stalk and heat some red currants as for jelly, pour off three parts of the juice, which can be used for that preserve, and press the remainder, with the pulp of the fruit, closely through a hair-sieve reversed; boil it briskly, keeping it stirred the whole time, until it forms a dry paste; then for each pound (when first weighed) add seven ounces of pounded sugar, and boil the whole from twenty-five to thirty minutes longer, taking care that it shall not burn. This paste is remarkably pleasant and refreshing in cases of fever, and acceptable often for winter-desserts.

Red currants boiled from 5 to 7 minutes, pressed with one-fourth of their juice through a sieve, boiled from 1½ to 2 hours. To each pound, 7 oz pounded sugar: 25 to 30 minutes.

Obs. Confectioners add the pulp, after it is boiled dry, to an equal weight of sugar at the candy height: by making trial of the two methods, the reader can decide on the better one.

† ['*Pastes*' *or* '*cheeses*' *of fruit are much used in country districts in France as dessert and served with cream cheese.*]

BLACK CURRANT JAM AND MARMALADE

No fruit jellies so easily as black currants when they are ripe; and their juice is so rich and thick that it will bear the addition of a very small quantity of water sometimes, without causing the preserve to mould.

To six pounds of the fruit, stripped carefully from the stalks, add four pounds and a half of sugar. Let them heat gently, but as soon as the sugar is dissolved boil the preserve rapidly for fifteen minutes. A more common kind of jam may be made by boiling the fruit by itself from ten to fifteen minutes, and for ten minutes after half its weight of sugar has been added to it.

Black currants, 6 lb; sugar, 4½ lb: 15 minutes. Or: fruit, 6 lb: 10 to 15 minutes. Sugar, 3 lb: 10 minutes.

Obs. There are few preparations of fruit so refreshing and so useful in illness as those of black currants, and it is therefore advisable always to have a store of them, and to have them well and carefully made.

NURSERY PRESERVE

Take the stones from a couple of pounds of Kentish cherries, and boil them twenty minutes; then add to them a pound and a half of raspberries, and an equal quantity of red and of white currants, all weighed after they have been cleared from their stems. Boil these together quickly for twenty minutes; mix with them three pounds and a quarter of common sugar, and give the preserve fifteen minutes more of quick boiling. A pound and a half of gooseberries may be substituted for the cherries; but they will not require any stewing before they are added to the other fruits. The jam must be well stirred from the beginning, or it will burn to the pan.

Kentish cherries, 2 lb: 20 minutes. Raspberries, red currants, and white currants, of each 1½ lb: 20 minutes. Sugar, 3¼ lb: 15 minutes.

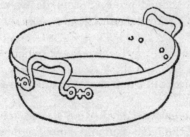

GROSEILLÉE
(*Another good preserve*)

Cut the tops and stalks from a gallon or more of well-flavoured ripe gooseberries, throw them into a large preserving-pan, boil them for ten minutes, and stir them often with a wooden spoon; then pass both the juice and pulp through a fine sieve, and to every three pounds' weight of these add half-pint of raspberry-juice, and boil the whole briskly for three-quarters of an hour; draw the pan aside, stir in for the above portion of fruit, two pounds of sugar, and when it is dissolved renew the boiling for fifteen minutes longer.

Ripe gooseberries, boiled 10 minutes. Pulp and juice of gooseberries, 6 lb; raspberry-juice, 1 pint: ¾ hour. Sugar, 4 lb: 15 minutes.

Obs. When more convenient, a portion of raspberries can be boiled with the gooseberries at first.

DAMSON JAM

(*Very good*)

The fruit for this jam should be freshly gathered and quite ripe. Split, stone, weigh, and boil it quickly for forty minutes; then stir in half its weight of good sugar roughly powdered, and when it is dissolved, give the preserve fifteen minutes additional boiling, keeping it stirred, and thoroughly skimmed.

Damsons, stoned, 6 lb: 40 minutes. Sugar, 3 lb: 15 minutes.

Obs. A more refined preserve is made by pressing the fruit through a sieve after it is boiled tender; but the jam is excellent without.

EXCELLENT DAMSON CHEESE

When the fruit has been baked or stewed tender, as directed above, drain off the juice, skin and stone the damsons, pour back to them from a third to half of their juice, weigh and then boil them over a clear brisk fire, until they form quite a dry paste; add six ounces of pounded sugar for each pound of the plums; stir them off the fire until this is dissolved, and boil the preserve again without quitting or ceasing to stir it, until it leaves the pan quite dry, and adheres in a mass to the spoon. If it should not stick to the fingers when lightly touched, it will be sufficiently done to keep very long; press it quickly into pans or moulds; lay on it a paper dipped in spirit when it is perfectly cold; tie another fold over it, and store it in a dry place.

Bullace cheese is made in the same manner, and almost any kind of plum will make an agreeable preserve of the sort.

To each pound of fruit, pared, stoned, and mixed with the juice and boiled quite dry, 6 oz of pounded sugar: boiled again to a dry paste.

QUINCE JELLY

Pare, quarter, core, and weigh some ripe but quite sound quinces, as quickly as possible, and throw them as they are done into part of the water in which they are to be boiled, as directed at page 267, allow one pint of this to each pound of the fruit, and simmer it gently until it is a little broken, but not so long as to redden the juice, which ought to be very pale. Turn the whole into a jelly-bag, or strain the liquid through a fine cloth, and let it drain very closely from it but without the slightest pressure. Weigh the juice, put it into a delicately clean preserving pan, and boil it quickly for twenty minutes; take it from the fire and stir in it, until it is entirely dissolved, twelve ounces of sugar for each pound of juice, or fourteen ounces if the fruit should be very acid, which it will be in the earlier part of the season; keep it constantly stirred and throughly cleared from scum, from ten to twenty minutes longer, or until it jellies strongly in falling from the skimmer; then pour it directly into glasses or moulds. If properly made, it will be sufficiently firm to turn out of the latter, and it will be beautifully transparent, and rich in flavour. It may be made with an equal weight of juice and sugar mixed together in the first instance, and boiled from twenty to thirty minutes. It is difficult to state the time precisely, because from different causes it will vary much. It should be reduced rapidly to the proper point, as long boiling injures the colour: this is always more perfectly preserved by boiling the juice without the sugar first.

To each pound pared and cored quinces, 1 pint water: ¾ to 1½ hour. Juice, boiled 20 minutes. To each pound, 12 oz sugar: 10 to 20 minutes. Or, juice and sugar equal weight: 20 to 30 minutes.

This is delicious used instead of red currant jelly with meat.

QUINCE MARMALADE

When to economize the fruit is not an object, pare, core, and quarter some of the inferior quinces, and boil them in as much water as will nearly cover them, until they begin to break; strain the juice from them and for the marmalade put half a pint of it to each pound of fresh quinces: in preparing these, be careful to cut out the hard stone parts round the cores. Simmer them gently until they are perfectly tender, then press them, with the juice, through a coarse sieve; put them into a perfectly clean pan, and boil them until they form almost a dry paste; add for each pound of quinces and the half-pint of juice, three-quarters of a pound of sugar in fine powder, and boil the marmalade for half an hour, stirring it gently without ceasing: it will be very firm and bright in colour. If made shortly after the fruit is gathered, a little additional sugar will be required; and when a richer and less dry marmalade is better liked, it must be boiled for a shorter time, and an equal weight of fruit and sugar may be used.

Quinces, pared and cored, 4 lb; prepared juice, 1 quart: 2 to 3 hours. Boiled fast to dry, 20 to 40 minutes. Sugar, 3 lb: 30 minutes.

Richer marmalade: quinces, 4 lb; juice, 1 quart; sugar, 4 lb.

GENUINE SCOTCH MARMALADE†

Take some bitter oranges, and double their weight of sugar; cut the rind of the fruit into quarters and peel it off, and if the marmalade be not wanted very thick, take off some of the spongy white skin inside the rind. Cut the chips as thin as possible, and above half-inch long, and divide the pulp into small bits, removing carefully the seeds, which may be steeped in part of the water that is to make the marmalade, and which must be in the proportion of a quart to a pound of fruit. Put the chips and pulp into a deep earthen dish, and pour the water boiling over them; let them remain for twelve or fourteen hours, and then turn the whole into the preserving pan, and boil it until the chips are perfectly tender. When they are so, add by degrees the sugar (which should be previously pounded), and boil it until it jellies. The water in which the seeds have been steeped, and which must be taken from the quantity apportioned to the whole of the preserve, should be poured into a hair-sieve, and the seeds well worked in it with the back of a spoon; a strong clear jelly will be obtained by this means, which must be washed off them by pouring their own liquor through the sieve in small portions over them. This must be added to the fruit when it is first set on the fire.

Oranges, 3 lb; water, 3 quarts; sugar, 6 lb.

Obs. This receipt, which we have not tried ourselves, is guaranteed as an excellent one by the Scottish lady from whom it was procured.

† [*This is the receipt I use with great success. It makes an excellent, dark, rather bitter preserve.*]

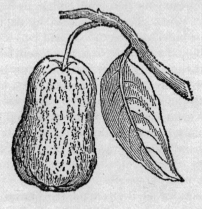

25

Mango

PICKLES

OBSERVATIONS ON PICKLES

With the exception of walnuts, which, when softened by keeping, or by the mode of preparing them, are the least objectionable of any pickle, with Indian mangoes, and one or two other varieties, these are not very wholesome articles of diet,* consisting, as so many of them do, of crude hard vegetables, or of unripe fruit. In numerous instances, too, those which are commonly sold to the public have been found of so deadly a nature as to be eminently dangerous to persons who partake of them often and largely. It is most desirable, therefore, to have them prepared at home, and with good genuine vinegar, whether French or English. That which is home made can at least be relied on; and it may be made of excellent quality and of sufficient strength for all ordinary purposes. The superiority of French vinegar results from its being made of wine; no substitute producing any equal to that derived from the unmixed juice of the grape.

Pickles should always be kept quite covered with their liquor, and well secured from the air and from the influence of damp; the last of which is especially detrimental to them. We can quite recommend to the reader the rather limited number of receipts which follow, and which might easily be multiplied did the size of our volume permit. Pickling is so easy a process, however, that when in any degree properly acquired, it may be extended to almost every kind of fruit and vegetable successfully. A few of the choicer kinds will nevertheless be found generally more acceptable than a greater variety of inferior preparations. Mushrooms, gherkins, walnuts, lemons, eschalots, and peaches, for all of which we have given minute directions, will furnish as much choice as is commonly required. Very excellent Indian mangoes too may be purchased at the Italian warehouses, and to many tastes will be more acceptable than any English pickle.

* Flavoured vinegars or mustard are more so, and are equally appetizing and pungent.

TO PICKLE PEACHES, AND PEACH MANGOES

Take, at their full growth, just before they begin to ripen, six large or eight moderate-sized peaches; wipe the down from them, and put them into brine that will float an egg. In three days let them be taken out, and drained on a sieve reversed for several hours. Boil in a quart of vinegar for ten minutes two ounces of whole white pepper, two of ginger slightly bruised, a teaspoonful of salt, two blades of mace, half a pound of mustard-seed, and a half-teaspoonful of cayenne tied in a bit of muslin. Lay the peaches into a jar, and pour the boiling pickle on them: in two months they will be fit for use.

Peaches, 6 or 8: in brine three days. Vinegar, 1 quart; whole white pepper, 2 oz; bruised ginger, 2 oz; salt, 1 teaspoonful; mace, 2 blades; mustard-seed, ½ lb: 10 minutes.

Obs. The peaches may be converted into excellent mangoes by cutting out from the stalk-end of each, a round of sufficient size to allow the stone to be extracted: this should be done after they are taken from the brine. They may be filled with very fresh mustard-seed, previously washed in a little vinegar; to this a small portion of garlic, or bruised eschalots, cayenne, horse-radish, chilies (the most appropriate of any), or spice of any kind may be added, to the taste. The part cut out must be replaced, and secured with a packthread crossed over the fruit.

SWEET PICKLE OF MELON
(*Foreign Receipt – To serve with Roast Meat*)

Take, within three or four days of their being fully ripe, one or two well-flavoured melons; just pare off the outer rind, clear them from the seeds, and cut them into slices of about half-inch thick; lay them into good vinegar, and let them remain in it for ten days; then cover them with cold fresh vinegar, and simmer them very gently until they are tender. Lift them on to a sieve reversed, to drain, and when they are quite cold stick a couple of cloves into each slice, lay them into a jar (a glass one, if at hand) and cover them well with cold syrup, made with ten ounces of sugar to the pint of water, boiled quickly together for twenty minutes. In about a week take them from the syrup, let it drain from them a little, then put them into jars in which they are to be stored, and cover them again thoroughly with good vinegar, which has been boiled for an instant, and left to become quite cold before it is added to them.

This pickle is intended to be served more particularly with roast mutton, hare, and venison, instead of currant jelly, but it is very good with stewed meat also. Small blades of cinnamon, and a large proportion of cloves are sometimes stuck into the melon, but their flavour should not prevail too strongly. We have found the receipt answer extremely well as we have given it, when tried with small green melons, cut within four days of being fit for table.

Melons not quite ripe, pared from hard rind and sliced, 1 or 2: in vinegar 10 days. Simmered in it until tender. In syrup 6 to 7 days. In fresh vinegar to remain. Ready to serve in a month.

A common Sweet Pickle of Melon. – Prepare the fruit as above. In a fortnight simmer it until tender; drain, and lay it into jars, and pour on it while just warm, a pickle made with a pound and two ounces of coarse brown sugar, twenty cloves, and half a drachm of cinnamon to the pint of vinegar, boiled together for ten minutes.

TO PICKLE WALNUTS

The walnuts for this pickle must be gathered while a pin can pierce them easily, for when once the shell can be felt, they have ceased to be in a proper state for it. Make sufficient brine to cover them well, with six ounces of salt to the quart of water; take off the scum, which will rise to the surface as the salt dissolves, throw in the walnuts, and stir them night and morning; change the brine every three days, and if they are wanted for immediate eating, leave them in it for twelve days; otherwise, drain them from it in nine, spread them on dishes, and let them remain exposed to the air until they become black: this will be in twelve hours, or less. Make a pickle for them with something more than half a gallon of vinegar to the hundred, a teaspoonful of salt, two ounces of black pepper, three of bruised ginger, a drachm of mace, and from a quarter to half an ounce of cloves (of which some may be stuck into three or four small onions), and four ounces of mustard-seed. Boil the whole of these together for about five minutes; have the walnuts ready in a stone jar or jars, and pour it on them as it is taken from the fire. When the pickle is quite cold, cover the jar securely, and store it in a dry place. Keep the walnuts always well covered with vinegar, and boil that which is added to them.

Walnuts, 100; in brine made with 12 oz salt to 2 quarts water, and changed twice or more, 9 to 12 days. Vinegar, full ½ gallon; salt, 1 teaspoonful; whole black pepper, 2 oz; ginger, 3 oz; mace, 1 drachm; clove, ¼ to ½ oz; small onions, 4 to 6; mustard-seed, 4 oz: 5 minutes.

PICKLED ONIONS

Take the smallest onions that can be procured, just after they are harvested, for they are never in so good a state for the purposes as then; proceed, after having peeled them, to throw them into boiling vinegar, and when they begin to look clear, which will be in three or four minutes, put them into jars, and pour the pickle on them. The vinegar should be very pale, and their colour will then be exceedingly well preserved. Any favourite spices can be added to it.

Onions, 1 quart; vinegar, 1 quart; salt, 1 dessertspoonful; whole white pepper, 1 oz.

TO PICKLE NASTURTIUMS

These should be gathered quite young, and a portion of the buds, when very small, should be mixed with them. Prepare a pickle by dissolving an ounce and a half of salt in a quart of pale vinegar, and throw in the berries as they become fit, from day to day. They are used instead of capers for sauce, and by some persons are preferred to them. When purchased for pickling, put them at once into a jar, and cover them well with the vinegar.

TO PICKLE RED CABBAGE

Strip off the outer leaves, wipe, and slice a fine sound cabbage or two extremely thin, sprinkle plenty of salt over them, and let them drain in a sieve, or on a strainer for twelve hours or more; shake or press the moisture from them; put them into clean stone jars, and cover them well with cold vinegar, in which an ounce of black pepper to the quart has been boiled. Some persons merely cover the vegetable with strong unboiled vinegar, but this is not so well.

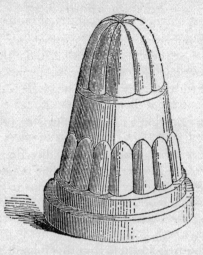

26

Modern Cake Mould

CAKES

GENERAL REMARKS ON CAKES

We have inserted here but a comparatively limited number of receipts for these '*sweet poisons*', as they have been emphatically called, and we would willingly have diminished still further even the space which has been allotted to them, that we might have had room in their stead for others of a more really useful character; but we have felt reluctant to withdraw such a portion of any of the chapters as might materially alter the original character of the work, or cause dissatisfaction to any of our kind readers; we will therefore content ourselves with remarking, that more illness is caused by habitual indulgence in the richer and heavier kinds of cakes than could easily be credited by persons who have given no attention to the subject.

Amongst those which have the worst effects are almond, and plum *pound* cakes, as they are called; all varieties of the *brioche* and such others as contain a large quantity of butter and eggs.

The least objectionable are simple buns, biscuits, yeast and sponge cakes, and *meringues*; these last being extremely light and delicate, and made of white of egg and sugar only, are really not unwholesome.

TO PREPARE BUTTER FOR RICH CAKES

For all large and very rich cakes the usual directions are, *to beat the butter to a cream*; but we find that they are quite as light when it is cut small and gently melted with just so much heat as will dissolve it, and no more. If it be shaken round in a saucepan previously warmed, and held near the fire for a short time, it will soon be liquefied, which is all that is required: it must on no account be *hot* when it is added to the other ingredients, to which it must be poured in small portions after they are all mixed, in the way which we have minutely described in the receipt for a Madeira cake, and that of the Sutherland puddings (Chapter 21). To *cream* it, drain the water well from it after it is cut, soften it a little before the fire should it be very hard, and then with the back of a large strong wooden spoon beat it until it resembles thick cream. When prepared thus, the sugar is added to it first, and then the other ingredients in succession. For plum cakes it is better creamed than liquefied, as the fruit requires a paste of some consistence to prevent its sinking to the bottom of the mould in which it is baked. For plain seed-cakes the more simple plan answers perfectly.

ALMOND MACAROONS

Blanch a pound of fresh Jordan almonds, wipe them dry, and set them into a very cool oven to render them perfectly so; pound them to an exceedingly smooth paste, with a little white of egg, then whisk to a firm solid froth the white of seven eggs, or of eight, should they be small; mix with them a pound and a half of the finest sugar; add these by degrees to the almonds, whisk the whole up well together, and drop the mixture upon wafer-paper, which may be procured at the confectioner's: bake the cakes in a moderate oven a very pale brown. It is an improvement to their flavour to substitute an ounce of bitter almonds for one of the sweet. They are sometimes made with an equal weight of each; and another variety of them is obtained by gently browning the almonds in a slow oven before they are pounded.

Jordan almonds blanched, 1lb; sugar, 1½lb; whites of 7 or 8 eggs: 15 to 20 minutes.

IMPERIALS
(Not very rich)

Work into a pound of flour six ounces of butter, and mix well with them half a pound of sifted sugar, six ounces of currants, two ounces of candied orange-peel, the grated rind of a lemon, and four well-beaten eggs. Flour a tin lightly, and with a couple of forks place the paste upon it in small rough heaps quite two inches apart. Bake them in a very gentle oven, from a quarter of an hour to twenty minutes, or until they are equally coloured to a pale brown.

Flour, 1 lb; butter, 6 oz; sugar, 8 oz; currants, 6 oz; candied peel, 2 oz; rind of 1 lemon; eggs, 4: 15 to 20 minutes.

FINE ALMOND CAKE

Blanch, dry, and pound to the finest possible paste, eight ounces of fresh Jordan almonds, and one ounce of bitter; moisten them with a few drops of cold water or white of egg, to prevent their oiling; then mix with them *very* gradually twelve fresh eggs which have been whisked until they are *exceedingly* light; throw in by degrees one pound of fine, dry, sifted sugar, and *keep* the mixture light by constant beating, with a large wooden spoon, as the separate ingredients are added. Mix in by degrees three-quarters of a pound of dried and sifted flour of the best quality; then pour gently from the sediment a pound of butter which has been just melted, but not allowed to become hot, and beat it very gradually, but very thoroughly, into the cake, letting one portion entirely disappear before another is thrown in; add the rasped or finely-grated rinds of two sound fresh lemons, fill a thickly-buttered mould rather more than half full with the mixture, and bake the cake from an hour and a half to two hours in a well-heated oven. Lay paper over the top when it is sufficiently coloured, and guard carefully against its being burned.

Jordan almonds, ½ lb; bitter almonds, 1 oz; eggs, 12; sugar, 1 lb; flour, ¾ lb; butter, 1 lb; rinds lemons, 2: 1½ to 2 hours.

Obs. Three-quarters of a pound of almonds may be mixed with this cake when so large a portion of them is liked, but an additional ounce or two of sugar, and one egg or more, will then be required.

PLAIN POUND OR CURRANT CAKE
(*Or rich Brawn Brack, or Borrow Brack*)

Mix, as directed in the foregoing receipt, ten eggs (some cooks take a pound in weight of these), one pound of sugar, one of flour, and as much of butter. For a plum cake, let the butter be worked to a cream; add the sugar to it first, then the yolks of the eggs, next stir lightly in the whites, after which, add one pound of currants and the candied peel, and, last of all, the flour by degrees, and a glass of brandy when it is liked. Nearly or quite two hours' baking will be required for this, and one hour for half the quantity.

To convert the above into the popular Irish 'speckled bread', or *Brawn Brack* of the richer kind, add to it three ounces of carraway-seeds: these are sometimes used in combination with the currants, but more commonly without.

Rasp on some lumps of well-refined sugar the rind of a fine sound lemon, and scrape off the part which has imbibed the essence, or crush the lumps to powder, and add them to as much more as will make up the weight of eight or ten fresh eggs in the shell; break these one by one, and separate the whites from the yolks; beat the latter in a large bowl for ten minutes, then strew in the sugar gradually, and beat them well together. In the mean time let the whites be whisked to a quite solid froth, add them to the yolks, and when they are well blended sift and *stir* the flour gently to them, but do not beat it into the mixture; pour the cake into a well-buttered mould, and bake it an hour and a quarter in a moderate oven.

Rasped rind, 1 large lemon; fresh eggs, 8 or 10; their weight of dry, sifted sugar; and half their weight of flour: baked, 1¼ hour, moderate oven.

A GOOD MADEIRA CAKE

Whisk four fresh eggs until they are as light as possible, then, continuing still to whisk them, throw in by *slow* degrees the following ingredients in the order in which they are written: six ounces of dry, pounded, and sifted sugar; six of flour, also dried and sifted; four ounces of butter just dissolved, but not heated; the rind of a fresh lemon; and the instant before the cake is moulded, beat well in the third of a teaspoonful of carbonate of soda: bake it an hour in a moderate oven. In this, as in all compositions of the same nature, observe particularly that each portion of butter must be beaten into the mixture until no appearance of it remains before the next is added; and if this be done, and the preparation be kept light by constant and light whisking, the cake will be as good, if not better, than if the butter were creamed. Candied citron can be added to the paste, but it is not needed.

Eggs, 4; sugar, 6 oz; flour, 6 oz; butter, 4 oz; rind of 1 lemon; carbonate of soda, ⅓ of teaspoonful: 1 hour, moderate oven.

Take for these whites of eggs and sugar in the proportion of six to the pound, or half that quantity for a small number of *meringues*. Boil the sugar with a pint of water until it whitens, and begins to fall in flakes from the skimmer; have the eggs whisked to a perfectly solid froth quite ready at the proper moment, and when the sugar has stood for two or three minutes, and been worked well from the sides of the pan, mingle them gradually, but very quickly, until they become firm enough to retain their shape perfectly when moulded with a teaspoon; lay out the cakes on paper, and place them in an oven so slow as to harden without giving them colour. As they are not to be filled, but merely fastened together, they may be baked on tins. Part of them may be varied by the addition of three or four ounces of pounded almonds mixed thoroughly with the remainder of the eggs and sugar, when a portion of the *meringues* have been moulded: these, however, will require to be much longer baked than the others; but they will be excellent. They should be lightly browned, and crisp quite through.

Sugar, 1 lb; water, 1 pint; whites of eggs, 6: *very* slow oven, 20 to 30 minutes, or longer.

ACTON GINGERBREAD

Whisk four strained or well-cleared eggs to the lightest possible froth and pour to them, by degrees, a pound and a quarter of treacle, still beating them lightly. Add, in the same manner, six ounces of pale brown sugar free from lumps, one pound of sifted flour, and six ounces of good butter, *just* sufficiently warmed to be liquid, and no more, for if hot, it would render the cake heavy; it should be poured in small portions to the mixture, which should be well beaten up with the back of a wooden spoon as each portion is thrown in: the success of the cake depends almost entirely on this part of the process. When properly mingled with the mass, the butter will not be perceptible on the surface; and if the cake be kept light by constant whisking, large bubbles will appear in it to the last. When it is so far ready, add to it one ounce of Jamaica ginger and a large teaspoonful of cloves in fine powder, with the lightly grated rinds of two fresh full-sized lemons. Butter thickly, in every part, a shallow square tin pan, and bake the gingerbread slowly for nearly or quite an hour in a gentle oven. Let it cool a little before it is turned out, and set it on its edge until cold, supporting it, if needful, against a large jar or bowl. We have usually had it baked in an American oven, in a tin less than two inches deep; and it has been excellent. We retain the name given to it originally in our own circle.

GOOD COMMON GINGERBREAD†

Work very smoothly six ounces of fresh butter (or some that has been well washed from the salt, and wrung dry in a cloth) into one pound of flour, and mix with them thoroughly an ounce of ginger in fine powder, four ounces of brown sugar, and half a teaspoonful of beaten cloves and mace. Wet these with three-quarters of a pound of cold treacle, or rather more, if needful; roll out the paste, cut the cakes with a round tin cutter, lay them on a floured or buttered baking tin, and put them into a very slow oven. Lemon-grate or candied peel can be added, when it is liked.

Flour, 1 lb; butter, 6 oz; sugar, ¼ lb; ginger, 1 oz; cloves and mace, ½ teaspoonful; treacle, ¾ lb: ½ to ¾ hour.

† [*If you use cutters shaped like little men, this is how to make gingerbread men, with currant eyes and buttons.*

QUEEN CAKES†

To make these, proceed exactly as for the pound currant cake of page 314, but bake the mixture in small well-buttered tin pans

† [*These, in some books are called simply 'Heart Cakes' and were, with cider, a speciality of some of the inns near London in the eighteenth century.*]

(heart-shaped ones are usual), in a somewhat brisk oven, for about twenty minutes.

JUMBLES

Rasp in some good sugar the rinds of two lemons; dry, reduce it to powder, and sift it with as much more as will make up a pound in weight; mix with it one pound of flour, four well-beaten eggs, and six ounces of warm butter: drop the mixture on buttered tins, and bake the jumbles in a *very* slow oven from twenty to thirty minutes. They should be pale, but perfectly crisp.

A GOOD SODA CAKE

Break down half a pound* of fresh butter into a pound of fine dry flour, and work it into very small crumbs; mix well with these half a pound of sifted sugar, and pour to them first, a quarter of a pint of boiling milk, and next, three well-whisked eggs; and some grated nutmeg, or fresh lemon-rind, and eight ounces of currants, cleaned and dried; beat the whole well and lightly together, then strew in a very small teaspoonful of good carbonate of soda in the finest powder, which has been rubbed through a sieve and well mixed with a little sugar, and again beat the cake well and lightly for three or four minutes; put it into a buttered mould, and bake it from an hour to an hour and a quarter; or divide it in two, when three-quarters of an hour will be sufficient for each part.

Flour, 1 lb; butter, ½ lb; sugar, ½ lb; boiling milk, full ¼ pint; eggs, 3; currants, ½ lb; good carbonate of soda, 1 very small teaspoonful: 1 to 1¼ hours. Or: divided in two, ½ to ¾ hour.

Obs. This, if carefully made, resembles a pound cake, but is much less expensive, and far more wholesome, while it has the advantage of being very expeditiously prepared, Great care, how-

* Six ounces would to many tastes be quite sufficient, and the less butter the cake contains the better.

ever, must be taken to avoid mixing with it too large a proportion, or a coarse quality of soda; as either will impart to it a far from agreeable flavour.

THREADNEEDLE STREET BISCUITS

Mix with two pounds of sifted flour of the very best quality three ounces of good butter, and work it into the smallest possible crumbs; add four ounces of fine, dry, sifted sugar, and make them into a firm paste with new milk; beat this forcibly for some time with a rolling-pin, and when it is extremely smooth roll it the third of an inch thick, cut it with a small square cutter, and bake the biscuits in a very slow oven until they are crisp to the centre: no part of them should remain soft. Half a teaspoonful of carbonate of soda is said to improve them, but we have not put it to the test. Carraway-seeds can be added when they are liked.

Flour, 2 lb; butter, 3 oz; sugar, 4 oz; new milk, 1 pint or more: biscuits *slowly* baked until crisp.

AUNT CHARLOTTE'S BISCUITS

These biscuits, which are very simple and very good, may be made with the same dough as fine white bread, with the addition of from half to a whole ounce of butter to the pound kneaded into it after it has risen. Break the butter small, spread out the dough a little, knead it in well and equally, and leave it for about half an hour to rise; then fold it a quarter of an inch thick, prick it well all over, cut out the biscuits, and bake them in a moderate oven from ten to fifteen minutes: they should be crisp quite through, but not deeply coloured.

White-bread dough, 2 lb; butter, 1 to 2 oz; to rise ½ hour. Baked in moderate oven 10 to 15 minutes.

Obs. To make the biscuits by themselves, proceed as for Bordyke bread; but use new milk for them, and work three ounces of butter into two pounds of flour before the yeast is added.

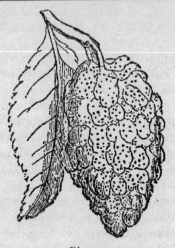

27

Citron

CONFECTIONARY

CARAMEL
(The quickest way)

Put into a brass skillet, or preserving-pan, some sifted sugar of the finest quality, and stir it softly with a wooden spoon or spatula, over a very gentle fire until it has become liquid; a pale or a deep tint may then be given to it, according to the purpose for which it is required: so soon as it is entirely melted, and looks clear, it is ready for use. Pastry-cooks glaze small pastry by just dipping the surface into it; and they use it also for *nougat*, and other confectionary, though it is not in general quite so brilliant as that which is made by other methods. When the sugar first begins to melt, it should be stirred only just in that part, or it will not be equally coloured.

This is a preparation of barley sugar, and almonds, filberts, or pistachio-nuts, of which good confectioners, both foreign and English, make a great variety of highly ornamental dishes. We must, however, confine our directions to the most common and simple mode of serving it. Blanch twelve ounces of fine Jordan almonds in the usual way, wipe them very dry, split them in halves, and spread them upon tins or dishes; dry them in a very gentle oven, without allowing them to brown; or if the flavour be liked better so, let them be equally coloured to a pale gold tint: they should then be often turned while in the oven. Boil to barley sugar in a small preserving-pan six ounces of highly-refined sugar, throw in the almonds, mix them with it well without breaking them, turn the nougat on to a dish slightly rubbed with oil, spread it out quickly, mark it into squares, and cut it before it is cold; or pour it into a mould, and with an oiled lemon spread it quickly, and very thin over it, and turn it out when cool. It must at all times be carefully preserved from damp; and should be put into a dry tin box as soon as it is cold.

Sugar, 6 oz; almonds, 12 oz.

Another and more expeditious way of making it, is to boil the sugar to caramel without any water, as previously directed: the proportion of almonds can be diminished at pleasure, but the nougat should always be well filled with them.

EVERTON TOFFIE

No. 1 – Put into a brass skillet or small preserving-pan three ounces of very fresh butter, and as soon as it is just melted add a pound of brown sugar of moderate quality; keep these stirred gently over a very clear fire for about fifteen minutes, or until a little of the mixture, dropped into a basin of cold water, breaks clean between the teeth without sticking to them: when it is boiled to this point, it must be poured out immediately, or it will burn. The grated rind of a lemon, added when the toffie is half done, improves it much; or a small teaspoonful of powdered ginger moistened with a little of the other ingredients as soon as the sugar is dissolved and then stirred to the whole, will vary it pleasantly to many tastes. The real Everton toffie is made with a much larger proportion of butter, but it is the less wholesome on that very account. If dropped upon dishes first rubbed with a buttered paper, the toffie when cold can be raised from them easily.

Butter, 3 oz; sugar, 1 lb: 15 to 18 minutes. Or, sugar, 1 lb; butter, 5 oz; almonds, 2 oz: 20 to 30 minutes.

No. 2 – Boil together a pound of sugar and five ounces of butter for twenty minutes; then stir in two ounces of almonds blanched, divided, and thoroughly dried in a slow oven, or before the fire. Let the toffie boil after they are added, till it crackles when dropped into cold water, and snaps between the teeth without sticking.†

Sugar, 1 lb; butter, 5 oz; almonds, 2 oz: 20 to 30 minutes.

† [*This must still be the first introduction to 'cooking' for many children.*]

CHOCOLATE DROPS

Throw into a well heated metal mortar from two to four ounces of the best quality of cake-chocolate broken small, and pound it with a warm pestle until it resembles a smooth paste or very thick batter; then add an equal weight of sugar in the finest powder, and beat them until they are thoroughly blended. Roll the mixture into small balls, lay them upon sheets of writing-paper or upon clean dishes, and take them off when they are nearly cold. The tops may be covered with white nonpareil comfits [*or sugar strands*], or the drops may be shaken in a paper containing some of these, and entirely encrusted with them; but it must be recollected that they will not adhere to them after they become hard. More or less sugar can be worked into the chocolate according to the taste; and a Wedgwood mortar may be used for it when no other is at hand, but one of bell-metal will answer the purpose better.

28

DESSERT DISHES

A well-selected and well-arranged dessert, however simple in its character, may always be rendered agreeable to the eye and to the taste: but in no department of the table can so much that is attractive to both be more readily combined; and at the present day an unusual degree of luxury is often displayed in it, the details of which, however, would be out of place here.

For common occasions, a few dishes of really fresh fruit taste-fully disposed and embedded in large green leaves, will be all that is required for a plain summer or autumn dessert; and at other parts of the year such as are appropriate to the season; but from the immense variety of cakes, biscuits, confections, ices, *bonbons*, and other *sucreries* (some of them extremely brilliant in appearance), and of fruit native and foreign, fresh, dried and preserved in every possible manner which are adapted to them, desserts may be served in any kind of style.

PEARLED FRUIT, OR FRUIT EN CHEMISE

Select for this dish very fine bunches of red and white currants, large ripe cherries, and gooseberries of different colours, and strawberries or raspberries very freshly gathered. Beat up the white of an egg with about half as much cold water, dip the fruit into this mixture, drain it on a sieve for an instant, and then roll it in fine sifted sugar until it is covered in every part; give it a gentle shake, and lay it on sheets of white paper to dry. In England, thin gum-water is sometimes used, we believe, for this dish, instead of the white of egg; we give, however, the French method of preparing it. It will dry gradually in a warm room, or a sunny window, in the course of three or four hours.

Obs. This is an inexpensive dish, which if well prepared has the appearance of fine confectionary. The incrustation of sugar much increases too the apparent size of the fruit. That which is used for it should be of the best quality, and fine and dry. When it becomes moist from the fruit being rolled in it, it will no longer adhere to it as it ought.

SALAD OF MIXED SUMMER FRUITS

Heap a dessert-dish quite high with alternate layers of fine fresh strawberries stripped from the stalks, white and red currants, and white or red raspberries; strew each layer plentifully with sifted sugar, and just before the dish is sent to table, pour equally over the top two wine-glassesful of sherry, Madeira, or any other good white wine. Very thick Devonshire cream may be laid entirely over the fruit, instead of the wine being mingled with it. Currants by themselves are excellent prepared in this way, and strawberries also. The fruit should be gently stirred with a spoon when it is served. Each variety must be picked with great nicety from the stalks.

Pare and slice half a dozen fine ripe peaches, arrange them in a dish, strew them with pounded sugar, and pour over them two or three glasses of champagne: other wine may be used, but this is best. Persons who prefer brandy can substitute it for wine. The quantity of sugar must be proportioned to the sweetness of the fruit.

BAKED COMPÔTE OF APPLES
(*Our little lady's Receipt*)

Put into a wide Nottingham jar, with a cover, two quarts of golden pippins, or of the small apple which resembles them in appearance, called the orange pippin (this is very plentiful in the county of Kent), pared and cored, but without being divided; strew amongst them some small strips of very thin fresh lemon-rind, throw on them, nearly at the top, half a pound of good Lisbon sugar, and set the jar, with the cover tied on, for some hours, or for a night, into a very slow oven. The apples will be extremely good, if not too quickly baked: they should remain entire, but be perfectly tender, and clear in appearance. Add a little lemon-juice when the season is far advanced.

Apples, 2 quarts; rind, quite small lemon; sugar, ½ lb: 1 night in slow oven; or some hours baking in a *very* gentle one.

Obs. These apples may be served hot as a second-course dish; or cold, with a boiled custard poured round or over them. They will likewise answer admirably to fill *Gabrielle's pudding*, or a *vol-au-vent à la crême*.

TO BAKE PEARS

Wipe some large sound iron pears, arrange them on a dish with the stalk end upwards, put them into the oven after the bread is withdrawn, and let them remain all night. If well baked, they will be excellent, very sweet, and juicy, and much finer in flavour than those which are stewed or baked with sugar: the *bon chrétien* pear also is delicious baked thus.

STEWED PEARS

Pare, cut in halves, and core a dozen fine pears, put them into a close shutting stewpan with some thin strips of lemon-rind, half a pound of sugar in lumps, as much water as will nearly cover them, and should a very bright colour be desired, a dozen grains of cochineal, bruised, and tied in a muslin; stew the fruit as gently as possible, four or five hours, or longer should it not be perfectly tender. Wine is sometimes added both to stewed pears and to baked ones. If put into a covered jar, well tied down and baked for some hours, with a proper quantity of liquid and sugar, they will be very good.

BOILED CHESTNUTS

Make a slight incision in the outer skin only, of each chestnut, to prevent its bursting, and when all are done, throw them into plenty of boiling water, with about a dessertspoonful of salt to the half gallon. Some chestnuts will require to be boiled nearly or quite an hour, others little more than half the time: the cook should try them occasionally, and as soon as they are soft through, drain them, wipe them in a coarse cloth, and send them to table quickly in a hot napkin.

Obs. The best chestnuts are those which have no internal divisions: the finest kinds are quite *entire* when shelled.

RED CURRANT ICE

Strip from the stalks and take two pounds' weight of fine ripe currants and half a pound of raspberries; rub them through a fine sieve, and mingle thoroughly with them sufficient cold syrup to render the mixture agreeably sweet, and – unless the pure flavour of the fruit be altogether preferred – add the strained juice of one large or of two small lemons, and proceed at once to freeze the mixture.

Currants, 2 lb; raspberries, ½ lb; sugar, ¾ to 1 lb: boiled for 6 or 8 minutes in ½ pint of water and left till quite cold. (Juice of lemon or lemons at pleasure.)

Strawberry and raspberry water-ices are made in precisely the same manner.

To convert any of these into English ice-creams, merely mingle the juice and pulp of the fruit with sufficient pounded sugar to sweeten them, or with the syrup as above, and then blend with them gradually from a pint and a half to a quart of fresh sweet cream, and the lemon-juice or not at choice.

29

Antique Wine Vase

SYRUPS, LIQUEURS, ETC.

FINE CURRANT SYRUP, OR SIROP DE GROSEILLES

Express the juice from some fine ripe red currants, which have been gathered in dry weather, and stripped from the stalks; strain, and put it into a new, or a perfectly clean and dry earthen pitcher, and let it stand in a cellar or in some cool place for twenty-four hours, or longer, should it not then appear perfectly curdled. Pour it gently into a fine hair-sieve, and let the clear juice drain through without pressure; pass it through a jelly-bag, or a closely-woven cloth, weigh it, and add as much *good* sugar broken small as there is of the juice, and when this is dissolved turn the syrup into a preserving-pan or stewpan, and boil it gently for four or five minutes being careful to clear off all the scum. In twelve hours afterwards the syrup may be put into small dry bottles, and corked and stored in a cool, but dry place. It is a most agreeable preparation, retaining perfectly the flavour of the fresh fruit; and mixed with water, it affords, like strawberry or raspberry vinegar, a delicious summer beverage, and one which is peculiarly adapted to invalids. It makes also a fine isinglass jelly, and an incomparable sweet-pudding sauce. A portion of raspberry or cherry-juice may be mixed with that of the currants at pleasure.

CHERRY-BRANDY
(*Tappington Everard Receipt*)

Fill to about two-thirds of their depth, some wide-necked bottles with the small cherries called in the markets brandy-blacks; pour in sufficient sifted sugar to fill up more than half of the remaining space, and then as much good French brandy as will cover the fruit, and reach to the necks of the bottles. Cork them securely, and let them stand for two months before they are opened: the liqueur poured from the cherries will be excellent, and the fruit itself very good.

OXFORD RECEIPT FOR BISHOP

'Make several incisions in the rind of a lemon, stick cloves in these, and roast the lemon by a slow fire. Put small but equal quantities of cinnamon, cloves, mace, and allspice, with a race of ginger, into a saucepan with half a pint of water: let it boil until it is reduced one-half. Boil one bottle of port wine, burn a portion of the spirit out of it by applying a lighted paper to the saucepan; put the roasted lemon and spice into the wine; stir it up well, and let it stand near the fire ten minutes. Rub a few knobs of sugar on the rind of a lemon, put the sugar into a bowl or jug, with the juice of half a lemon (not roasted), pour the wine into it, grate in some nutmeg, sweeten it to the taste, and serve it up with the lemon and spice floating in it.'

Obs. Bishop is frequently made with a Seville orange stuck with cloves and slowly roasted, and its flavour to many tastes is infinitely finer than that of the lemon.

CAMBRIDGE MILK PUNCH

Throw into two quarts of new milk the very thinly-pared rind of a fine lemon, and half a pound of good sugar in lumps; bring it slowly to boil, take out the lemon-rind, draw it from the fire, and stir quickly in a couple of well-whisked eggs which have been mixed with less than half a pint of cold milk, and strained through a sieve; the milk must not of course be allowed to boil after these are mixed with it. Add gradually a pint of rum, and half a pint of brandy; mill the punch to a froth, and serve it immediately with quite warm glasses. At the University the lemon-rind is usually omitted, but it is a great improvement to the flavour of the beverage. The sugar and spirit can be otherwise apportioned to the taste; and we would recommend the yolks of three eggs, or of four, in preference to the two whole ones.

New milk, 2 quarts; rind, 1 large lemon; sugar, ½ lb; fresh eggs, 2; cold milk, ⅓ pint: rum, 1 pint; brandy, ½ pint.

TO MULL WINE
(An excellent French Receipt)

Boil in a wineglassful and a half of water, a quarter of an ounce of spice (cinnamon, ginger slightly bruised, and cloves), with three ounces of fine sugar, until they form a thick syrup, which must not on any account be allowed to burn. Pour in a pint of port wine, and stir it gently until it is on the *point* of boiling only: it should then be served immediately. The addition of a strip or two of orange-rind cut extremely thin, gives to this beverage the flavour of Bishop. In France light claret takes the place of port wine in making it, and the better kinds of *vin ordinaire* are very palatable thus prepared.

Water, 1½ wineglassful; spice, ¼ oz, of which fine cloves, 24, and of remainder, rather more ginger than cinnamon; sugar, 3 oz: 15 to 20 minutes. Port wine or claret, 1 pint; orange-rind, if used, to be boiled with the spice.

Obs. Sherry, or very fine raisin or ginger wine, prepared as above, and stirred hot to the yolks of four fresh eggs, will make good egg-wine.

AN ADMIRABLE COOL CUP

Weigh six ounces of sugar in lumps, and extract the essence from the rind of a large fresh lemon by rubbing them upon it; then put them into a deep jug, and add the strained juice of one lemon and a half. When the sugar is dissolved, pour in a bottle of good cider, and three large wineglassesful of sherry; add nearly half a small nutmeg lightly grated, and serve the cup with or without some sprigs of fresh balm or borage in it. Brandy is sometimes added to it, but is, we think, no improvement. If closely covered down, and placed on ice for a short time, it will be more agreeable as a summer beverage.

331

'Strip the tender leaves of mint into a tumbler, and add to them as much wine, brandy, or any other spirit, as you wish to take. Put some pounded ice into a second tumbler; pour this on the mint and brandy, and continue to pour the mixture from one tumbler to the other until the whole is sufficiently impregnated with the flavour of the mint, which is extracted by the particles of the ice coming into brisk contact when changed from one vessel to the other. Now place the glass in a larger one, containing pounded ice: on taking it out of which it will be covered with frost-work.'

Obs. We apprehend that this preparation is, like most other iced American beverages, to be imbibed through a reed; the receipt, which was contributed by an American gentleman, is somewhat vague.

DELICIOUS MILK LEMONADE

Dissolve six ounces of loaf sugar in a pint of boiling water, and mix with them a quarter of a pint of lemon-juice, and the same quantity of sherry; then add three-quarters of a pint of cold milk, stir the whole well together, and pass it through a jelly-bag till clear.

EXCELLENT PORTABLE LEMONADE

Rasp, with a quarter-pound of sugar, the rind of a very fine juicy lemon, reduce it to powder, and pour on it the strained juice of the fruit. Press the mixture into a jar, and when wanted for use dissolve a tablespoonful of it in a glass of water. It will keep a considerable time. If too sweet for the taste of the drinker, a very small portion of citric acid may be added when it is taken.

First boil the water which is to be used for the wine, and let it again become perfectly cold; then put into a sound sweet cask eight pounds of fine Malaga raisins for each gallon that is to be used, taking out only the quite large stalks; the fruit and water may be put in alternately until the cask is full, the raisins being well pressed down in it; lay the bung lightly over, stir the wine every day or two, and keep it full by the addition of water that has, like the first, been boiled, but which must always be quite cold when it is used. So soon as the fermentation has entirely ceased, which may be in from six to seven weeks, press in the bung, and leave the wine untouched for twelve months; draw it off then into a clean cask, and fine it, if necessary, with isinglass, tied in a muslin and suspended in it. We have not ourselves had this receipt tried; but we have tasted wine made by it which had been five years kept, and which so much resembled a rich foreign wine that we could with difficulty believe it was English-made.

To each gallon of water (boiled and left till cold) 8 lb of fine Malaga raisins; to stand 12 months; then to be drawn off and fined.

Obs. The refuse raisins make admirable vinegar if fresh water be poured to them, and the cask placed in the sun. March is the best time for making the wine.

THE COUNSELLOR'S CUP

Rub a quarter of a pound of sugar upon the rinds of two fine China oranges,† put it into an enamelled stewpan, and pour on it a pint of water; let these boil gently for two or three minutes, then pour on half a pint of China orange-juice mixed with that of one lemon, and previously strained through muslin; the moment this begins to boil, pour it into a hot jug, and stir to it half a pint of the best Cognac brandy. Serve it immediately. When preferred cold, prepare the syrup with the juice of the fruit, cover it down in the jug, set it into ice, or into a very cool place, and add the spirit only just before the cup is wanted for table. Should the fruit be very acid, increase the proportion of sugar. A few slight strips of the rind of a Seville orange cut very thin, would to many tastes be an agreeable addition to the beverage; which should be made always with fresh sound fruit.

Sugar, 4 oz (6 if needed); rasped rinds of China oranges, 2; water, 1 pint: 3 minutes. Strained juice of China oranges mixed with that of 1 large lemon, ½ pint; best Cognac brandy, ½ pint.

Obs. For a large cup these proportions must be doubled. Sherry or Madeira substituted for the brandy, will make a pleasant cool cup of this kind; and equal parts of well made lemonade, and of any good light white wine, thoroughly cooled down, will give another agreeable beverage for warm weather; but a much smaller proportion of wine would better adapt it to many tastes.

† [*'China' oranges are sweet oranges as opposed to the bitter Seville ones.*]

30

Patent Percolator, with Spirit Lamp

COFFEE, CHOCOLATE, ETC.

COFFEE

There is no beverage which is held in more universal esteem than good coffee, and none in this country at least, which is obtained with greater difficulty (unless indeed it be *pure* wine). We hear constant and well-founded complaints both from foreigners and English people, of the wretched compounds so commonly served up here under its name, especially in many lodging houses, hotels, and railway refreshment rooms;* yet nothing can be easier than to prepare it properly. Some elaborate and various fanciful modes of making it have been suggested at different times by writers fond of novelty, but they have in general nothing to recommend them beyond the more simple processes which follow, and of which we believe the result will seldom prove unsatisfactory to our readers, unless it be to such of them as may have been accustomed to the spiced or other peculiar Oriental preparations of the fragrant berry, or simply to the exquisite quality of it, which would appear to be obtainable only in the East; or which, at all events, is beyond the reach of the mass of English consumers, and of their near Continental neighbours.

* At some of the principal stations on lines connected with the coast, by which an immense number of strangers pass and repass, the coffee is so bad, that great as the refreshment of it would be to them, particularly in night travelling, in very cold weather, they reject it as too nauseous to be swallowed. A little *national pride* ought surely to prevent this, if no higher principle interfered to do so; for to exact the full price of a good commodity, and habitually to supply only trash for it, is a commercial disgrace.†

† [*These comments, written more than a century ago, seem to remain as true now as they did then.*]

A FEW GENERAL DIRECTIONS FOR MAKING COFFEE

When good coffee is desired, let it be procured if possible of a first-rate London house which can be depended on; and we would recommend that it should be of the finest quality that can be obtained; for there is no real economy in using that which is nominally cheaper, as a larger quantity will be required to give the same amount of strength, and the flavour will be very inferior. It should always be *freshly roasted*; but when a constant and large demand for it exists, it will be easy to have it so. When it has been stored for any length of time it will be much freshened and improved by being gently heated through, either in the oven or in a stewpan held high above the fire. It should be often turned while it is warming, and ground as soon as it is cold again. *Never purchase it ready ground* unless compelled to do so. When no proper mill for it is fitted up in the house, a small portable one, which may be had at a trifling expense, will answer tolerably well for grinding it, though it cannot be used with quite the same facility as those which are fastened firmly to a wall; but whatever form of mill may be used it should be arranged so as to reduce the berries to a moderately fine powder; for if it be too coarse the essence will be only partially extracted from it by filtering; and if it be extremely fine the water will not percolate through it, and it will not be clear.

Always serve hot milk or cream, or hot milk and cold cream, if preferred, with breakfast coffee. In the evening, when milk is served at all with it, it should likewise be boiling.

Do not, *in any way*, make use of the residue of one day's coffee in preparing that of the next; you would but injure the purity of its flavour by doing so, and effect *next to nothing* in the matter of economy.

EXCELLENT BREAKFAST COFFEE

A simple, well-made English filter, or *percolator*, as it is called, will answer perfectly for making coffee, but from amongst the many of more recent invention which are on sale, the reader who prefers one of ornamental appearance, and of novel construction, will easily be suited. The size of the filter must be adapted to the number of persons for whom the coffee is to be prepared; for if a large quantity of the powder be heaped into an insufficient space for it, there will not be room for it to swell, and the water will not pass through. Put three ounces of coffee into one which will contain in the lower compartment, two pints and a half; shake the powder quite level and press it closely down; remove the presser, put on the top strainer, and pour round and round, so as to wet the coffee equally, about the third part of a measured pint of fast boiling water. Let this drain quite through before more is added; then pour in – still *quite boiling* – in the same manner, as much more water, and when it has passed through, add the remainder; let it drain entirely through, then remove the top of the filter, put the cover on the part which contains the coffee, and serve it immediately. It will be very strong, and perfectly clear. Fill the breakfast cups two parts full of new boiling milk, and add as much of the infusion as will give it the degree of strength which is agreeable to those for whom it is prepared. When it is liked extremely strong, the proportion of milk must be diminished, or less later be poured to the coffee.

Good breakfast coffee (for three persons). Best Mocha, in moderately fine powder, ground at the instant of using it, 3 oz; boiling water added by degrees, 1 pint (more at pleasure). Boiling milk served with it, 1½ pint to 1 quart. Cream in addition to either of the above, at choice.

BURNT COFFEE, OR COFFEE À LA MILITAIRE†
(*In France vulgarly called Gloria*)

Make some coffee as strong and as clear as possible, sweeten it in the cup with white sugar almost to syrup, then pour the brandy on the top gently over a spoon, set fire to it with a lighted paper, and when the spirit is in part consumed, blow out the flame, and drink the *gloria* quite hot.

† [*This must be the forerunner of Irish coffee (made with Irish whiskey) and Gaelic – perhaps originally Gallic – coffee made with brandy, but not as rich as no cream is added.*]

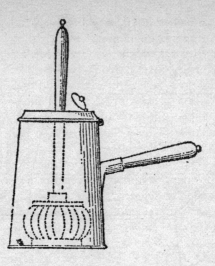

TO MAKE CHOCOLATE

An ounce of chocolate, if good, will be sufficient for one person. Rasp, and then boil it from five to ten minutes with about four tablespoonsful of water; when it is extremely smooth add nearly a pint of new milk, give it another boil, stir it well, or mill it, and serve it directly. For water-chocolate use three quarters of a pint of water instead of the milk, and send rich hot cream to table with it.

Chocolate, 2 oz; water, quarter-pint, or rather more; milk, ¾ pint: ½ minute.

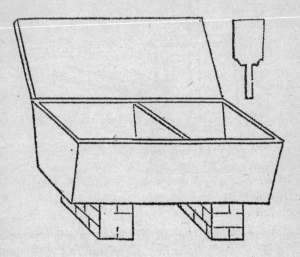

31

BREAD†

A FEW RULES TO BE OBSERVED IN MAKING BREAD

Never use too large a proportion of yeast, as the bread will not only become dry very speedily when this is done, but it will be far less sweet and pleasant in flavour than that which is more slowly fermented, and the colour will not be so good: there will also be a great chance of its being bitter when brewer's yeast is used for it.

Remember that milk or water of *scalding* heat poured to any kind of yeast will render the bread heavy. One pint of either added quite boiling to a pint and a half of cold, will bring it to about the degree of warmth required. In frosty weather the proportion of the heated liquid may be increased a little.

When only porter-yeast – which is dark-coloured and bitter – can be procured, use a much smaller proportion than usual, and allow *much* longer time for it to rise. Never let it be sent to the oven until it is evidently *light*. Bitter bread is unpalatable, but not really unwholesome; but heavy bread is *particularly* so.

Let the leaven be kneaded up quickly with the remainder of the flour when once it is well risen, as it should on no account be allowed to sink again before this is done, when it has reached the proper point; and in making the dough, be particularly careful not to render it too lithe by adding more liquid than is requisite. It should be quite firm, and entirely free from lumps and crumbs throughout the mass, and on the surface also, which ought to be *perfectly smooth*.

In winter, place the bread while it is rising sufficiently close to the fire to prevent its becoming cold, but never so near as to render it *hot*. A warm thick cloth should be thrown over the pan in which it is made immediately after the leaven is mixed, and kept on it until the bread is ready for the oven.

† [*Eliza Acton was much interested in the subject of home baking, and wrote the 'English Bread Book', which was published in 1857.*]

BORDYKE BREAD
(*Author's Receipt*)

Mix with a gallon of flour a large teaspoonful of fine salt, make a hollow in the centre, and pour in two tablespoonsful of solid, well purified yeast, gradually diluted with about two pints and a half of milk, and work it into a thick batter with the surrounding flour, strew a thick layer over and leave it to rise from an hour to an hour and a half; then knead it up with as much more warm skimmed milk, or half new milk and half water, as will render it quite firm and smooth without being very stiff; let it rise another hour, and divide it into three loaves; put them into square tins slightly buttered, or into round baking pans, and bake them about an hour and a quarter in a well-heated oven. The dough can be formed into household loaves if preferred, and sent to the oven in the usual way. When a finer and more spongy kind of bread is required for immediate eating, substitute new milk for skimmed, dissolve in it about an ounce of butter, leave it more liquid when the sponge is set, and let the whole be lightly kneaded into a lithe dough: the bread thus made will be excellent when new, and for a day or so after it is baked, but it will become dry sooner than the other.

Flour, 1 gallon; salt, 1 teaspoonful; yeast, 2 tablespoonsful; skimmed milk, 2½ pints: to rise from 1 to 1½ hour. Additional milk, 1 to 2 pints: to rise 1 hour. 3 loaves, baked 1¼ hour.

Obs. 1. A few spoonsful of cream will wonderfully improve either of the above receipts, and sweet butter-milk, substituted for the other, will give to the bread the shortness of a cake: we would particularly recommend it for trial when it can be procured.

Obs. 2. Shallow round earthen pans answer much better, we think, than tins for baking bread; they should be *slightly* rubbed with butter before the dough is put into them.

POTATO BREAD

One pound of good mealy potatoes, steamed or boiled very dry, in the ordinary way, or prepared by Captain Kater's receipt (see Chapter 17), and rubbed quite hot, through a coarse sieve, into a couple of pounds of flour, with which they should be well mixed, will produce excellent bread, which will remain moist much longer than wheaten bread made as usual. The yeast should be added immediately after the potatoes. An ounce or two of butter, an egg and some new milk, will convert this bread into superior rolls.

GENEVA ROLLS, OR BUNS

Break down into very small crumbs three ounces of butter with two pounds of flour; add a little salt, and set the sponge with a large tablespoonful of solid yeast, mixed with a pint of new milk, and a tablespoonful or more of strong saffron water; let it rise for a full hour, then stir to a couple of well-beaten eggs as much hot milk as will render them lukewarm, and wet the rolls with them to a light, lithe dough; leave it from half to three-quarters of an hour longer, mould it into small rolls, brush them with beaten yolk of egg, and bake them from twenty minutes to half an hour. The addition of six ounces of good sugar, three of butter, half a pound or more of currants, the grated rind of a large lemon, and a couple of ounces of candied orange-rind, will convert these into excellent buns. When the flavour of the saffron is not liked, omit it altogether. Only so much should be used at any time as will give a rich colour to the bread.

Flour, 2 lb; butter, 3 oz; solid yeast, 1 large tablespoonful (saffron, 1 teaspoonful; water, less than a quarter pint); new milk, 1 pint: 1 hour, or more. 2 eggs, more milk: ¾ hour: baked 20 to 30 minutes.

EXCELLENT DAIRY-BREAD MADE WITHOUT YEAST†

(Author's Receipt)

When we first heard unfermented bread vaguely spoken of, we had it tried very successfully in the following manner; and we have since been told that an almost similar method of preparing it is common in many remote parts both of England and Ireland, where it is almost impossible to procure a constant supply of yeast. Blend well together a teaspoonful of pounded sugar and fifty grains of the purest carbonate of soda; mix a saltspoonful of salt with a pound of flour, and rub the soda and sugar through a hair-sieve into it. Stir and mingle them well, and make them quickly into a firm but not *hard* dough with sour buttermilk. Bake the loaf well in a thoroughly heated but not *fierce* oven. In a brick, or good iron oven a few minutes less than an hour would be sufficient to bake a loaf of similar weight. The buttermilk should be kept until it is quite acid, but it must never be in the slightest degree rancid, or otherwise bad. *All* unfermented bread should be placed in the oven directly it is made, or it will be heavy.

† [*This kind of bread, though usually made with wholemeal flour, is still commonly to be found in Ireland today, with local variations in style.*]

TO FRESHEN STALE BREAD (AND PASTRY, ETC.) AND PRESERVE IT FROM MOULD

If entire loaves be placed in a gentle oven and heated quite through, *without* being previously dipped into cold water, according to the old-fashioned plan, they will eat almost like bread newly baked: they should not remain in it long enough to become hard and dry, but they should be made hot throughout. In very damp localities, when large household bakings take place but once in eight or ten days, it is sometimes necessary to use precautions against the attack of mould, though the bread may have been exceedingly well made; and the method recommended above will be the best for warding it off, and for preserving the bread eatable for several days longer than it would otherwise be. If *large* loaves be just dipped into cold water and then placed in a quick oven until they are again thoroughly dried, they will resemble *new* bread altogether.

Pastry, cakes, and biscuits, may all be greatly improved when stale, by heating them in a gentle oven.

TO KNOW WHEN BREAD IS SUFFICIENTLY BAKED

When the surface is uniformly browned, and it is everywhere *firm to the touch*, and the bottom crust of the loaf is hard, it is generally certain that it is thoroughly baked. To test bread that has been cut (or yeast-cakes), press down the crumb lightly in the centre with the thumb; when it is elastic and rises again to its place, it is proof that it is perfectly done; but if the indentation remains, the heat has not sufficiently penetrated the dough to convert it into wholesome eating.

32

FOREIGN AND JEWISH COOKERY

It is not clear on what principle Eliza Acton divides her 'Foreign Cookery' from the rest. Many of the receipts in the main part of the book are French, and there is a separate chapter on Curries, as Indian food had been familiar to the English middle classes ever since the establishment of the East India Company, from which time onwards there were few families that did not have some connection, near or remote, with the Far East. In this chapter, it seems to be only the Jewish dishes, already referred to in the Introduction, that are particularly 'foreign'.

REMARKS ON JEWISH COOKERY

From being forbidden by their usages to mingle butter, or other preparations of milk or cream with meat at any meal, the Jews have oil much used in their cookery of fish, meat, and vegetables. Pounded almonds and rich syrups of sugar and water agreeably flavoured, assist in compounding their sweet dishes, many of which are excellent, and preserve much of their oriental character; but we are credibly informed that the restrictions of which we have spoken are not at the present day very rigidly observed by the main body of Jews in this country, though they are so by those who are denominated strict.

TO FRY SALMON AND OTHER FISH IN OIL
(To Serve Cold)

Turn into a small deep frying-pan, which should be kept for the purpose, a flask of fresh olive oil, place it over a clear fire, and as soon as it ceases to bubble lay in a pound and a half of delicate salmon properly cleansed and well dried in a cloth, and fry it gently until it is cooked quite through. The surface should be only lightly browned, and when the proper colour is attained the pan must be lifted so high from the fire as to prevent it being deepened. Drain the fish well when it is done, and when it is perfectly cold, dish, and garnish it with light foliage. The Jews have cold fried fish much served at their repasts.† Fillets of sole, plaice, brill, small turbots, or other flat fish, may be fried as above, and arranged in a symmetrical form round a portion of a larger fish, or by themselves. We would recommend as an accompaniment one of the Mauritian chatnies which are to be found in this chapter.

Olive oil, 1 small flask; salmon, about 1½ lb: ½ hour or rather more. Fillets of fish, 5 to 10 minutes.

Obs. The oil should be strained through a sieve, and set aside as the fish is done; it will serve many times for frying if this be observed.

† [*Jewish fried fish is still a great speciality nowadays and eaten either hot or cold.*]

We have not thought it necessary to test this receipt ourselves, as we have tasted the puddings made by it more than once, and have received the exact directions for them from the Jewish lady at whose house they were made. They are extremely delicate and excellent. The almonds for them were procured ready ground from a Jew confectioner, but when they cannot be thus obtained they must be pounded in the usual manner. With half a pound of sweet, mingle six or seven bitter almonds, half a pound of sifted sugar, a little fine orange-flower water, with the yolks of ten and the whites of seven well whisked eggs, and when the whole of the ingredients are intimately blended, bake the pudding in a rather quick oven for half an hour, or longer should it not be then sufficently firm to turn out of the dish. Sift sugar thickly over, or pour round it a rich syrup flavoured with orange-flower water, noyau or maraschino.

Obs. We think a fruit syrup – pine-apple or other – or a compôte of fruit would be an excellent accompaniment to this pudding, which may be served hot or cold. We conclude that the dish in which it is baked, if not well buttered, must be rubbed with oil. The above proportions will make two puddings of sufficient size for a small party.

THE LADY'S OR INVALID'S NEW BAKED APPLE PUDDING
(Author's Original Receipt – Appropriate to the Jewish table)

This pudding, which contains no butter, is most excellent when made with exactness by the directions which follow, but any variation from them will probably be attended with entire failure, especially in the crust, which if properly made will be solid, but very light and crisp; whereas, if the proportion of sugar for it be diminished, the bread will not form a compact mass, but will fall into crumbs when it is served. First weigh six ounces of the crumb of a light stale loaf, and grate it down small; then add to, and mix thoroughly with it three ounces and a half of pounded sugar, and a slight pinch of salt. Next, take from a pound to a pound and a quarter of russets, or of any other good baking apples; pare, and then take them off the cores in quarters without cutting the fruit asunder, as they will then, from the form given to them, lie more compactly in the dish. Arrange them in close layers in a deep tart-dish which holds about a pint and a half, and strew amongst them four ounces of sugar and the grated rind of a fine fresh lemon; add the strained juice of the lemon, and pour the bread-crumbs softly in a heap upon the apples in the centre of the dish, and with the back of a spoon level them gently into a very smooth layer of equal thickness, pressing them lightly down upon the fruit, which must all be perfectly covered with them. Sift powdered sugar over, wipe the edge of the dish, and bake the pudding in a somewhat quick oven for rather more than three-quarters of an hour. We have had it several times baked quite successfully in a baker's oven, of which the heat is in general too great for puddings of a delicate kind. Very pale brown sugar will answer for it almost as well as pounded. For the nursery, some crumbs of bread may be strewed between the layers of fruit, and nutmeg or cinnamon may be used instead of lemon.

Obs. We insert this receipt here because the pudding has been so much liked, and found so wholesome by many persons who have partaken of it at different times, that we think it will be acceptable to some of our readers, but it belongs properly to another work which we have in progress, and from which we extract it now for the present volume. An ounce or more of ratifias crushed to powder, may be added to the crust, or strewed over the pudding before it is served, when they are considered an improvement.

A FEW GENERAL DIRECTIONS FOR THE JEWISH TABLE

As a substitute for milk, in the composition of soufflés, puddings, and sweet dishes, almond-cream as it is called, will be found to answer excellently. To prepare it, blanch and pound the almonds, and then pour very gradually to them boiling water in the proportion directed below; turn them into a strong cloth or tammy, and wring it from them with powerful pressure, to extract as much as possible of it from them again.

The fruit custards of page 287 and the *meringues* of fruit of page 288 are perfectly suited to the tables of Jewish families; and sweet or savoury *croustades* or fried patties may be supplied to them from the receipts in the present work, by substituting clarified marrow for the butter used for them in general cookery. The reader will easily discover in addition, numerous dishes distributed through this volume which may be served to them without departing from their peculiar usages.

Almond-cream: (for puddings, etc.) almonds, 4 oz; water, 1 pint. For blancmanges, and rich *soufflés*, creams and custards: almonds, ½ to whole pound; water, 1 to 1½ pint.

Obs. As every cook may not be quite aware of the articles of food strictly prohibited by the Mosaic law, it may be well to specify them here. Pork in every form; all varieties of shell-fish, without exception; hares, rabbits, and swans.

TOMATA AND OTHER CHATNIES
(*Mauritian Receipts*)

The composition of these favourite oriental sauces varies but little except in the ingredient which forms the basis of each. The same piquant or stimulating auxiliaries are intermingled with all of them in greater or less proportion. These are, young onions, chilies (sometimes green ginger), oil, vinegar, and salt; and occasionally a little garlic or full grown onion, which in England might be superseded by a small portion of minced eschalot. Green peaches, mangoes, and other unripe fruits, crushed to pulp on the stone roller, shown at the head of this chapter; ripe bananas, tomatas roasted or raw, and also reduced to a smooth pulp; potatoes cooked and mashed; the fruit of the egg-plant boiled and reduced to a paste; fish, fresh, salted, or smoked, and boiled or grilled, taken in small fragments from the bones and skin, and torn into minute shreds, or pounded, are all in their turn used in their preparation.* Mingle with any one of these as much of the green onions and chilies chopped up small, as will give it a strong flavour; add salt if needed, and as much olive oil, of pure quality, with a third as much of vinegar, as will bring it to the consistence of a thick sauce. Serve it with currie, cutlets, steaks, pork, cold meat, or fish, or aught else to which it would be an acceptable accompaniment.

* We are indepted for these receipts to a highly intelligent medical man who has been for twenty years a resident in Mauritius.

AN INDIAN BURDWAN
(*Entrée*)

This is an Oriental dish of high savour, which may be made either with a young fowl or chicken parboiled for the purpose, or with the remains of such as have already been sent to table. First, put into a stewpan about a tablespoonful of very mild onion finely minced, or a larger proportion with a mixture of eschalots, for persons whose taste is in favour of so strong a flavour; add rather more than a quarter of a pint of cold water, about an ounce of butter smoothly blended with a very small teaspoonful of flour, a moderate seasoning of cayenne, and a tablespoonful of essence of anchovies. Shake or stir this sauce over a clear fire until it boils, then let it stand aside and merely simmer for ten or fifteen minutes, or until the onion is quite tender, then pour to it a couple of wineglassesful of Madeira (Sherry or Teneriffe will do), and a tablespoonful of chili-vinegar. Lay in the fowl after having carved it neatly, divided all the joints, and stripped off the skin; and let it remain close to the fire, but without boiling, until it is perfectly heated through; bring it to the point of boiling and send it immediately to table. A dish of rice, boiled as for currie, is often, but not invariably, served with it. Should the fowl have been parboiled only – that is to say, boiled for a quarter of an hour – it must be gently stewed in the sauce for fifteen or twenty minutes; longer, even, should it not then be quite tender. Cold lamb, or veal, or calf's-head, or a delicate young rabbit, may be very advantageously served as a *rechauffé*, in a sauce compounded as above. The various condiments contained in this can be differently apportioned at pleasure; and pickled capsicum, or chilies minced, can be added to it at choice either in lieu of, or in addition to the chili-vinegar. The juice of a fresh lime should, if possible, be thrown into it before it is served. Except for a quite plain family dinner, only the superior joints of poultry should be used for this dish. Care should be taken not to allow the essence of anchovies to predominate too powerfully in it.

THE KING OF OUDE'S OMLET

Whisk up very lightly, after having cleared them in the usual way, five fine fresh eggs; add to them two dessertspoonsful of milk or cream, a small teaspoonful of salt, one – or half that quantity for English eaters – of cayenne pepper, three of minced mint, and two dessertspoonsful of young leeks, or of mild onions chopped small. Dissolve an ounce and a half of good butter in a frying-pan about the size of a plate, or should a larger one of necessity be used, raise the handle so as to throw the omlet entirely to the opposite side; pour in the eggs, and when the omlet, which should be kept as thick as possible, is well risen and quite firm, and of a fine light brown underneath, slide it on to a very hot dish, and fold it together 'like a turnover', the brown side uppermost: six or seven minutes will fry it. This receipt is given to the reader in a very modified form, the fiery original which we transcribe being likely to find but few admirers here we apprehend: the proportion of leeks or onions might still be much diminished with advantage: 'Five eggs, two tolahs of milk, one masha of salt, two mashas of cayenne pepper, three of mint, and two tolahs of leeks.'

KEDGEREE OR KIDGEREE, AN INDIAN BREAKFAST DISH

Boil four ounces of rice tender and dry as for currie, and when it is cooled down put it into a saucepan with nearly an equal quantity of cold fish taken clear of skin and bone, and divided into very small flakes or scallops. Cut up an ounce or two of fresh butter and add it, with a full seasoning of cayenne, and as much salt as may be required. Stir the kedgeree constantly over a clear fire until it is very hot; then mingle quickly with it two slightly beaten eggs. Do not let it boil after these are stirred in; but serve the dish when they are just set. A Mauritian chatney may be sent to table with it. The butter may be omitted, and its place supplied by an additional egg or more.

Cold turbot, brill, salmon, soles, John Dory, and shrimps, may all be served in this form.†

† [*The best of all 'Kidgerees' to my mind is made with smoked haddock, in which case no 'Chatney' is needed.*]

SIMPLE TURKISH OR ARABIAN PILAW
(*From Mr Lane,† the Oriental Traveller*)

'Pilaw or pilau is made by boiling rice in plenty of water for about twenty minutes, so that the water drains off easily, leaving the grains whole, and with some degree of hardness; then stirring it up with a little butter, just enough to make the grains separate easily, and seasoning it with salt and pepper. Often a fowl, boiled almost to rags, is laid upon the top. Sometimes small morsels of fried or roasted mutton or lamb are mixed up with it; and there are many other additions; but generally the Turks and Arabs add nothing to the rice but the butter, and salt, and pepper.'

Obs. We are indebted to the courtesy of Mr Lane for this receipt which was procured from him for us by one of his friends.

† [*Edward William Lane, translator of a* Thousand and One Nights *and a well known Arabic scholar.*]

Take the fish from the bones, and cut it into inch and half squares; lay it into a stewpan with sufficient hot water to barely cover it; sprinkle some salt over, and boil it gently until it is about half cooked. Lift it out with a fish-slice, pour the liquor into a basin, and clear off any scum which may be on it. Should there be three or four pounds of fish, dissolve a quarter of a pound of butter in a stewpan, and when it has become a little brown, add two cloves of garlic and a large onion finely minced or sliced very thin; fry them until they are well coloured, then add the fish; strew equally over it, and stir it well up with from two to three tablespoonsful of Bengal currie powder; cover the pan, and shake it often until the fish is nicely browned; next add by degrees the liquor in which it was stewed, and simmer it until it is perfectly done, but not so as to fall into fragments. Add a moderate quantity of lemon-juice or chili vinegar, and serve it very hot.

RISOTTO À LA MILANAISE

Slice a large onion very thin, and divide it into shreds; then fry it slowly until it is equally but not too deeply browned; take it out and strain the butter, and fry in it about three ounces of rice for every person who is to partake of it. As the grain easily burns, it should be put into the butter when it begins to simmer, and be very gently coloured to a bright yellow tint over a slow fire. Add it to some good boiling broth lightly tinged with saffron, and stew it softly in a copper pan for fifteen or twenty minutes. Stir to it two or three ounces of butter mixed with a small portion of flour, a moderate seasoning of pepper or cayenne, and as much grated Parmesan cheese as will flavour it thoroughly. Boil the whole gently for ten minutes, and serve it very hot, at the commencement of dinner as a *potage*.

Obs. The reader should bear in mind what we have so often repeated in this volume, that rice should always *be perfectly cooked*, and that it will not become tender with less than three times its bulk of liquid.

(Entrée – German Receipt – Good)

Skin, open, and cleanse one fine eel (or more), cut it into finger-lengths, rub it with a mixed seasoning of salt and white pepper, and leave it for half an hour. Wipe it dry, wrap each length in sage leaves, fasten them round it with coarse thread, roll the eel in good salad oil or clarified butter, lay it on the gridiron, squeeze lemon-juice over, and broil it gently until it is browned in every part. Send it to table with a sauce made of two or three ounces of butter, a tablespoonful of chili, tarragon, or common vinegar, and one of water, with a little salt; to keep this smooth, proceed as for the Norfolk sauce of Chapter 5. Broiled fish is frequently served without *any* sauce. A quite simple one may supply the place of that which we have indicated above; eels being of so rich a nature, require no other.

COMPÔTE DE PIGEONS (STEWED PIGEONS)

The French in much of their cookery use more bacon than would generally be suited to a very delicate taste, we think. This bacon, from being cured without saltpetre, and from not being smoked, rather resembles salt pork in flavour: we explain this that the reader may, when so disposed, adapt the receipts we give here to an English table by omitting it. Cut into dice from half to three-quarters of a pound of streaked bacon, and fry it gently in a large stewpan with a morsel of butter until it is very lightly browned; lift it out, and put in three or four young pigeons trussed as for boiling. When they have become firm, and lightly coloured, lift them out, and stir a large tablespoonful of flour to the fat. When this thickening (*roux*) is also slightly browned, add gradually to it a pint, or something more, of boiling veal-stock or strong broth; put back the birds and the bacon, with a few small button-onions when their flavour is liked, and stew the whole very gently for three-quarters of an hour. Dish the pigeons neatly with the bacon and onions laid between them; skim all the fat from the sauce, reduce it quickly, and strain it over them. The birds should be laid into the stewpan with the breasts downwards.

The third, or half of a bottle of small mushrooms is sometimes added to this dish. It may be converted into a *compôte aux petits pois* by adding to the pigeons when the broth, in which they are laid, first begins to boil, a pint and a half of young peas. For these, a pint and a quarter at the least, of liquid will be required, and a full hour's stewing. The economist can substitute water for the broth. When the birds can be had at little cost, one, two, or more, according to circumstances, should be stewed down to make broth or sauce for the others.

Obs. Pigeons are excellent filled with the mushrooms *au beurre*, of page 199, and either roasted or stewed. To broil them proceed as directed for a partridge (French receipt), page 170.

MAI TRANK (MAY-DRINK)

(*German*)

Put into a large deep jug one pint of light white wine to two of red, and dissolve in it sufficient sugar to sweeten it agreeably. Wipe a sound China orange, cut it in rather thick slices, without paring it, and add it to the wine; then throw in some small bunches of faggots of the fragrant little plant called *woodruff*; cover the jug closely to exclude the air and leave it until the following day. Serve it to all *May-day visitors*. One orange will be sufficient for three pints of wine. The woodruff should be washed and well drained before it is thrown into the jug; and the quantity of it used should not be *very* large, or the flavour of the beverage will be rather injured than improved by it. We have tried this receipt on a small scale with lemon-rind instead of oranges, and the mixture was very agreeable. Rhenish wine should properly be used for it; but this is expensive in England. The woodruff is more odorous when dried gradually in the shade than when it is fresh gathered, and imparts a pleasant fragrance to linen, as lavender does. It grows wild in Kent, Surrey, and other parts of England, and flourishes in many suburban gardens in the neighbourhood of London.

INDEX